SCHOHARIE
UNITED
PRESBYTERIAN
CHURCH

The Eighth Book

of

Mr. Jeremiah Burroughs

Being a Treatise of the

EVIL OF EVILS,

or the

Exceeding Sinfulness of Sin

Wherein is Shown

1. That there is more evil in the least sin than there is in the greatest affliction.
2. Sin is most opposite to God.
3. Sin is most opposite to man's good.
4. Sin is most opposite to all good in general.
5. Sin is the poison or evil of all other evils.
6. Sin has a kind of infiniteness in it.
7. Sin makes a man comfortable to the devil.

All these several heads are branched
out into very many particulars.

(Edited by Don Kistler)

Soli Deo Gloria Publications
"...for instruction in righteousness..."

Soli Deo Gloria Publications
P.O. Box 451, Morgan, PA 15064
(412) 221-1901/FAX 221-1902

*

The Evil of Evils was first published in 1654.
This Soli Deo Gloria reprint, in which
stylistic and spelling changes have
been made, is © 1992.

*

ISBN 1-877611-48-4

*

THE CONTENTS

The First Part

tion between Father, Son, and Holy Ghost, (3) in His counsels, (4) in the end for which God had done all He has done. First, sin wrongs God's attributes: (1) His all-sufficiency, showed in two particulars. (2) It wrongs His omnipresence and omniscience. (3) Sin wrongs His wisdom. (4) Sin wrongs His holiness. (5) Sin wrongs God in settings man's will above God. (6) Sin wrongs God's dominion. (7) Sin wrongs God's justice. (8) Sin wrongs God in His truth.

Me." Thirdly, there are eight considerations of Christ's sufferings.

The Second Part

Sin is most opposite to man's good, and far more opposite to the good of man than affliction.

the heart against God and the means of grace.

The Third Part

The Fourth Part

The Fifth Part

come it. Second, sin has a kind of infiniteness because it has an infinite desert in it expressed in three particulars: (1) the desert of the loss of an infinite Good; (2) it deserves to put an infinite distance between you and God; (3) it deserves infinite misery. Third, sin has a kind of infinite evil because an infinite price is required to make an atonement between God and man. Fourth, there is a kind of infinite evil in sin because we must hate it infinitely. Fifth, sin is an infinite evil because it is the universal cause of all evil. Sixth, the Scripture makes use of evil things to set out the evil of sin. Seventh, there's an infiniteness in sin because the Scripture sets out sin by sin itself.

The Sixth Part

afflicted with temptation from the devil.

thoughts of trouble of conscience for sin are (1) a high degree of blasphemy, and (2) a degree towards the unpardonable sin.

mercy to get the pardon of sin.

under affliction, are more sensible of affliction than of sin. Also, there are five discoveries whether men's afflictions or sins trouble them. Fifthly, it reprehends those who get out of affliction by sinful courses, and yet think they are doing well. Sixthly, it reprehends those who, after being delivered from affliction, can bless themselves in their sin.

To The Reader

Reader, the creature's vanity and emptiness, the abounding sinfulness of sin, and Christ's all-sufficiency and fulness, and how to live the life of faith in Christ, are subjects containing the sum and substance of religion, and much treated on promiscuously among divines. And I think among all the treatises of this blessed man, Mr. Jeremiah Burroughs (now triumphing in glory above all sin and sorrow), which have been received with so much acceptance among the saints, there has not been presented to your view a more practical piece than this now in your hands. And though various divines have written and spoken much concerning this subject, yet, in my poor judgment, this out-does all of this nature that ever my eyes beheld, setting forth with life and spirit the subject in hand and bringing it down powerfully in a practical way to convince the judgment and work upon the affections of the weakest reader. That which is the undoing of those who think themselves no small Christians, is resting in a bare notion of the creature's emptiness, sin's filthiness, Christ's fulness, and having some high, towering speculations concerning the nature and object of faith. And to be able to discourse on these things in company, and upon occasion, is the religion of the world and, more especially, of our formal professors.

Now the reality of these confessed principles are not made powerful upon the conscience by the clearest, most naturally acquired light in the world, but when the Lord is pleased to set home those over-aweing, soul-balasting thoughts of eternity, then, and never until then, shall we live, act, and walk as a people who acknowledge these principles of Christianity to be true. While the things of religion and thoughts of eternity lie swimming only in our brains, they never conquer, command, and subdue the heart in a way of practical obedience. Many men's thoughts, language, and lives are such that, if they were certain there is no God, no sin, no hell, no wrath to be feared, no grace to be minded and attained, no judgment day when they must give an account, they could not be worse than they are nor do worse than they do.

O the horrid atheism bound up in men's hearts and they see it not! How else dare men be so profane in their lives under gospel light? How dare they sit so stupidly under the powerful awakening means of grace? How else could such vile thoughts be cherished and such cursed practices and principles be maintained? How else dare men choose sin rather than affliction when they are brought into straits? How otherwise are men more afraid of open shame than of secret sins? In a word, how dare men walk without God in the world, at least without secret prayer and communing with their own hearts for days, weeks, months, and years together?

I am persuaded that more men drop down to hell in our day under the abuse of gospel light than ever did in the gross darkness of popery. Then, they better improved their talents according to the light afforded, and walked better and more suitably to the light they received, whereas these gospel truths which now shine more fully and clearly in the faces of so many thousands are not so much improved in a more circumspect, holy, and humble walking, but rather abused to a more loose and wanton carriage and censorious judging of one another, men sinning the more because grace abounds so much. How could the saints then love and embrace with singleness of heart? But now the foundations of love are shaken and a perverse spirit is mingled among us.

O how heavily does the wrath of God lie upon the professors of our age for the abuse of gospel light and they do not feel it, God's administrations in this latter age of the world being more subtle and spiritual and, therefore, more undiscernible than in former ages! O how many have we nowadays who think they walk clearly in the midst of gospel light, magnifying and exalting free grace, triumphing in their

Christian liberty, looking upon others as kept in bondage who do not come up to their pitch and practice, and yet are no better than Solomon's fools who make a mockery of sin, being conceitedly set at liberty, but really are slaves to sin and Satan.

Certainly, until men's consciences are made tender and fearful of the least touches and appearances of evil, they have good cause to suspect not only the strength, but the soundness of their hearts in grace. While men are bold with sin and can put it off at an easy rate of sorrow, let their attainments seem never so high in understanding the mysteries of the gospel, they never yet knew truly what it is to exalt Christ and free grace. Look, in what measure we slight sin, in the same measure we slight God Himself in His person and attributes. And how can that great gospel duty of walking humbly with God be expressed, and how can Christ be rightly lifted up and advanced in our souls without a right sight and sense of sin? Never will Christ be wonderful Christ, and never will grace be wonderful grace until sin is wonderful sin and experimentally apprehended as out of measure sinful. Never, until sin is seen and sorrowed for as the greatest evil, will Christ be seen and rejoiced in as the greatest Good.

Were we once thoroughly convinced of the infinite evil in sin, as containing in it the evil of all evils (nothing being an evil indeed properly, but as it has the bitter ingredient and cursed sting of sin in it), how would sin be hated and shunned more than the most deadly poison, and feared more than the devil, more than hell itself? Nothing has made and founded hell but sin, nor made the devil such a black fiend but sin. Nay, nothing is so much a hell, I mean a torment, as sin itself. Nothing binds the creature in such chains of misery as when it is held in the cords of its own sin, Proverbs 5:22. Men look upon sin through false mediums, and believe the reports and interpretations which the world and the flesh gives of sin, and thus are cheated to their own destruction.

Could we but lay our ears to hell and hear the howlings and yellings of those damned spirits aggravating sin, we should then have a true comment upon the subject in hand.

Afflictions in this world now and then awaken the conscience, reviving the fight and sense of sin by some grievous pains, but one half hour in hell, being separated from the comfortable presence of all good and blessedness will make the evil of sin rightly understood. Certainly there's an evil in sin beyond what the largest created understanding is able to fathom, sin being one of those things which can never be punished enough, which appears in that all those unspeakable, insufferable torments inflicted upon the damned through all eternity is but a continual paying of this sad debt, and giving satisfaction to divine justice for the wrong which sin has done. Divine justice shall not, otherwise, have sufficiently taken its due out of the sinner. Now the Judge of all the world, who is the standard of justice itself, neither can, nor will, do any wrong to His creature in punishing it more than its iniquity deserves.

Reader, I shall say no more now, but beseech the Lord to carry home these truths by His Spirit into your bosom, that there may be a Divine impression made upon your heart in reading suitable to the author's in preaching, and that you may (out of love to holiness) so fear and hate sin now that you may never suffer the vengeance of eternal fire (the wages of sin) hereafter; which is the unfeigned and earnest desire of

Your Soul's Well-Wisher in Christ Jesus,

John Yates

The Evil of Evils
or
The Exceeding Sinfulness of Sin

For this hast thou chosen rather than affliction.
Job 36:21 (latter part)

Chapter 1

That it's a very evil choice to choose sin rather than affliction.

(Reader, this treatise was first preached at Stepney, near London, on the Lord's Day mornings. It was begun November 29, 1641, and finished February 27, 1643. It is thought good to give the reader notice hereof, in respect to some expressions used in this treatise.)

In these words is drawn up Elihu's false charge against holy Job, wherein he shamefully scandalized this man of God, concerning whom the Lord Himself gives in this letter a testimony that *he was perfect and upright, one that feared God and eschewed evil,* Job 1:1. And yet Elihu speaks here to this effect against him, that he chose iniquity rather than affliction; that he should see less evil in sin than he did in affliction; that for his affliction he was troubled, but for his sin he was not afflicted; that the burden of his affliction lay heavy as a talent of lead upon him, but his sin was lighter than a feather. Or thus, "you have chosen iniquity rather than affliction, whereas God requires of you to give Him glory in your humble submission unto Him in your patience under His mighty hand. You have behaved yourself stubbornly and stoutly, and have denied to give God the glory of His sovereignty, majesty, holiness, justice, and purity; and this you have chosen rather than to be content to lie under the afflicting hand of God."

Whichever way it is taken, it was a heavy charge had it been true. So, for it to be alleged against any soul, that they choose iniquity rather than affliction, is a great and heavy charge.

The doctrinal truth which arises from the words thus opened is this: **That it is a very evil choice for any soul under heaven to choose the least sin rather than the greatest affliction.** Better be under the greatest affliction than be under the guilt or power of any sin. It is true that neither sin nor affliction is to be chosen. Affliction in itself is an evil, and sin is an evil, but the object of the will is good and choice is of the will. Therefore, neither (barely considered as in themselves) can be chosen; but, because of some evils, the lesser in comparison of the greater may come under a notion of good, and so may be sometimes chosen. The will cannot choose anything but, under the notion of good, either real or in appearance; and, though affliction is in itself an evil, yet in regard of sin it may come under the notion of good, and that's to be chosen rather than sin. Now this is the work I have to do, to make out this conclusion to you, that any affliction is to be chosen rather than any sin; that there is more evil in any sin, the least sin, than in the greatest affliction.

My principal business is to charge men's consciences with the evil of their sin and show to them how much evil there is in sin. All men are afraid of afflictions and troubled at affliction, but where's the man or woman that fears sin and flies from it as from a serpent, and is troubled at sin more than any affliction? That there is more vile in sin than in affliction, in general (I suppose), is granted by all. None dare deny it; but, because they do not see how this is, they do not have convincing arguments to bring this truth to their souls with power. But I hope, before I have done with this point, that I shall make it clear to everyone's conscience.

There is more evil in sin than in outward trouble in the world; more evil in sin than in all the miseries and torments of hell itself.

Suppose that God should bring any of you to the brink of that bottomless gulf and open it to you, and there you should see those damned creatures sweltering under the wrath of the infinite God, and there you should hear the dreadful and hideous cries and shrieks of those who are under such soul-amazing and soul-sinking torments through the wrath of the Almighty. Yet, I say, there is more evil in one sinful thought than there is in all these everlasting burnings, and that is what I shall endeavor to clear and prove to every man's conscience, that we shall not only see it as an ill choice to choose sin rather than affliction, but (if it comes in competition) to choose sin rather than all the tortures and torments of hell, however many of you give in to sin upon very easy terms. Yet, the truth is, that if it should come into competition whether we would endure all the torments that there are in hell to all eternity rather than to commit one sin, I say, if our spirits were as they should be, we would rather be willing to endure all these torments than commit the least sin.

And, brethren, do not think this is a high strain, for I who come to speak in the name of God do not come to speak hyperbolically, to raise expressions higher than these things are in reality. No, I do not come for that end, and I should take the name of God in vain if I should do so. Therefore, I dare not raise things beyond that which they are in reality themselves. Therefore know, whatever I shall say unto you in this thing is not words or expressions, but I speak as in the name of God, as I would take it upon my own conscience, having to deal between God and you in that great work, and in this place to deliver this truth, that there is more evil in the least sin than in all the miseries that a creature is capable of, either here or in hell besides. I hope if I shall make this out to you, you will then believe that you have not

yet understood the sinfulness of sin, that the burden of sin
has not lain upon you to be felt as the burden of sin. Now,
then, that I may fully convince you, there is more evil in the
least sin than in any affliction.

Chapter 2

The servants of God have chosen the most dreadful afflictions rather than the least sin.

First, those servants of God, who have been guided by the wisdom of God to make their choice, have rather chosen the sorest and most dreadful afflictions in this world than willingly commit the least sin. For example, if you would but turn your thoughts to what you have read or heard of the martyrs, what hideous and grievous torments they suffered, the boiling of their bodies in scalding lead, laying their naked backs on hot gridirons, rending and tearing their members in pieces with horses, pulling their flesh off with pinchers, and others by red-hot burning tongs, enduring their flesh to be scorched by being broiled, first on one side, then on the other side. Yes, weak women have endured this, to have their flesh harrowed with stones and sharp irons, to have their bodies slayed and then thrown into rivers of cold ice, and a thousand more things, whatever hell and wicked men could devise. They were content to endure all this, and certainly could they have devised ten thousand times more exquisite torments than they did, they would have been content to have endured that, and whatever else, rather than to act against their consciences and commit the least sin. And they accounted this to be a good choice when, as they saw sin against their consciences on the one hand and all their torments on the other, they rather embraced these tortures than embrace that sin.

For this choice of theirs, they are renowned in the hearts of the saints to all generations. Yes, the Holy Ghost witnesses that they have a good report, Hebrews 11. Those who suffered sawing asunder and scourging, those who went up and down in sheepskins and goatskins, in leather breeches and doublets, suffering the spoiling of their goods

and of all that they had, these had a good report, and the
Holy Ghost commends them for their choice.

Many of you, when it comes to it, will be more loathe to
loose a coin than commit a sin, more loath to endure the least
shame or a nick-name than to commit a sin. Are there not
many servants here, or children, who will tell a lie (when
they have done an evil) rather than suffer a little shame in the
family from their parents or masters, fellow-servants and
children? What a difference is there between your hearts and
the heart of the martyrs!

They could endure all the tortures on their bodies that
could be devised rather than to commit any known sin
against their consciences, and you will venture to commit a
known sin against your conscience rather than to be found
out in some fault and have an angry word or a little shame! If
it is only to gain two pence, they will tell a lie, and are willing to choose sin rather than endure the least trouble. A
mighty difference between you and them.

You know how it was with Paul. When he speaks of
afflictions, these are his expressions: they are but *light and
momentary;* they are but for a moment, but *they work an exceeding weight of glory.* Mark it. Light afflictions. What
were they? You would count them heavy if they were upon
you. Blessed Paul (that great vessel to bear the name of God
as great an instrument of God's glory as any in the world
except Christ Himself) was whipped up and down as if he
had been a rogue. He was put into the stocks. He did not
have clothes to cover his nakedness; he had not bread to eat,
and he was accounted the off-scouring of the world, and yet
he accounts all this but light.

But when he comes to sin, that is heavy! *O wretched
man that I am!* Thus he gives a dreadful shriek at sin. See
what a difference he makes between affliction and sin, and
accounts it abundantly more evil to be in sin than to be in
affliction. And so it was Christ Himself, who is the Wisdom
of the Father, and therefore could not choose but judge right.

Yet He was content for the sake of poor souls to come and undergo all kinds of affliction and pain and sorrow so as to be made a man of sorrows, as the Scripture speaks. How was He content to have His body whipped and scourged? He was laughed at and scorned, and, though He was a possessor of heaven and earth, yet He did not have a house to put His head in; yes, to bear the wrath of God for the sin of man, to be made a curse for man under the curse of the law, and to be under that pain and extremity through the wrath of His Father when He sweat great drops of blood?

All this Christ would endure. But now, if it had been to have committed the least sin to have saved all the world, Christ would never have done it. Though Christ could be content to suffer all kinds of miseries, yes, even the wrath of His Father, yet had it been to have committed the least sin, Christ would have let all the world be damned eternally rather than that he would have done that, there being so much evil in it. Afflictions taken in the strength and latitude of them, yet they have no greater evil in them than Christ is capable of. I say, take them in the strength and latitude of them, certainly there was never any affliction since the world began endured like Christ's, and yet these are no other than Christ, God, and man is capable of. And it may stand with the blessedness of His divinity that that person, both God and man, could be under such afflictions. Christ was content with these, *He made His soul an offering for sin.* But sin is so great an evil that Christ is not capable of it.

Christ never entertained the least thought of it, but cast it off if it came to Him. Therefore, certainly, there is more evil in the least sin than there is in the greatest affliction. The afflictions that Christ endured, though they were not every way the same with the damned in hell, yet certainly there was the wrath of God as really and truly upon Christ as truly upon the damned in hell, as really, though I say not in every kind, in the same way and manner. And, therefore, see that Christ was capable of that evil, of the wrath of the Almighty upon His soul, and yet not capable of sin. He was willing to undergo that, and yet not to have the least guilt of sin applied to Him. And therefore, certainly, there is more evil in the least sin than in the greatest affliction.

Chapter 3

There is some good in affliction, but none in sin.

Well, for further arguments, though this one thing were enough to stop all mouths in the world and make every soul subscribe and acknowledge that there is greater evil in the least sin than in any affliction, I shall be large in this argument, because it is of wonderful concernment to stop men in their course of sin, to humble them for their sin, to make them resolve against sin, to see their miserable estate in sin, and so see their need of Christ.

I shall fully make it out, that affliction is to be chosen rather than sin. First, because there is some good in affliction, but none in sin. Second, because sin has more evil in it than affliction.

First, affliction has some good in it, but sin has none. You know what David said in Psalm 119:71, *It is good for me that I have been afflicted.* That is how he spoke of affliction. But when St. Paul speaks of sin, he said, *In me, that is in my flesh, dwelleth no good,* Romans 7:18. It is as if he should say, "As far as I am unregenerate, in my unregenerate part there is no good at all." He calls sin by the name of flesh. There is no good at all in sin.

1. There is no good of entity or being. All things that have a being have some good in them, for God has a being, and everything that has a being has some good in it because it is of God. But sin is a non-entity, a no-being. It is rather the deprivation of a being than any being at all, and here is a great mystery of iniquity. That which is a non-entity in itself yet has such a might efficacy to trouble heaven and earth. This is a great mystery.

2. Secondly, it has no good of causality. That is, sin is so evil that it can bring forth no good. Afflictions bring forth good. Sin is such an evil as it cannot be made good, it is not

an instrument for good. Afflictions are made instrumental for good.

OBJECTION. "No," you will say, "cannot God bring good out of sin? And does not God bring good out of sin?" ANSWER. To this I answer, it is true. God brings good out of sin, that is occasionally, but not instrumentally. He may take occasion to bring good out of sin committed, but (mark it) God never makes sin an instrument for good, for an instrument comes under somewhat as efficient. An instrument gives some power towards the effect, but God never uses sin like this. God never made sin an instrument of any good, that is, that sin should have any power or any influence into that good effect that God brings out of it as afflictions have. God does not only take occasion by afflictions to do His people good, but He makes them channels to convey the mercies to their souls. And thus afflictions have an instrumental efficacy in them to do men good. Therefore, says the Holy Ghost in Hebrews 12:10, *He chastens them for their profit that they might be partakers of His holiness.* Affliction is, oftentimes, made the instrument to convey the greatest good the creature is capable of. And in Isaiah 27:9, *By this the iniquity of Jacob shall be purged.* That is, by this as an instrument; but sin is never thus. Sin is never sanctified by God to do good to a soul. Afflictions are sanctified by God to do good; therefore, sin is a greater evil than affliction. Sin is so evil that it is not capable of any work of God to sanctify it for good. But no afflictions are so evil but that they are capable of a work of God to sanctify them for abundance of good. This is the second.

Thirdly, sin has greater evil than affliction in the rise of it. There is no good principle when sin comes, but there are good principles from when afflictions arise. For example, whom God loves He chastens. He chastens every son He receives. So, then, chastisement has a principle of love, but it cannot be said that whom God loves He suffers to fall into sin. It cannot be said that this is a fruit of His love. It can never be said that it is a fruit of God's love that such a man or woman commits sin, but it may be said that it is a fruit of God's love that such a man or woman is afflicted. Therefore, there is more good in affliction than there is in sin.

Nay, observe this. Many times, God does not afflict a man or woman because He does not love them, but it can never be said that God does not suffer a man or woman to sin because He does not love them. I say, there is many a man or woman who goes on prosperously and does not meet with such afflictions as others meet with; and the reason is because God does not have such a love to them as to other men. But it cannot be said thusly, that there are such men who keep themselves from such sins that others wallow in and, therefore, they do it because God does not have such a love for them as for others. It cannot be said to be so, but it may be said that such are not as afflicted as others because God does not love them as well as others.

It is a dreadful fruit of God's hatred that He does not afflict them, but it is not a fruit of His hatred not to let them fall into sin. I remember a speech an Ancient had on Hosea 4:14, *I will not punish their daughters when they commit adultery.* He said, "O dismal wrath of God, that God will not afflict them and punish them!" But now, if it is true that lack of afflictions come from God's wrath, and being put into afflictions may come from God's love, certainly, then, there is not as much evil in affliction as is in sin, for it can never be said so of sin.

Fourthly, there is no good annexed to sin as is to affliction. For example, there is not the good of promise, not the good of evidence, and not the good of blessing annexed to sin as is to affliction.

1. Afflictions have the good of promise. *I will be with you in the fire and in the water; And by this shall the iniquity of Jacob be purged.* And I could spend the remainder of this book opening to you the great promises God has annexed to

afflictions. But God has not annexed any promises of good to sin. When God afflicts, then you may challenge God's promise. David said, in Psalm 119:75, *In very faithfulness hast Thou afflicted me, O Lord.* "This is but a fruit of Your promise in afflictions. And You are faithful in afflicting, but sin has no promise annexed to it."

"Yet it may be," you will say, "that all shall work together for the good of them who love God." But this is not given by way of a promise. This Scripture will not bear it, though it is true that God may occasionally work good to His people by sin. But this Scripture cannot bear it, that there is any promise for it in that place, for, first, it is against the scope of that text. The scope of that place is to uphold the hearts of God's people in affliction. He said, *All things,* but sin is no thing, and *all things work together.* And so He speaks of that which has an efficacy in it. That will, together with God, work for good; but sin has no efficacy to work on, for God will not work by that. That is one thing, then. Affliction has the good of the promise annexed to it, but sin has none. Therefore, there is some good in affliction, but none in sin.

2. Affliction has the good of evidence. God makes our afflictions to be signs of our sonship and adoption. If you are not afflicted, then you are bastards and not sons. We have Philippians 1:28, *Be not troubled or terrified.* Trouble for the saints is an evidence of salvation for them, but a token of perdition for those who are the terrifiers or troublers of them. Afflictions are a sign of your salvation, but that is not true of sin.

3. Further, there is a blessing propounded to afflictions. Blessed are those who mourn, and blessed is the man whom God chastises and teaches His law; but there is no blessing allowed to sin. It is not capable of it. The good is not annexed to sin that is to affliction and, therefore, affliction is to be chosen rather than sin.

And, from this, see the different working of the hearts of

the saints under their sin and under their affliction. That follows from this head: There is some good annexed to affliction that is not annexed to sin.

First, it follows that the saints can cry to God with liberty of spirit under affliction, but they cannot under sin. They can go to God and tell God their afflictions, and challenge God with a holy boldness in afflictions, but who can go to God and challenge God because he has told a lie, or the like? Does this make me go with a holy boldness to God and challenge God's promise, because I have committed such and such a sin?

Secondly, when affliction comes, a gracious heart can kiss the rod and accept the punishment of his sin, but now a gracious heart can never be well-pleased with his sin, can never accept his sin. Though God punishes one sin with another, sometimes, yet there cannot be a well-pleasedness with sin and a kissing of that.

Thirdly, a gracious heart may rejoice in affliction and have an abundance of comfort in afflictions. *Count it all joy,* said the Holy Ghost, *when you fall into trials* and afflictions; but now we can never rejoice in sin. No man can rejoice in sin, though God should turn sin to never so much good. One cannot rejoice in sin and have that comfort which he may in affliction.

Fourthly, a gracious heart may bless God for afflictions, bless God that ever He did call him into an afflicted state; but he can never bless God for putting him into a sinful state, though God works good out of it. Nay, further, the good a gracious heart has, sometimes, by afflictions may encourage him to be more willing to go into affliction again when God calls him to it, but if a gracious heart should get good occasionally by sin, yet this good cannot encourage him to fall into sin again. This would be a desperate wickedness if it did.

Fifthly, a gracious heart may desire that God not take away the affliction until it is sanctified, and that He would continue it until it is sanctified; but no man may or ought to pray thus, "Lord, continue me in this sin until I am humbled." Therefore, you see, there is an abundance of difference between affliction and sin. One has a great deal of good annexed to it, and the other has none at all.

4. Sin is so evil that it is not capable of any good at all. Though the air is never so dark, yet it is capable of light. That would be a dismal darkness that was not capable of light coming in to it. That which is bitter, though never so bitter, yet is capable of receiving that which will sweeten it. That which is never so venomous is yet capable of such things as will make it wholesome; but sin is so dark that it is incapable of light, so bitter that there is no way to make it sweet, so venomous that there is no way to make it wholesome.

Now for the clearing of this, consider these three things. Put all the good in heaven and earth, and in all the creatures in heaven and earth together. Suppose the quintessence of all the good of all the creatures of heaven and earth were put together and bring that to sin and add it to it. It would not make it good. No, sin would remain as evil as it was before. Now that must be poison, indeed, that is not at all diminished by the addition of every sovereign thing in the world. So it is with sin.

Therefore (I beseech you, brethren, observe it), those men and women are mightily mistaken who think that by adding some good to their former sinful lives it will make them good. They think, "I have been a sinful creature, indeed, but now I will amend and reform and be better." O know that there is so much evil in sin that the addition of all the good of all the creatures in heaven and earth cannot make it less evil than before. For that, you must not only now think to live better and add good to your former self, but you must take a course for the taking away of the former evil, for delivering you from the guilt, stain, and filth of your former sin.

Sin is not capable of good. All those good ends that any men have in the commission of sin do not make their sin better. They cannot make sin good just because they have good ends. Some may think they have good ends in the commission of sin. They may think, perhaps, that by commission of some sin they may further some grace, do good to others, or glorify God. There may be such deceit in the heart as this:

(1.) They may think such a sin will help such a grace and help against such a temptation. They may think that such a sin may help their humility. It is a common temptation (when in trouble of conscience) to do away with yourself, because then you will sin no more. A man thinks thusly, "As long as I live, I shall sin against God. Therefore, if I do away with myself, I will cease to sin."

But know, if you lay violent hands upon yourself and think you shall have good by it to sin no more, yet your sin is wicked and abominable though you place a good end upon it, such as sinning no more. Though it were possible to increase grace never so much by the least sinful thought, we must not commit this least sinful thought for never so good an end as to help forward such a grace.

(2.) A second end may be to do good to others and, I say, if it were possible, if a man might be a means to save the whole world if he would commit one sin, if he could save the whole world from eternal torments by the commission of one sin, you should suffer the whole world to perish rather than commit one sin. There is that much evil in sin.

Augustine wrote, in a tract of his, concerning an officious lie. A friend of his wrote to him to answer this question about telling a lie, "Would you not tell a lie to do good to another man?"

Many think, "What's the harm? Though I tell a lie, I do another person good. Indeed, if I may do hurt, then I must not, but if I may do good, may I not tell a lie?" This question was brought to Augustine, and he said, "You must not tell a lie to save the whole world." This was his answer.

Suppose that the soul of your father, mother, or child (this is but a supposition), or the like, would be saved or damned if you will commit one sin. Suppose such a temptation should come. You must not commit one sin though the soul of your father or mother, or all the world rested on it!

It is one thing to commit a sin to gain a coin. "Oh, now, by a deceitful word I may have this gain, perhaps twenty shillings." You must not venture upon sin to save the world; therefore, not to gain six pence or shilling. Certainly, these are the truths of God, and for one to come and speak these things in a solemn manner in the presence of God, if it were not upon deliberation and good search, it would be a great boldness and, therefore, certainly, believe that there is such an evil in sin. And though you pass by a thousand idle thoughts and evil actions, and they are gone with you and you make little of them, if you but knew what the evil of sin was, you would look upon them with amazement and cry out, "Lord, what have I done!"

Men and women go abroad, and before they come home they meet with company and there swear many oaths, commit lewdness, tell lies and do wickedness. O did they but know what they have done that day they would come home wringing their hands and ready to pull their hair and lie tumbling upon the very ground for the evil they have done!

(3.) Further, we must not commit sin though it be for the glory of God. Many put this end upon it. This is the principle of the Papists. To advance the Catholic cause, they think they may do any wickedness: murder princes, blow up parliaments, keep no faith, promises, or oaths, take liberty to rise in rebellion, to commit all outrages and cut all the Protestant's throats; and to advance the Catholic cause they take the Sacrament upon it, and yet think because it is for so good an end (as they conceive), therefore, they may commit any wickedness.

It is certain that God does not need the devil to help His

cause, but suppose that by sin God's glory might be furthered in some particular. We must not commit the least sin
for the greatest glory of God that can be imagined! So much
evil there is in sin. And, therefore, for such who many times
strain their conscience to do that which their consciences regret, and their conscience told them that they should not do
it, yet merely upon this pretense, that they might do service
in the church.

O their ministry is dear, to do good to souls, to preach to
so many souls. By this means God may have glory, and
hereupon they venture to strain their consciences to have liberty to preach. This certainly is a great evil. We must not
strain our consciences in any thing to commit the least sin
upon imagination of the greatest glory that can be brought to
God. Good ends put upon sins cannot make them better.
This is the second thing.

5. Fifth, all the good that God Himself can bring from
sin can never make sin good. Such evil there is in it that the
infinite power and goodness of God can never make sin
good. True, God may destroy sin. Yet that which is sin cannot be made good by all the power of God. Such evil there is
in sin. This is a fifth thing.

6. There is no good in sin, not comparatively. That is,
though it is true that one sin is less than another, yet no sin is
good in comparison of another. In affliction, as one affliction is less than another, so one affliction is good in comparison to another. A less affliction is good in comparison to a
greater, and all affliction is good in comparison to sin. But in
sin, though one sin is less than another, yet the least sin is
not good in comparison of the greatest, and take the least sin
of all, and it is not good in comparison of any affliction. And
you shall see how this is useful to us.

Chapter 4

Nine Consequences of Excellent Use

Hence we see for our instruction that this maxim which many have has nothing to do in point of sin, to wit, "of two evils you must choose the least." True, in regard of the evil of affliction, comparing one affliction with another, we may choose the least; but this cannot be the case in the matter of sin, that of two sins we may choose the least because, though one sin is less than another, yet the least sin can never come under the notion of good comparatively. As all other evils are good comparatively, though never so great evils, yet comparatively they may be good. Yet sin can have no goodness any way comparatively. Therefore, of two evils, we must not choose the least, and that in this sense:

1. Because sin is, in itself, sinful.

2. And, because choosing the least can never be a means to prevent the greater, but rather to make way for the greater. And, brethren, observe it (for it may be useful in the course of our lives), God never brings any man or woman to such straits who, of necessity, must choose this or the other sin. When two sins shall stand in competition, we may conceit such straits to ourselves, yet there are no such real straits. God brings men into such straits that, of necessity, they must choose either this or that affliction. So David was brought into such a strait. He must choose famine, sword, or pestilence. Yet God never brings men into such straits that they must, of necessity, chose this or that sin. You deceive your own heart if you think that you are brought into such a strait.

Therefore, this is a vain thing and savors of an exceedingly carnal heart, that when men are doing that which is evil for them to say, "It is better to do this than something worse." For example, suppose some stay home on the

Lord's Day and mend their clothes. If anyone rebukes them they will say, "Better to do this than something worse. Better to do this than go to the ale-house."

This is true, but this savors of a carnal heart to think that you must choose one sin rather than another. You must not choose any of them! Both of them are evil, though one may be less evil than another. Or, if some spend their time in play, when they are rebuked they put it off with this shift, "Better to do this than something worse." And so they go abroad and spend their time in seeing plays and say, "Better to do this than something worse." It is yet true that, though this is not as great a sin as others, if it is a sin it must not be done on any terms! And you deceive your own heart in this if you think it is better to do this than something worse, for sin cannot be good, and so it is not to be chosen at any time. Thus we see there is no good in sin, and a great deal of good from affliction.

Hence, there follows these nine consequences of excellent use for us.

First Consequence

If there is no good in sin, then certainly sin is not the work of God, for God saw all His works and they were very good. But sin has no goodness in it and, therefore, it is not of God. God disclaims it.

Second Consequence

If this is so, then whatever promises sin makes to anyone, they are all but delusions. Why? Because sin is not good in any kind. Sin can bring no good to any soul. If anyone says, "Oh, but sin brings pleasure, and does it not bring profit and honors in the world? Do not many live in high esteem in the world by sinful courses? Have they not pleasures and delights in sinful courses?" But cursed are the pleasures, honors, and profits that come in by sin. Certainly, if sin promises any good, it deludes you and your seduced heart deceives you, and you are feeding on ashes, for there is no good in sin.

Third Consequence

Hence it follows that no sin can be the object of the will of a rational creature, because the true object of the will, for it to close with, is good. O the desperate deceit in the hearts of men in the world that, whereas God has made the will (and put a rational soul into it) to be of that nature, that the only object of it is good one way or another, yet they are so miserably mistaken that they choose sin under color of good. Certainly there is no good in sin.

Fourth Consequence

Hence it follows that nothing that is good should be ventured for sin. Why? Because sin has no good, and will you venture the loss of good to get that which has no good? Surely if sin has no good in it, then there should not be the loss of any good ventured for it. You would not venture, at sea or land, any good for that which has no good. O how infinitely men are deceived who venture the loss of God, peace of conscience, loss of credit, health, estate, loss of all for their lusts! O this is a mighty mistake! You have ventured the loss of a great deal of good for that which has no good at all. Know this day that God presents to your soul the desperate delusions of it. What, will you lose God, heaven, and Christ, and all for that which has no good? But thus do many venture all the good in God, in Christ, in heaven, and in eternal life. They are laid on the one side, as it were, and their lusts on the other, and they will venture the loss of all that good so that they might obtain the supposed good in sin. What have you done, O man or woman, who has ventured the loss of all good for that which has no good at all, nay, all evil in it?

Fifth Consequence

It follows, then, that if there is no good at all in sin, then we ought to make nothing that is good to be in any way serviceable to our sin. For example, we must not take the good creatures of God and make them serviceable to our lusts which have no good at all. Do not take the faculties of your souls and the members of your bodies to make them serviceable to your lusts. O how men and women abuse the good things of God to make them serve their corruptions! Yes, brethren, there are many who abuse the ordinances of God, the duties of God's worship, the graces of God's spirit, to make them serviceable to their lusts, their pride, self-ends, and self-seekings.

Just think of it. If it is a great wickedness to take meat and drink, or any of God's good creatures, and make them serviceable to your lusts, how great a wickedness is it to take the graces of God's spirit, the working of God's spirit, enlargement in prayer and following of sermons, and profession of religion, to make them serve your lusts which have no good in them at all?

Sixth Consequence

Hence (if sin has no good at all in it) this follows: how are they mistaken who make sin their chief good as thousands upon thousands in the world do? The chief good that their hearts are set upon is satisfying themselves in some base lust. I put it to your souls this day in the name of God, what is it that your heart is set upon as your chief good? Is it not that height of wickedness I speak of? Such a secret lust you live in? That you venture your eternal state upon? O wickedness above measure?

Seventh Consequence

Hence follows this, then, that all the time we spend in a sinful state is all lost time. O look to this, you young ones. All the time you spend in the vanity of your youth is all lost time, and you who have lived until you are old and have been a long time in a sinful state, you have lost all your time. O the time upon which eternity depends is all lost, for you have spent it in the ways of sin, which has no good in it at all!

Eighth Consequence

If sin has no good in it, then all wicked men who live in the ways of sin are useless members of the world. They are burdens upon the earth, unprofitable members who go on in the ways of sin who neither have, nor can have, any good.

Ninth Consequence

Lastly, if sin has no good at all in it, then, when there is a temptation to sin, there does not need to be any deliberation about it as to whether or not it should be admitted. If once you know it to be a sin, you need not reason the condition of admission or not, or what will follow. You immediately reject it without deliberation. Why? Because there is no good in it. We may deliberate about anything that has even a little good in it (though a greater good is offered), before we accept the one and cast off the other, but, if there is no good, there does not need to be any deliberation.

If anything is pronounced to be sin, to be prejudicial to the estate of your soul, this must not be deliberated upon. Therefore, this is a vain plea that men have, "What kind of government must we have if this is taken away?" First examine if this is evil or not evil that we have. If it is evil, it must be rejected, without deliberation, and we know what we must have in its stead. Indeed, if it was good, we might deliberate; but if it is evil and a sin, it must be cast off without deliberation. Brethren, this I am speaking of is of great use, because the strength sin usually has is from deliberating about it.

I beseech you to observe this. Take heed forever of reasoning with temptation, of consulting and casting about in your thoughts questions like "What will become of it? What trouble may come by this if I do not harken to this?"

Take heed of reasoning. If the devil can but get you to reason about it, he has got it half granted already. You need not reason with any temptation. Cast it off immediately because sin has no good in it. O that God would convince all our hearts of these things!

Chapter 5

There is more evil in the least sin than in the greatest affliction opened in six particulars, being the general scope of the whole treatise.

Now secondly, there is more evil in the least sin than in the greatest affliction. I am now to make this out unto you in these six particulars.

First, sin is most opposed unto God Himself, the Chief Good.

Second, sin is most opposite unto man's good. Affliction is not so opposed to the good of the creature as sin is.

Third, sin is opposed unto all good in general, and so will be revealed to be a universal evil.

Fourth, sin is the evil of all other evils. It is that which is the very venom and poison of all other evils whatsoever, and is, therefore, the greatest.

Fifth, there is a kind of infiniteness in sin, though not properly infinite, it cannot be so. Yet in the nature of it, it has a kind of infiniteness.

Sixth, the evil of it is revealed in the conformity sin has with the devil. There is no creature that conspires against God but only devils and sinful men.

These are the six things to be opened for the discovery of the evil of sin. And, I beseech you, seriously attend to what shall be delivered in these, for I hope before I have done to make it appear to everyone's conscience who shall vouchsafe to read, attend, and consider what I say, that sin is another manner of business than the world thinks it to be. O that your hearts might come to see yourselves to be as you are, in an ill case, in a worse condition than you imagine. And I beseech you to give way to this and be willing to hear it, for though it seems a hard doctrine, yet it is a soul-saving doctrine; and, for lack of this, many thousands upon thousands of souls perish because they never understood what sin meant.

Had many thousands in hell known what sin was, it might have delivered them from everlasting flames. God has reserved you alive, and who knows but for this end: to understand what sin is that your hearts may be humbled, and so everlastingly saved through Christ. Brethren, the way to understand sin is the way to be humbled for sin, and to be humbled for sin is to have sin pardoned and the soul saved.

I should never treat upon such a doctrine as this is. Therefore, I beseech you to mark what I say and see whether or not I make out these things I undertake.

Chapter 6

Sin most opposite to God the Chief Good opened in four heads.

First, it is most opposite to God who is the Chief Good. The lowest capacity for understanding may easily understand this. That which is most opposite to the Chief Good must be the chief evil. I suppose the weakest in this congregation will understand this way of reasoning. That evil which is most opposite to the Chief Good must be the chief evil; but sin is that which is most opposite to God, who is the Chief Good, and, therefore, must be the chief evil. That, then, is that I must make good.

QUESTION. How does it appear that sin is most opposite to the Chief Good?

ANSWER. Brethren, when I have made out this, I shall show sin to be very sinful, and the greatest venom of sin lies in this one thing I am now opening. Should I tell you never so much of the evil of sin, in the danger that comes from it, hell that follows it, should I write a book about hell and damnation for sin, it does not have as much to humble the soul in a saving manner as this I am now treating.

Perhaps I might scare you in preaching of hell and damnation, but revealing this I now speak of, the opposition sin has to God, has more in it to humble the soul in a saving manner and to cause the soul to feel sin to be the most evil where it is evil, to be the greatest burden where it is most weighty. This point, I say, has more power in it than any other. Therefore, let me set upon this, and see how I make this good. Sin is most opposite to God, the Chief Good. There are these four things which reveal the truth of this.

First, sin, in its own nature, is most opposite to the nature of God.

Second, sin, in the working of it, is a continued working

against God. The nature of sin is opposite to God's nature, and the working of sin is most opposite to God.

Third, sin wrongs God more than anything else.

Fourth, sin strikes at the very being of God as far as it can do.

So then, let us sum it up again. That which, in its own nature, is most opposite to God; that which, in its working, is continually working against God; that which most wrongs God; and that which strikes at the very being of God Himself, must be the greatest evil. Sin does all of these things.

Chapter 7

Sin in itself opposite to God showed in five things.

First, that sin in itself is most opposite to God. To understand this, take these five things and they, rightly understood, will make it as clear as the sun at noon day.

1. The nature of sin is so opposite to God that there is nothing so contrary to Him as sin. God has nothing but sin contrary to Him (take it so); therefore, it must be opposite, for God has nothing contrary to His own nature but sin. It is the only contrary, the only opposite to God. There is nothing perfectly contrary to another but it is so contrary as there is nothing but that which is so contrary as that is; for that is the rule of contraries. There may be diversity and difference of many things to one, but an absolutely perfect contrariety can be only of one to one.

Now there is nothing contrary to God's nature but sin. God has no object that He can look upon contrary to Himself in all the world but sin alone; for there is nothing else, except sin, that is not from God, and by God, and for God. Now that which is from Him and by Him and for Him cannot have a contrariety to Him; but sin is neither from Him, nor by Him, nor for Him. Sin is directly contrary to Him. Therefore, there is more evil in sin than in any other thing.

It is not so with affliction. Affliction is from God, and by God, and for God, and is not contrary to God because it is from God Himself.

2. Sin is so opposite to God that, if it were possible that the least drop of it could get into God's nature, God would instantly cease to be a God. He could not continue one moment to be a God any longer. Such evil there is in sin. If there should be such a poison that, if one drop of it should come into the ocean, all the ocean would be instantly poisoned, you would say that was a very fearful poison. If a

drop of poison should be so poisonous that if one drop of it got in to heaven then immediately the sun, moon, and stars would fall down and be annihilated, you would say this was a venomous poison. Certainly, if but one drop of sin should get into God, the infinite Being of God would instantly cease to be.

The sea, though vast, is not infinite. The heavens, though vast, are not infinite. The infinite God would have no being at all if sin should get into God. Therefore, it is very evil. Therefore, also, we ought to have holy thoughts of God, seeing sin is so infinitely contrary to His nature.

3. So opposite is sin to God that, if God should be but the cause of any sin in any other, He would instantly cease to be a God. It strikes at the very life of God. He would cease to be God, He could be God no longer if He should be the cause of sin in any other. We need to take heed, therefore, how we father sin upon God, saying that He could be the cause of sin, for such is the evil of sin that God must cease to be if He should be but any cause to give any efficacy to sin in us. Indeed, for afflictions, God will own that. He said, in Amos 3:6, *Is there any evil in a city and the Lord hath not done it?* And in Micah 2:3, it is said there that *God deviseth evil.* If there is no evil in the city but God does it, yes (said the Prophet) God devises evil; there is no evil of punishment, but God devises it. God will be content to own that. To be the Author of all the torments of all the damned in hell, God will own that. God will say, "I have done it, and I am the Author of all the torments of all the damned in hell." But such is the evil of sin that, if God were the Author of it, He could not be God any longer, but would cease to be God.

4. Such is the evil of sin that, if God should but approve of it and like it, if He should be like it when another has committed it, even that would cause Him to cease to be God. Wicked men are ready to think that, because God is patient and long-suffering, He is of the same judgment as them-

selves. Psalm 50:21, *Because I held My peace, thou thoughtst that I was altogether such an one as thyself; but I will reprove thee, and set them in order before thine eyes.* It is the just temper and frame of wicked and ungodly men to this day that, because God holds His peace and does not come upon them to get revenge for sin immediately, they are ready to think that God approves of sin and is of their judgment.

"Indeed," said a wicked man, "many ministers cry out against sin that is very grievous, but I hope God will give liberty to my ways and walkings. Surely God is not against them. He approves of them. Why else would God suffer me in them and be so patient towards me in them?"

Oh! Know that when you have any such thoughts of God as these, you blaspheme God! If that were true that you are thinking, that God approved of your wicked ways, God must cease to be God; God would be God no longer.

QUESTION. Why? How does this appear?

ANSWER. This is the reason for it. Because then God would not be infinitely holy, and holiness is God's being. And if God is not infinitely holy, He is not God at all, but ceases to be immediately, which is impossible and blasphemous to think.

5. Such is the evil of sin, so opposite to God's nature, that if God did not hate sin as much as He does, He would cease to be God, not only if He allowed it and liked it; for He may permit it in His creatures and not like it. But, I say, if God did not hate sin as much as He does, if it could be conceived that God could hate sin somewhat less than He does, He would instantly cease to be God. He could not remain God one moment if He ceased to hate sin in any degree less than He does.

QUESTION. Why? How does this appear?

ANSWER. Thus, if God ceased to hate sin (I do not speak of the manifesting of His hatred, but that which is His nature, that is proportionable to hatred, as we say), if God did not hate it as much as He does, then He did not hate sin infinitely, for there cannot be anything infinite and less than infinite standing together. These two cannot ever stand. If it is infinite, it remains so. If there should be a degree under that, it must be finite.

Now if God's hatred for sin were less than it is, it would be but a finite hatred and, if it were a finite hatred, then God could not be infinitely holy, for infinite holiness must have infinite hatred against sin.

I beseech you to observe this, for you are ready to think, "Though God is against sin and hates it, yet I hope God does not hate it as much as many ministers make Him out to hate it. God is not so much against sin as they speak of. It is true that, when we do amiss, we must cry out to God for mercy and pray to God to forgive us; yet to make so much of sin as they do, and to say that God sets Himself so much against it as they say is but their opinion."

O brethren, take heed of this opinion! If God should hate sin less than He does, He should cease to be. Either He must hate sin with infinite hatred or He ceases to be God, so evil and opposite is sin to God's nature.

If these things are true, there is a great deal of evil in sin. If there is nothing so opposite to God as sin, and if but the least drop of sin should get into God it would make God cease to be God; and if He should be but the cause of any sin in His creature, He would cease to be God; and if He should hate it less than He does, He could not be God; and all these things are true, then we need to take heed to ourselves and think, "Certainly there is more evil in my heart, more opposition in my heart to God than I have been aware of." What do you say now? Will you venture to commit sin for a coin or six pence if there is so much opposition to God in it? Would it not be better to be under any affliction than under the guilt of sin, if there is such opposition to God in it? This is the first general head, nothing is so opposite to God as sin. I say, sin is most opposite to God.

Chapter 8

The workings of sin are always against God.

Secondly, as the nature of sin is opposite to God, so in the workings of sin there is a continual working against God. A sinful heart that is always stirring and working is always working against God. Therefore, you shall observe these several expressions the Holy Ghost has concerning sin.

1. The Holy Ghost calls it *enmity to God*, Romans 8:7. The wisdom of the flesh (the best part the flesh has) is enmity against God.

2. Yes, the Holy Ghost says it is *walking contrary to God*, Leviticus 26. You have it in several places, verse 21 and verse 28, and several others.

3. It is *fighting against God*, Acts 5:39 and Acts 23:9. In these two places, rejecting the gospel is called fighting against God.

4. In Acts 7:51, *You do always resist the Holy Ghost.* There is a company of men who naturally walk contrary, resisting and fighting against God. We see that we must take heed of opposing the ministry of the gospel for, while you do that, you fight against God. You think you only oppose such and such men, but opposing the gospel is not fighting against us men, but against God. You may turn it off with what names you will, and put what pretences you will upon it, but let me tell you, they who strike upon the lantern do violence to the candle within.

5. Sin, in Scripture, is called *striving against God*, Isaiah 45:9. *Woe unto him that striveth with his Maker: Let the potsheard strive with the potsheards of the earth.* As far as sin prevails in your heart or life, so far you are guilty of striving with your Maker.

6. It is also called *rising against God*. By sin, the soul

rises against God. And for that you have an expression in Micah 2:8, *Even My people of late are risen up as an enemy.* These are strange expressions: enmity, walking contrary, striving, fighting, resisting, rising against God, and yet these are all in sin. But that I may open it further, I shall show how sin fights, strives, and rises against God.

Chapter 9

How sin resists God.

First, sin resists God in His authority, in His sovereignty, and in His dominion over the creature. The language of sin is, "God shall not reign!" It is the setting of the will of a base, wretched creature against the will of the infinite, eternal, glorious God. And is there not evil in this? Though it may be that you do not, on purpose, set your will against God, yet it is so in sin. There is the setting of your will against the will of the infinite, eternal God, resisting the sovereignty and majesty and dominion of the infinite God. Yes, you resist God in His Law; you resist and oppose God in that righteous Law of His which He gave you to obey.

QUESTION. But how is this in every sin? It may be so in some great and notorious sins, but is this fighting against God, striving, rising, and walking contrary to Him in every sin?

ANSWER. For that I answer: (1) that every sin comes from the same root, and look what venom there is in any one sin. As far as its nature, it is in every sin, though not to the same degree. It is true, one sin may have a higher degree of evil in it than another, but every sin is envenomed with the same evil. That which is the venom of any one sin is the venom of all. All comes from the same root.

In a tree, there is more sap in an arm of the tree than in a twig, but the twig has the same kind of sap that the arm of the tree has, and it all comes from the same root. So, though there is more venom in some gross, crying sins than in others, yet there is no sin that does not have the same sap and the same kind of venom that the worst sin has.

(2) Yes, consider further, that God does not count sin only according to man's intentions in sinning, what man intends, but what the nature of the sin tends unto; not what I

aim at in my sinning, but what my sin aims at. There is the end of the agent and the end of the act. Now, it is true that, though the end of a sinner is not always to strive against God and fight with God, yet the end of his sin is so, though not always the end of the sinner. I beseech you to observe how God may lay grievous sins to their charge, and that he does not count a man's sins according to his intentions, but according to that which is in the nature of his sin.

For example, you would think it a strange sin to charge any man in the world with hating God. Come to any man, though he is the greatest sinner in the world, the most notorious villain, and charge him thusly, "You are a vile wretch and you hate the living God!" He would revile you and be ready to spit in your face. And yet it is said in Scripture that he hates God. In Romans 1, the Apostle, in his catalogue of sins (when he would show the state of all men by nature, for the first seven chapters of Romans are to show the nature of the Jews and Gentiles), tells them that there were those who were haters of God. Among other notorious sins, being a hater of God is one. But I will show it in a more plain way in the Second Commandment.

The worst villain in the nation would spit in your face if you should say that he hates God. What do you say to him who seems devout, and worships God in a more glorious way than He has appointed? The Scripture says that he hates God. See the Second Commandment. *Thou shalt not make unto thyself any graven image. Thou shalt not bow down thyself to them, nor worship them, etc. For I will visit the sins of the fathers upon the children, unto the third and fourth generation of them that HATE Me.* Why is this set in the Second Commandment rather than any other, that God will visit the sins of them that HATE Him? Those that sin against the Second Commandment seem to honor God, and to love God more than any other. They are not only content to worship God in that ordinary way that others do, but in a more glorious, pompous way. Well, it may be that the breaker of the Second Commandment pretends more love to God than any, and yet there God says that they are those who hate Him. So you see that God does not reckon sin according to a man's intentions.

Certainly the worshippers of images do not intend to hate God, but God accounts sin according to what it is in its own nature. It is as if God should say, "If you will not worship Me according to My way of worship, if you will not be content with that but will set up a new devised worship of your own, call it what you will, I account it to be hatred of Me!"

Secondly, sin is rebellion. What man in the world would be convinced that He does anything by way of rebellion against God? Yet mark, God charges sin with rebellion even in that which they pretend they are doing, and all for God's glory. See that in the example of Saul, I Samuel 15. You find there that Saul spared Agag and the fat of the cattle, and pretended to offer sacrifice to God. Samuel came to him in the name of God and said, "Rebellion is as the sin of witchcraft."

"Why," Saul might say, "Lord, have mercy upon me! Is this such rebellion? I did it for the honor of God. I did it to sacrifice to God." And yet the prophet of God, in God's name, charged Saul with rebellion.

Now, brethren, you see that sin has, in its own nature, things men do not intend in their sinning. Therefore, while I speak of the nature of sin, some may say, "Indeed, this may be true of sinful, wicked, notorious wretches, but is this true of me?"

Yes, it may be true of the most civil man or woman in God's presence this very day. God may charge them with hatred and rebellion.

Thirdly, sin is a despising of God. Who would acknowledge in their sin that they despise God? Scarcely any in the world is so wicked as to acknowledge they despise God. And yet mark it, God charges David with this for the

commission of that one sin. See 2 Samuel 12:9. David de-
spised God.

Well, though neither hatred, nor rebellion, nor despising
God are in the intent of the man in committing sin, yet God
sees it in the nature of them. So, then, if sin is despising
God, rebellion against God, walking contrary, and enmity
against God, if all this is in sin (though in every sin the
creature does not intend this, but God sees this in the root of
every sin, in the venom of every sin), therefore, you that
have gone on in the course of sin, lay this second thing to
heart. You are those who have walked in the course of your
lives in opposition against the dreadful God of all the world,
against the infinite God. This has been the course of your
life.

Truly, brethren, that of which I have spoken is enough
to pluck down the stoutest heart, the most wicked and
wretched heart in the world.

Think of what it would be like to have a minister of God
to come and charge these people in God's name like this.
"You have gone on in all your life up until now, ever since
you were born, in a continual opposition to God Himself;
unto the infinite Lord, the eternal First Being of all the
World. Your life has been nothing but enmity to this God.
You have as directly opposed and striven against and resisted Him as every man opposed, resisted, and strove with
another man, and this you have done in the whole course of
your life." Certainly there is more in this to humble a man
than anything that can be spoken to show him the evil of sin.

When Christ would humble Saul's heart, what did He
do? He came and said, *Saul, Saul, why persecutest thou
Me?*

What was Paul's response? *Who art thou, Lord?* It is as
if he had said, "Lord, I did not think I had to deal with You.
Who are You, Lord?"

Christ said, "I am He who you are persecuting." Though
Christ said no more, it is as if He had said, "Look upon Me.

I am that great and glorious God that has you at an advantage
and can tread you under My feet."

Immediately, Saul fell down trembling and astonished
and said, *Lord, what wilt Thou have me to do?*

O that it might be so this day, that some heart might fall
down trembling and astonished. And when you get alone
and think on what has been said, say, "Lord, in the ways of
sin I have opposed, resisted, and been an enemy to You. O
Lord! I never thought it, O now Lord, forgive me."

It is time, it is time, brethren, to cease resisting God, for
He is above you and will have the victory and the glory over
all creatures. O perhaps you have been an old enemy, an old
sinner. Perhaps all your days you have walked in a course of
sin. Yes, perhaps your father has been an enemy; you his
enemy and your father God's enemy. Perhaps you have
been an old adulterer, a swearer, a wicked man opposed to
God. Perhaps you have nourished up children to be enemies
to God. You nourish and breed a company of brats to be enemies to God. You breed them in ways of sin and wickedness, and so there is a generation of enemies against God.

O brethren, that God would stir your hearts and make
you fall down before Him, that you would see yourselves
guilty of so great an enmity!

Many are ready to excuse themselves thusly. "He is nobody's enemy but his own, a good-natured man. And I am
nobody's enemy but my own."

Yes, besides your own, you are an enemy to the eternal
God, and your ways have been quite contrary to the eternal
God. And you are guilty of this and the Lord charges you
with it today. I remember when Daniel came to Belshezzar.
He came to him and thought that he had enough to humble
that proud King Belshezzar when he said to him, "That God
in whose hands the breath of your nostrils and all your ways
are, you have not glorified."

It has a great deal of power to bring down the most
proud, most stout spirit on the earth when God shall give

commission to conscience to come and charge him and say, "O you wicked wretch! Remember that the God in whose hands are all your ways and the breath of your nostrils, you have not glorified."

And suppose conscience has commission to come thus and say, "That God in whose hands the breath of your nostrils and all your ways are, you have walked contrary to all your life." I say, it would have a great deal of power in it to humble the proudest heart in the world. And this is the second particular of the operations of sin's workings. It is going cross to God.

There are two more in this branch, how sin is opposite to God. Sin wrongs God, and sin is striking at God. But because the fourth is shorter than the third, I shall begin with the fourth and make the third last. I said before, sin was continually working against God; but now I say sin is striking against God.

Chapter 10

Sin is a striking against God.

Thirdly, sin is a striking against God. I told you sin was an opposing of God and all His ways, but now I say that sin is striking at the very life of God. A man may fight with another and yet not seek to take away his life, to destroy him; but sin strikes at the very being of God. I remember an expression in Leviticus 24:16, speaking of the blasphemer that blasphemed the name of God. The words translated from the Latin are, "he did strike through the name of God." Certainly sin is a striking of God.

Indeed, God is not a body that we can strike Him with our hands; but God is a Spirit, and so the spirits of men may, by their sins, strike at God Himself. So strike at God (observe this) and you wish God would cease to be God. This is a horrible wickedness indeed, you will say.

What will you say to such a wickedness as this, that it should enter into the heart of any creature, "O that I might have my lust and, rather than I will part with my lust, I would rather that God should cease to be God than that I would leave my lust. I would rather God should be no more." This is a horrible wickedness!

But what will you say if I convince your consciences that this is in your bosoms, that you have been guilty of this sin? Yes, in some measure, every sin may justly be charged with this, that rather than the sin should not be committed, you would rather have God to cease to be.

You will say, "Lord, have mercy on us. Though you have told us some other things that are hard and strict, yet they seem to be true, but you shall never make me believe this. All the men in the world shall never make me to believe this, that I should be guilty of so much wickedness as to desire that God would not be God at all rather than to lose my lust. I hope there is not this much wickedness in me."

I beseech you, harken, and I hope to convince you that there is so much wickedness in the heart of man that they would rather God were not God at all than that they would lose their lusts. To this end, observe these two things.

1. First, do you not think it is in the nature of a sinner (so far as sin prevails in his heart) to come to this, that he could wish God were not as holy as He is? That God did not hate sin as much as He does? That He was not as just and as strict and severe against sin as He is? Is this not in every sinner's heart in the world? Certainly you deceive yourselves if you do not own this.

I say, as far as sin prevails in your hearts, could you not wish that God were not so holy as to hate those sins you love, and not so just as to be severe against sin as He is? Is not this in your hearts? It is impossible for any creature to love any thing and yet not with that another did not hate it as much as he does. Well, if this is in you, that you love such a sin, that you could wish God did not hate it as much as He does, that he was not as just, holy, and severe against sin as He is, this is to wish in your heart that God was not God at all, that the life and being of God were gone.

It is the work of the heart wishing that God was not God, for if He did not (as I told you) hate sin as much as He does, He could not be God at all. Now this is plain, and there is scarcely any one bosom that is not guilty of this; scarcely any of you who may not lay your hand upon your hearts and say, "This breast of mine is guilty of this, that when my heart is set upon any evil way, I could wish that God was not so holy as to hate this. I would rather God should like this. I hear of God's justice, but does not my heart rise against God's justice? And I could wish that God was not as just as He is!"

Certainly, there is this in your heart to some degree. Therefore, charge your hearts with this, and know that, as far as you have been guilty of this, you have struck at the

being of God. And this horrible wickedness is charged upon
you, that your hearts have been set so far upon sin that you
could wish that God had not been God rather than that you
should lose your sin. You would think it is a horrible
wickedness for any man to be so deep in lust with another
woman as to wish the death of his wife. This would be a
horrible wickedness! And yet this is in your hearts, to wish
that God had no being so that you might have your sin. This
is especially true of profane persons. They, if they could
have their wish, would desire that there was no God at all.
The Scripture says, *The fool saith in his heart that there is no
God at all.* That man or woman who could wish that there
was no God at all so that he or she might have their lust, and
to wish God were not so holy, and did not hate sin as much
as He does, so that he or she might have their lust; this is a
horrible wickedness!

O that God would make you fall down and think, "O the
horrible wickedness and abomination of my heart, that I
should be set so far upon any base lust as to wish that God
was not God rather than that I not be satisfied with my lust,"
and yet this is in sin. Aye, and this is in every sin as far as it
prevails in your heart.

2. Secondly, it must be thus because it is the nature of
contrarieties to seek the destruction of one another. It is the
nature of fire to seek the destruction of water, and so it is the
nature of anything contrary to seek the destruction of that to
which it is contrary. But you have heard that there is nothing
contrary to God but sin alone. And if sin is the only contrary
that God has, then, certainly sin seeks the destruction of
God as much as it can.

It is true, however, that a sinner can never do God harm,
nor hinder God's working or being at all. Whatever becomes
of this wretch, though he is destroyed and perishes to all
eternity, God will remain blessed forever. But this is the
nature of sin, to seek the destruction of the eternal God of
glory. O charge your hearts with this! Do not wait until God

comes at the day of judgment to charge you with this, for there are many poor sinners who went on blindfolded all their days, and never saw sin for what it was until God came upon them at their death bed and charged them with this, and then their hearts were full of horror. And so, at the day of judgment, when God comes to charge them with this, they will be amazed and will see the truth of this. Therefore, seeing God does it now before the day of judgment, do you now charge it upon your own hearts that you may be humbled. This is the third particular, sin strikes at God.

Fourthly, sin wrongs God exceedingly. It does that wrong against God that all the angels in heaven, and all the men in the world, cannot make up for. Any one sin does this. Take the least sin that you commit. I say, it does that wrong to God that all the angels in heaven and men in the world can never make up for.

If all the angels in heaven and all the men in the world should come and say, "Lord God, this poor, wretched creature has committed this sin today. O Lord, we are content to suffer ten thousand years of torment in hell to satisfy You for that wrong done to You by this man or woman's sin," God would say, "It cannot be done by all men and angels. They can never make up for this wrong."

Yet know this, as I shall show hereafter, God will have this wrong made up or you must perish eternally. Many men plead thusly, "Who can challenge me and say that I have wronged them in all my life?" They think that this is enough. Well, suppose you have lived so that you have not wronged man in either word or deed, but you have still wronged God. The living, eternal God can charge you, even though man cannot, that you have done Him that wrong that all the creatures in the world cannot make good.

It would be a sad thing if a man had done that wrong to a kingdom that all the blood in his veins and in ten thousand generations more could not make up again. He would be weary of his life. You have done that wrong to the God of

heaven that all the angels in heaven and all the men in the
world can never make up again.

Well, to conclude, though these things are hard and sad
to think about, God knows I treat in tender bowels and compassion to you, and I do not know that I ever spoke to any
people in the world with more compassion. And know,
though I speak of these things now, yet, if God gives me
liberty, I shall be as glad and willing to be large in showing
you the riches of the grace of the gospel in Christ, and
God's mercy in Christ. And I hope your hearts will be as
free and large in this as I am in speaking of this. And if I
were now treating never so much of the riches of God's
mercy in Christ, I could not do it with more bowels of compassion than I do this.

I do this that you may come to know yourselves; that
you may come to know Christ; that Christ may be precious
in your thoughts; for the special end of Christ's coming was
to take away sin, to deliver from sin. Therefore, we must
know sin and charge our souls with sin that Christ may be
precious. Therefore, if any soul shall go away and say,
"Woe to me, what have I done?" then such a soul is fit to
hear of the doctrine of grace and mercy in Christ, and that in
due time (if God gives me liberty) may be declared to such a
soul.

But now, for the present, I believe this is a necessary
point for you to know, and this is that (though some may
rise up against it) which thousands upon thousands will have
cause to bless God for to all eternity, when it is preached
home upon their consciences by the Spirit of the Lord which
convinces of the fulness of sin.

Chapter 11

How sin wrongs God.

This was that which we proposed in the third place; but we shall handle it in this fourth place that we may enlarge upon it. But how does sin wrong God? The wrong you do to God by sin is such wrong that, if all the angels in heaven and all the men in the world would be content to endure thousands of years of torments in hell to make up that wrong, it could not be done. Any one sin that you commit does such wrong to God.

How does this appear? To make it out, I shall show you four things.

1. How sin wrongs God in all His attributes.

2. How it wrongs God in His personal relations: Father, Son, and Holy Ghost.

3. How it wrongs Him in His counsels in that order he has set in the world in all its creatures.

4. How it wrongs God in the very end for which He has done all that He has done in the end of all His works, even His glory.

First, sin wrongs God in His attributes. Sin holds forth this, that there is not a sufficiency of good in God for the satisfying of a soul. This language is apparent in every sin, and it holds this forth. As far as sin appears, it holds this forth before all and speaks this language: that there is not enough good in God, that is, the Blessed, Glorious, All-Sufficient, Eternal, Unchangeable Good and Fountain of all Good. Yet sin makes this profession, that there is not enough good in God to satisfy this soul, or else why does the soul depart from Him in any sinful way and go to the creature for any good if there is enough in God Himself?

Now there is great wrong done to that blessed God, who

is goodness itself, when any creature holds forth this idea that there is not sufficient good there but that the creature must be fain to seek for it somewhere out of God. As long as we seek comforts in the creature in order to [more fully bless] God, we seek for it in God, even though it is in the creature, if we seek it in order to [more fully bless] God. But when we come to seek for any good, any comfort in any way of sin (as no sin can be committed but there is this in it), though you do not say deliberately it, you do not think there is enough comfort in God. You are saying that you must have it in this sinful way, even though you do not say it out loud. But this is evident in your walking in the way of sin.

God sees this in the nature of every sin. Would not a father think it a wrong to him, would not a master think it a wrong, to have his son or his servant go and complain to his neighbor and say that he does not have enough meat? The wrong you think your child does to you by going to beg at your neighbor's door for meat is what you do to God when you go to sin. It is as if you should say, "Notwithstanding the fact that there is so much said of the infinite goodness of God and that infinite satisfaction in Him, for my part, I do not find enough in Him. I must have it elsewhere." This is a wrong to God's all-sufficiency in this first regard.

Secondly, a sinner going on in the ways of sin wrongs God thusly. He holds forth the idea that there is more good to be had in a sinful lust than there is to be had in all the glory and excellency in the infinite blessed God. You will say, "It is wrong to hold this forth, that there is more good to be had in a base, sinful lust than in all the glory in heaven and comfort in God."

Certainly this is so, and God sees it so and, unless God is satisfied for this sin in Christ, God will charge this upon your soul another day, you who have been guilty of this great sin. In every evil way, this is there.

Thus it appears because every sinful way is a departing from God and all the good that is in God. Now this, in the account of reason, may appear to the weakest capacity, that where there stands two goods propounded, and I depart from one and choose the other, by my choosing, though I say nothing when I choose the one and when I cannot enjoy both together, I do thereby profess that I account more good to be that which I choose than that from which I depart.

Thus it is in the ways of sin. God sets forth Himself to the soul and shows His goodness and excellency, as appears in all His glorious works. God appears in His Word to those who live under the gospel and He woos the soul, "My son, give My your heart. I am willing to communicate Myself to you, all the good that is in Me to your soul. If I have any good, anything in that infinite nature of Mine to comfort your soul and make you happy, I am willing to let it out and communicate it to you."

Thus God professes to all the world, to all the children of men, to all to whom the ministry of the gospel comes, that if your soul will come in and close with Him in that way He reveals to you, He is ready to communicate that goodness in Him to your soul to make you blessed.

But now, any man or woman who is in a sinful way, though they do not say so, yet they profess by their practice, "Though there is such goodness in You, yet here is such a sinful lust that I expect more goodness in this than in Your blessed majesty."

Certainly there is this in every sin, and God sees it and will deal with a sinner according to this if he comes to answer for his sin himself. For brethren, thus it stands. we cannot enjoy God and sinful ways both together. So far as any decline to sinful ways, so far they venture the loss of God eternally, and all the good that is in God. It may be that God will have mercy upon you and bring you into Christ, and Christ may satisfy God for the wrong you did to Him. This is nothing to you, but there is this evil in you.

Here is the evil of sin. There is not one sinful way that you close with but you venture the loss of all that infinite good that is to be enjoyed in the blessed God. And is this not wrong to God?

What is God if not better than a base lust? The devil himself is better than a base lust. That is, the devil has an entity in him. He is of God, though he is a devil by sin, yet he is a being created by God. But sin has no good, and therefore sin is worse than the devil. It is that which makes the devil as evil as he is, and yet you, in your sinful way, profess you account more good to be in sin than all the good of God Himself, as if sin were better than God Himself. For you venture the loss of God that you may have your sinful way!

O sinner! Stop in your way and consider what you are doing. Know that all your life has been nothing else but a continual profession before all the world by your sinful life that you find more good in a lust than all the good in the blessed God to be enjoyed to all eternity.

Second, you wrong God in the way of your sin thusly, in His omnipresence and omniscience. I put them both together.

You do it in that you dare do that before the very face of God which God infinitely hates. Is it not a wrong to any king for those who are your inferiors to do that before your face which you hate above all the things in the world? This a sinner does. All the ways of sin are before the very face of God, and they are such things as God infinitely hates, yet you dare do that before the face of God in some sin that you dare not do before the lowest boy or girl in your house! What a wrong this is to God's omniscience and omnipresence!

Perhaps you dare not do it before a six year old child, and yet you do it before the face of the infinite, blessed God. If a man should be afraid to do a thing before any servant in his house, the cook in his kitchen, and yet, when he comes before the king he does it there, would this not be a wrong to the king's majesty, that any dare to be so bold before him?

Again, you wrong His omnipresence in that you dare to

cast that which is filthy before His presence. To cast carrion, a dead dog, before a prince is wrong. Men in sinful ways do nothing but cast vomit and filth before the presence of a most holy God. Thus you wrong God in His omnipresence and omniscience.

Thirdly, you wrong God in His way of wisdom, because in sin you profess God's ways are not ways of wisdom, but you know better to provide for yourself than in the way God has set before you. How you cast folly on the ways of God and set your shallow way and heart before God's, as if you could provide for yourself and your own good more wisely than God has set you in a way to do.

The Word of God, and that which is revealed in the light of nature, is nothing else but beams of the infinite wisdom of God for the guiding of mankind into happiness and glory. The light of nature helps somewhat, though it does not reach far enough. The light of nature is made up of several beams of God's wisdom, but the light of the Word is made up of beams of wisdom a great deal more than the beams of nature. Now any sinner that forsakes the ways of God rejects these beams of wisdom as if they were dark. It is as if he should say, "I know how better to provide by this way."

Hence, carnal men account the ways of God to be foolishness, and the usual title they give to those who walk more strictly than others is this, "What fools they are, nothing but a company of fools who keep such a stir!"

It is an ordinary thing in the world for carnal hearts to cast folly upon the ways of God. They can sit home and applaud themselves in their wisdom. And why should they be such fools as others?

It is normal for parents who are carnal to come to their children and cast folly upon them when they look after the ways of God. Some do it openly, but every sin casts folly upon God and His blessed way, and in every sin you set your wisdom above God's wisdom.

Fourthly, in sin you cast dirt upon the holiness of God.

Holiness is the brightness of God's glory, and in the ways of sin you cast dirt upon the face of holiness itself. God's nature is pure, your sin is filthy and vile and contrary to Him. Your sin does what it can to darken the brightness of the infinite holiness of God.

Fifthly, you wrong God in sin in that you set up your will above the will of God. God's will is to be the rule of all the actions and ways of the creature, but you come and set up your will above God's. There is this hideous wickedness in every sin, at least in every willful sin when it comes into the will. Then the will of man is set up above the will of the infinite and glorious God.

Do you not account yourselves wronged when you want your way and a poor boy says he will have it otherwise? Do you not account yourselves wronged when he dares set his will above yours? O consider this, you who are willful. You cannot bear to have your will crossed, to have an inferior set their will against yours. You are not able to bear it. O consider what you do when you set your will against the will of the infinite God, nay, above it in two regards.

(1) Because when God's will is one way and yours another, you would rather have your way than that God should have His.

(2) Though God only wills that which is right and good, and is content to have His will satisfied in nothing but in things good, you will have your way whether it is right or wrong, good or bad. God will only have His way in that which is righteous and good. If you were set upon your will in that which was good, it would be another matter; but you will have your way whether it is right or wrong, good or bad. Come to men in their passion and say, "This is not right," and they will say, "I will it and that carries it!" What a proud spirit this is which dares set itself up against God's will. Good or bad, right or wrong, I must have it, and this attitude is in sin.

Sixthly, sin wrongs God in the dominion, power, and

sovereignty of God, which with men is a very tender thing. Where there is sovereignty, the least wrong cannot be endured. Men are mighty tender of power and sovereignty. And if they are so, God may be much more tender of His, which is as the apple of His eye. Let me suggest one consideration to you, which should make any man's heart bleed to consider how God is wrong in the world, and that is this; you shall have poor men and servants who dare not do anything to displease those who have power over them, whether it be a master, a landlord, or a justice of the peace. O how they shake and tremble if they are displeased! And, if anything goes against their mind, they dare not do it. But there is not the basest fellow, the vilest wretch alive, the poorest worm but he dares venture to sin against God, blaspheme the name of God, though he shakes at the word of a man of power, or even a man only a little above him.

He dares to fill his mouth with oaths even in the face of God Himself. There he has courage and valor, and he scorns to be be afraid. What is it to fear an oath! He has to brave a spirit to be afraid of that. O horrible wrong to the infinite God! What, is any superiority in man so great that men dare not offend them, and yet the poorest spirit that is dares to wrong and blaspheme the name of God!

Seventhly, there is wrong done to God in His justice. Sin wrongs God in His infinite justice (1) in that it is not afraid of God. God expects that all creatures should fear Him because of His justice.

(2) You do wrong to His justice in that, by ways of sin, you do as much as in you lies, even accuse the ways of God for being unjust and unequal, to say that your ways are more just and equal than God's. Therefore, God in Scripture reasons the case with His people, *What, are not My ways equal, are not your ways unequal?* Ezekiel 18:29. Certainly there is this in sin, for if you do not reckon your ways more equal, why do you choose them?

Eighthly, you wrong God in His truth. As if all God's

threatenings against the ways of sin in which you walk were
nothing but a tale and a lie, as if all the promises God has
made in His Word of grace and mercy to poor sinners who
will come in and repent were all but a lie. Thus sin wrongs
God in His truth.

Hence it is that a sinner is in a woeful state, because he
has thus wronged God. He has, therefore, all the attributes
of God pleading against him. Yes, they are continually
against you. Therefore, look to it. Until your sins are done
away in Christ, and your souls cleansed in Him, both night
and day all the attributes of God are pleading against you to
require that the wrong you have done to them may be righted
upon you.

A man is in a sad condition if he has thousands of men
coming to plead against him, crying out for justice upon
him. But if a man has a whole kingdom, and everyone
comes and cries for justice upon this man who has wronged
this kingdom, this man is in a woeful state! But I am speaking to every sinner before God. If your sins are not done
away with in Christ, know that it is not a whole kingdom
speaking against you, but all the divine attributes. All the attributes of God are continually before the Lord crying out
against you, calling for justice against this sin. "He has
wronged me" says one, "and me" says another, "and me"
says another, and so on and so on and, therefore, you are in
an evil condition. And it is much that you should sleep quietly when all God's attributes plead against you. It is a hard
case when the devil pleads against a man and accuses him,
and pleads against him before God, but when all the attributes of God plead against him (as I might show you more
at large), how woeful is his condition.

OBJECTION. But you will say, though all the other attributes plead against me, yet I hope mercy will plead for
me.

ANSWER. But that pleads against you, too, for you
wrong His mercy also. Indeed, there is no attribute more

wronged by sinners ordinarily than is the mercy of God. Do you think the mercy of God shall plead for you? That is especially wronged. Why? Because there is no attribute abused to be an abettor to sin more than is the mercy of God. It is abused and made to harden the hearts of men and women in sin. There is no attribute so abused.

You think that the justice of God pleads against you, but the mercy of God will plead for you. Justice is not as much wronged by sin as is mercy. The justice of God is not made an abettor of sin.

Now that is the greatest wrong that can be, for God's mercy to be made a means to abet sin, and to harden men's hearts in sin. It is a great wrong to make use of any creature to be serviceable to our sin. If a man makes meat, or drink, or clothes, or any creature serviceable to his lust, it is a wrong to that creature, and to God, the Creator of that creature, that you make it serviceable to your lust. But if it is a wrong to the creature, what is it to make the mercy of God serviceable to your lusts? And who is there who does not, in some degree or other, make the mercy of God serviceable to his lusts?

How do you think the mercy of God should plead for you when you do it such infinite wrong? When you venture upon sin because God is a merciful God? Thus you wrong the attributes of God by your sin.

Chapter 12

How sin wrongs God in His personal relations.

Secondly, now for the personal relations of God; Father, Son, and Holy Ghost, how they are wronged in the way of sin.

First, God the Father. Consider these in those operations most proper and especially attributed to them. For example, that attributed to the Father is the work of creation. Now you wrong God the Father in this special operation in that you abuse the gifts God has given you, that body and soul God has made. You abuse it to God's dishonor. You abuse His creatures; you take God's own creatures and abuse them to His dishonor. Yes, your own members that God made to honor Him with, you take them and fight Him with His own weapons. You not only fight against Him, but with His own weapons; and you fight against Him with the faculties and gifts He has given you. Thus you wrong God the Father in His work of creation.

Secondly, you wrong Christ in the work of redemption. Because the least sin you commit (if ever it is pardoned) is that which stabbed Jesus Christ to the very heart. I say, your sin was that which pierced Christ and brought forth blood and water from Him. It was that which whipped Christ; it was that which put Christ to death, which shed the blood of Christ, which crucified Christ.

I may say to every sinner who expects to be saved by Christ, as Peter did in Acts 2 when he said to those Jews, *Whom you have crucified,* and the text says that then they were pricked to their hearts. It is certain, you sinner (man or woman, whoever you are) that expects to have part in the blood of Christ, your sin crucified Christ, made Christ cry out upon the cross, *My God, My God, why hast thou forsaken Me?* What do you think of your sins now? And if you are such a one as has never been affected with the blood of Christ that was shed for your sins, then you wrong the blood of Christ more, for then you trample the blood of the everlasting covenant under your feet and account it as a common thing. Most men and women are such that live under the light of the gospel that, like swine, they trample the very blood of Christ under their feet and make nothing of it. They go to the Sacrament hand over head unprepared, and so come to be guilty of the body and blood of Christ. Certainly these are not strains of wit above the truth and reality of things. There is a reality in it, that your soul is charged from God this day of wronging Christ, the Second Person of the Godhead.

Thirdly, you wrong the Spirit of God in defacing the work of sanctification (as much as in you lies), in opposing the work of God's Spirit in your soul, in resisting the motions of God's Spirit. Who is there but is guilty of resisting the motions of the Holy Ghost? Who is there but at some time or other, when they have been in the Word, have not had some stirrings of the Spirit of God within them when they have heard such and such truths of God? But they have gone to company and laughed it away, drunk and played it away, talked it away. What a wrong is this to the Holy Ghost? You wrong the Holy Ghost by defiling your body, which should be the temple of the Holy Ghost.

Chapter 13

Sin wrongs the counsels of God in setting that order in the world that He has set.

Thirdly, you wrong the counsels of God in setting that order in the world which He has set. To understand it, know this. God, in His eternal counsel, has set a due order in all His creatures. They walk in an orderly way to fetch about that end that He Himself intended. Like a workman who makes a curious piece, he puts every wheel and piece in a right frame and due order, so that, by the order his art has placed in the work, the work may attain unto the end for which he has made it. This is what God has done.

He has made all things by weight and measure in due order. God made all things good, very good, and all that one creature might be serviceable to another as one wheel to a curious watch is serviceable to another, and all to bring about the end of the workman. So God, in His eternal will and counsel, has set all things in that proportion and order that He may fetch about His own end. But sin is the thing, and the only thing that breaks the order of God in the world and strikes at God's work to break it all to pieces, as much as lies in the sinner.

Suppose that all the cunning artificers in the whole nation, no, in all the world, should join together to make a carefully-made work in a carefully-made frame. Perhaps they spend seven years making it and, at length, bring it to perfection. They make it so exact that it is to be admired because of the order in the work. But suppose again that one should come and, through ignorance, give it a blow and strike it all to pieces. What a mischievous thing this would be!

Certainly this is in sin, for there is infinite depth of counsel and wisdom of God in setting all things in frame so that one thing should be serviceable to another, and, at length, all should come to be for God's glory.

Now there is no creature that can break the order God has made but men and angels, none but those creatures that are capable of sin. And certainly, sin does not only aim to break God's order, but actually does it. Sin brings disorder and breaks the order God has set. Only God, by His might power, knows how to bring sin into subjection so that He will have His glory by it, taking occasion by it to bring things into their right order again. But were it not that God was of infinite wisdom and power, sin would break all that curious work God has made and bring it all to confusion.

Now we know that art and wisdom adds to anything. For example, suppose some carefully-made building were all beaten to pieces and rubbish. There was no less material in the rubbish than in the building. The only difference is the art of the workman. The art and the order that makes the work beautiful makes a difference in excellency from a heap of rubbish.

So it is the order God has set in the world that makes the beauty of God's work, and sin does all it can to make all the work of God to be a heap of rubbish, a mere confusion. Indeed, when there is such a carefully-made piece of work-manship broken all in pieces, if a workman had enough skill and power to instantly put it together again, his art would be exceedingly admired and wondered at. Thus it is with God.

Certainly, were it not for God's infinite wisdom and power whereby He can bring all in order again, sin would bring all to rubbish, and know that you have a hand in this who have a hand in sin.

Chapter 14

Sin wrongs God in the end for which He has made all things.

Fourthly, sin wrongs God in the end for which He has made all things, which is His glory. Now we know that of all things, a man cannot endure to be wronged in his end. When he has an end to such and such a thing, and aims to bring such and such a thing to pass, though he should be frustrated in regard of some means, this does not trouble him. But when he comes to lose his end, this troubles him exceedingly.

Thus it is with a sinner. He sets himself against God to do what lies in him that God should lose His end of all that He has ever done. And if so be that God was not almighty to overpower things, certainly sin would quite frustrate God of His end for all of His works, for which He made all things, to wit, His glory.

Now a sinner does what he can to darken the glory of God. He, in effect, stands up and says, "If I can help it, God shall have no glory in the world."

I say, you who walk on in ways of sin, you are charged with this today in the name of God. You who are guilty of this have, in effect, stood up and said, as it were, "If I can help it, God shall have no glory in the world." And yet, it was for His glory that God made all things.

Truly, brethren, it cannot but be a soul-piercing consideration for any stout, stubborn sinner in the world to have this one thought (take it with you and work it upon your hearts, and see what it will do), "Had I never been born, God would never have been so dishonored." This one thought has a mighty power to pierce the most stout-hearted sinner in the world. Oh! Is not God infinitely worthy of all glory and honor in the world? Has He not made all creatures for His glory? And if I had never been born, and never had a being, God would never have been so dishonored. He would have had more glory if I had never been. If God had made me a dog, a toad, a snake or a serpent, God would have had more glory than by making me a man.

True, God will bring about His glory, and have more glory from you another way than if you had been made a dog or a toad, but no thanks to you. You do what you can in your way of sin to hinder His glory. God's almighty power brings this to pass. But if you go on in your ways of sin, it may be said of you that, if you had been made a dog or toad, God would have had more glory in the world than He now has in making you a man. Yes, you are so far from bringing God glory that you dishonor God as much as in you lies. And this, if it lies upon your heart as it should, is a sad consideration to humble the proudest heart in the world; to think that you live, and God has no glory by you, though this is the end for which God made the world.

Think thus: suppose God should have no more glory by all the world than He does by me. To what end was the world made? Suppose a person lives in a mere atheistical way and takes no notice of the majesty and glory of God, living only to eat, drink, play, and swear. Now, if his conscience tells him that this has been his way, I say to such a one, suppose God never had any more glory from any creature than from you. To what purpose has the world been made? For God, who has worked so wonderfully and gloriously in raising such a glorious edifice and frame, did it that He might have some glory from what He has done.

No man does anything unless it is for some end, and wisdom directs every man that his end is worth his labor, so that that at which he aims shall be worth all his work. Now God has some end, therefore, in making you, and He must have some excellent end; but now, what do I think in my conscience was the end of God in making the world and me? Was it for no other end but that men and women might live and eat and drink and lie and swear and commit other such wickednesses? Was this God's end?

I put it to your conscience. Every sinful man or woman, think how you have lived. What have you done in all your life? Look back to your former life and think how you have spent it. I have gotten money, and for what? Is it only to eat and drink and the like? And you have lived in a course of nature that now your conscience tells you, "Is this the end you live in the world for?"

Did God, when from all eternity He intended to make such a creature as you are to live in such a time in such a place, and preserved you all this while from such dangers at sea or at land, aim at no other end but that you should live to do as you do? Certainly your conscience will condemn you if you have but a heart to think of it.

You were upon your sickbed, and you cried to God to spare you. Do you think God spared you and gave you your life to live for no other end but this? Do you think this was the only end?

Take heed that you do not go on in ways of crossing God for His end, for God will have His end one way or the other. Suppose a man spends a great deal to deliver another man from misery and redeem him from captivity. Then, when he has brought him home, that former captive rails at him that he did this for him and does him all the mischief that he can. By anyone's account, that man has been greatly wronged. He has done so much for another and yet that man has been wronged and abused.

Certainly, then, God is wronged when He has given you a body, delivered you from such and such dangers, and you live to no other end but to satisfy your lusts. You exceedingly wrong God. This is so clear that a man would wonder where men's consciences are that they live quietly, and that their consciences do not fly in their faces continually.

Certainly, when God shall enlighten the conscience and bring these things with power to their souls, then sinners will stand amazed and wonder that they did not see this before. These things are so clear that it is a wonder I was so blind and did not have eyes to see these things before, and yet who lays these things to heart?

And thus we have done with the first thing in the explanation, the wrong that sin does to God in His nature, working against and striking at God in His relations. Now there are, I confess, those things I most aimed at in this work behind, therefore I will wind up in a word or two in some corollaries and consequences to be drawn from hence. Only this much, when I have told you sin is a greater evil than affliction, yes, a greater evil than all the torments of hell, as I said in the beginning. Then you may see, by what I have said, how this truth results out of these consequences, because it wrongs God, and God is so infinitely good.

If any man is afflicted or perishes in hell eternally, it is but the good of a creature, and the comfort of a creature, which has been crossed. But in sin there is the crossing of the good of an infinite God, and of His glory, and there is more good in God's glory than in all the peace and comfort of all creatures in the world. And, if so, then certainly there must be more evil in sin that is cross to God's glory than in all the pains and torments that are only cross to the peace and comforts that are in the creature. I say, hence follows these corollaries.

Chapter 15

(The First Corollary) It appears by this that but few men know what they do when they sin against God.

First, from this, certainly it appears that there are but few men who know what they do in sinning against God, nor have they known all this while. It was the complaint of the prophet Jeremiah, 8:6, that no man would say, *What have I done?* Certainly men in ways of sin never say, "Oh Lord, what have I done?"

Give me that man or woman who have gone on in ways of sin, who have imagined they have wronged God so much, that they have done so much against the infinite, eternal, glorious God. They think, indeed, that they have done amiss, done what they should not do, but it is a wrong to the infinite, glorious God and, therefore, certainly it appears but few men know God or know sin. Neither do they know who that God is with whom they have to deal. Neither do they know what sin is and how it works against that God with whom they have to deal.

If men only knew God, it would be enough to keep them from sin, and there is a notable place in I John 2:4, *He that saith I know Him and keepeth not His commandments is a liar, and the truth is not in him.* If there is any man in the congregation who says he knows God and does not keep His commandments, he lies, says the Holy Ghost. What, do you know God, man or woman? Sinner, man or woman, do you know God, that infinite, glorious, eternal God with whom you have to do? And do you not keep His commandments, but go on in ways of sin? Certainly you are a liar.

It may be that many of you are apt to say, "We know God. Why do we need to have so much of God preached?"

If you say that you know God and do not keep His commandments, you are a liar. But now join these together:

knowing what a glorious God this is and how sin works against this God.

Some know somewhat of God's attributes and can discourse of Him yet, perhaps, never knew before how sin made against this God. This is what people fail in. Certainly both together has not been known by most people. I remember a speech I read of a German divine upon his sickbed. He cried out thus, "In this disease I have learned what sin is, and how great the majesty of God is." These two he put together. We cannot know what sin is unless we know how great the majesty of God is. These two together will make men understand that they never considered before what their lives are and how people go on in a resolute, inconsiderate way. They do not know what they do, nor do they know what God is. Therefore, we may pray as Christ in another case, *Father forgive them for they know not what they do.* Poor creatures, they do not know what they do. They never imagined what the greatness of the glory of God is.

Chapter 16

(The Second Corollary) The necessity of our mediator being God and man.

Secondly, hence it appears the necessity that our mediator between God and us must be God as well as man. Great is the mystery of godliness that God is manifest in the flesh. Well, but what is the reason of this mystery of godliness? How does it come to pass that there is a necessity of such a mystery of godliness for saving poor souls? That God must be manifested in the flesh? That God must be man? That all the angels in heaven and men in the world could not be a mediator between God and us, but our mediator must be truly and verily God as well as man? What is the reason for this?

That of which I have been speaking gives a full reason of it. Our sins have so wronged God, have been so much against God, that it is only God can make up the wrong. Only such a mediator as Christ, who is both God and man, can make it up.

I suppose that most of you know from your catechism that Christ is God and man; but suppose I should put this question to you. You say Christ is God and man, but give me a sound reason. Why is it necessary that Christ must be God and man? Why can man not be saved by any Savior but such a one as must be verily and truly God and man? I suppose you will give me a sound, substantial reason and say, "God appointed it, and has ordained that it should be so." But, though it is God's will and God has ordained it, there is yet another reason, and this is it. You may say (when you hear Christ was God and man, that mighty Savior) here is the reason of all that, because sin so wrongs and strikes at God, and opposes God, that, of necessity, whoever comes to be a mediator between God and us must be God as well as man. Therefore, the Scripture says of Christ that His name shall be called, *Wonderful, Counsellor, the mighty God,* Isaiah 9:6.

Christ is the mighty God, and the mighty God in the work of reconciliation, in reconciling God and us together. Then He shows Himself mighty. If all the world had undertaken to mediate between God and us, the breach between God and us is so great that all the men in the world could have done no more than a piece of paper could to put out a flame. If a man had a mighty flame coming upon him, and he put a piece of paper around him to keep it off, we know that the fire will quickly burn the paper. He must put brass or iron between him and the fire.

The wrong done to God by the sin of man is such that, if all the men in the world, all the created powers in heaven and earth, had come to stand between God and us to satisfy God for the wrong sin did to Him, it would have been like a piece of brown paper against a mighty flame.

Whoever comes to stand between God and us must be one infinite, just like the Person is infinite whom we have offended, and that is Christ the Mediator, the mighty God, God and man. O know that the Mediator by which you must be saved must be very God, and the reason is because sin has done such infinite wrong to God.

Chapter 17

(The Third Corollary) There are but few that are humbled as they should be for sin.

Thirdly, that which follows from this is that, if sin is as much against God as we have showed, we see that there are very few who are humbled for sin aright. It will follow from hence. I shall make it out from the point that, if sin is of this nature and is as much against God as you have heard, certainly there are few people in the world who are humbled for sin aright.

There are many who are troubled for sin, and many who will cry out for their sin. There are many who are struck with many fears and terrors for sin, but these are never humbled for sin aright, and it is clear from what you have heard out of this point. Why? Because the humiliation for sin that is right must be a humiliation for it as it is the greatest evil of all; and it is the greatest evil as it is against God Himself.

Now the humiliation of most in the world is not so much for this, because sin is against God, or because it opposes God, or strikes at God, and wrongs God so much. This is not the thing that usually takes the hearts of men and women in their trouble for sin. It is the fear of the wrath of God, the fear of hell, and an accusing conscience that flashes the very fire of hell in their faces; this troubles them. And well it would be for many that they were troubled for this. This is the type of trouble that God blesses many times. There is great use of it, but this is not all; no, nor the chief trouble of the soul for sin.

These fears and horrors, I say, are not the chief one. The chief of all is the humiliation of the soul for sin as it is against God. Then is the heart humbled rightly for sin when it apprehends how, by sin, the soul has been against the infinite, glorious First-Being of all things. All other humiliations in the world are not sufficient without this. For (1) it is not deep enough. There can be no humiliation deep enough unless the soul is humbled for sin because it has sinned against God.

Yes, though the heart is so burdened with fears and horrors as to be sunk down into despair, yet I do not call that a depth of humiliation. It is not from the depth of humiliation that the soul despairs, for certainly (consider what I say, brethren) there is a mistake in this, to think that those who despair are overly humbled. No, despair is for lack of humiliation, for despair and pride may stand together.

The devil is proud. You will say that someone is "as proud as Lucifer." The devils despair. They are the most despairing creatures in the world and yet the most proud creatures in the world. Therefore, despair does not come from the depths of humiliation, but rather from the lack of humiliation. Certainly the hearts of men and women in despair fly against God, many times they fly desperately and proudly against God.

In despair, therefore, the heart is not humbled enough when it only has terrors and fears unless it is humbled for sin when it sees it as being against the majesty of God as has here been opened to you. Nothing casts down the soul so low in true humiliation as the sight of sin against God. "O what have I done against God? What has my life been against that infinite, glorious, eternal First Being of all things?"

When the soul comes to see that effectually, then it falls down, and falls down low, too. Certainly, brethren, the heart is never humbled thoroughly until it comes to feel the burden of sin to be heaviest there where it is heaviest. Mark, I say, until the heart feels the burden of sin to be heaviest where it is heaviest, it is not brought low enough. But the burden of sin is heaviest as it is against God rather than as it is against the good of the creature. Though it is a wonderful burden, yes, an intolerable burden if the conscience only apprehends sin as against the good of the creature. But the apprehension of sin as against God is a great deal more. It shows the burden of sin and makes the sin to be far more weighty than the other can possibly be.

(2) The apprehensions of sin any other way but this do not sanctify the name of God as this does. When the soul is cast down before the Lord for sin as it is against Himself, as it is against His glory, as it has wronged Him, this sanctifies the name of God a great deal more than any other humiliation does. If this is not in it, in other humiliation or other trouble (I will rather call it trouble for sin than humiliation), there may appear much self-love and a forced perplexity of spirit. But now the name of God is not as sanctified as when the heart shall fall down and be humbled because God has been wronged, because His attributes have been wronged, because He has been opposed in His glory. Now this humiliation especially lifts up the name of God and sanctifies it.

(3) Take any other humiliation, and it is not such an abiding humiliation as this is. This humiliation for sin will abide more upon the spirit than any other does. Many are troubled for sin, have a great deal of horror and perplexity of spirit in some fits, in some moods, at some times; but this trouble of theirs is but for a flash and it goes away, vanishes and comes to nothing. When trouble is only from the apprehension of danger and misery in itself, I say, it usually vanishes and comes to nothing. Why? Because when anything comes to make you think that this danger may be in any degree over, or that things are not as bad as you were afraid, the trouble immediately vanishes.

In times of sickness, the soul apprehends itself in danger of perishing. "I am now going, I see myself at the brink of the pit." Now the soul is troubled for sin, but when the danger appears to be over, the trouble for sin ceases. But when the soul is troubled for sin as being against God, this trouble cannot but abide though afflictions are gone. Though afflictions are gone, yet my trouble abides!

What's the reason many people on their sickbeds are so troubled for sin and cry out, "Oh! If God ever restores me, I will never do as I have done," and yet, as soon as they are well, they fall to their sin again? Here is the reason, because only their danger troubled them. But now, let the soul be kindly humbled for sin as against God and it will be this, "Oh! I have wronged God, that infinite Deity, that infinite, glorious First Being of all things." Let such a one be in sickness or in health, whatever condition such a one is in, the trouble abides upon the spirit. Yes, brethren, it abides upon the spirit even when the soul has hope that sin shall be pardoned.

Yes, when the soul knows for certain that sin shall be pardoned, yet the humiliation will abide upon the heart of such a man or woman. There's a great mistake in the world in the matter of trouble for sin. They think repentance or mourning for sin is but one act, that if once they have been troubled for sin they need never be troubled anymore. It is a dangerous mistake, for we need to know that true sorrow for sin, true repentance, is a continual act that must abide all our lives. And it is not only at that time when we are afraid that God will not pardon our sins, when we are afraid that we shall be damned for our sins, but when we come to hope that God will, yes, when we come to know that God has pardoned our sins. Yet then it will abide, only working in another manner, and it must be so if the heart is humbled for sin thus against God. For suppose God came in and graciously told the soul, "Though you have wronged Me, yet, through the mediation of My son, I will forgive you." Will this quiet the soul so as it will no longer be troubled and sorry for sin? No.

Now the sorrow comes in another way. "And is this the God I have wronged, the gracious, merciful God I have wronged, that, notwithstanding all the wrong I have done Him, that when He had my soul at an advantage and might have justly sent me down to the nethermost hell, and will He yet pardon me though there is no goodness in me? And will He yet have such thoughts of mercy as to send His own Son to make up that wrong and satisfy for the evil I have done?"

O now the heart bleeds afresh upon this, and mourns more than it ever did before. Many can say of this that, after they have apprehended their sin to be pardoned, their souls have mourned and melted more than ever they did before in the apprehension of horror and fear of God's wrath, and all upon this, because they did not see sin to be an evil except as it brings punishment, but they saw the evil of sin as being against God. "I have wronged God, struck at the infinite, glorious First Being of all things!" And this will abide upon the heart.

Therefore, this is another manner of trouble for sin than the other, and, because this trouble for sin is so effectual and so good, therefore it is that which I have endeavored the more to open unto you how sin is against God. Therefore, when I come to the other to show how it is against ourselves, I shall be brief in that because I know that this is the principal thing.

(4) The trouble for sin, if it is apprehended as evil any other way but this (or if this is not chief), cannot be as good because there is no trouble for sin but this that will ever make a divorce between sin and the soul. All other trouble will not do it unless this comes in. And, indeed, it is to admiration to consider how strong the union between sin and the soul is, and how hard to make the divorce. Take a man or a woman who apprehends never so much the wrath of God against sin. Take a man who lies, as it were, scalding in God's wrath, his conscience burning and bringing even hell to him so much that he cries and roars in the anguish of his soul for sin. One would certainly think that this man will never have anything more to do with sin. That is, in this horror and anguish and trouble for sin, he will certainly never keep company, be drunk, be unclean, or deceive anymore.

But this may be to the admiration of men and angels to see how men and women's hearts are set upon sin, that, notwithstanding all that anguish and horror that they have for it many times, they will do it again and as greedily as ever, yes, sometimes more greedily.

Once a man has overcome the trouble of conscience for sin and fallen into it again, he will then be more greedy. He will slight conscience, then, and make nothing of it once he has outlasted his conscience. He is like an unruly horse. If he has once cast off his rider, when that rider gets on his back again, he condemns him and will quickly throw him off again. So when the stubborn, unruly lusts of a man's heart have once cast off conscience so that a man who has once been under terrors of conscience for sin falls into it again, such a man's condition is very lamentable. I do not say wholly desperate. I dare not say so, for God's thoughts are higher than ours, as high as the heaven is above the earth; but this man's condition is very lamentable.

There is this strength in sin in the soul that all the terrors in the world will not breed a divorce between sin and the soul. But when once the soul can come to say with David, "Against Thee, against Thee only have I sinned; in my sins I have gone against that God who is so infinitely above all praise and glory," this is the humiliation. If anything will make a divorce between sin and the soul, this will do it.

This is the third corollary, that therefore there are very few humbled for sin aright, because they are not thusly humbled.

Chapter 18

(The Fourth Corollary) Admire the patience of God in seeing so much sin in the world and yet bearing it.

Fourthly, if it is so that sin is so much against God and so wrongs God, hence then we have all cause to stand and admire the infinite patience of the great God who shall behold so much sin in the world from such poor wretched, vile creatures, and yet shall bear it. It is true, those who do not know how sin strikes at God and wrongs Him are not so much taken with the patience and long-suffering of God; but now, that man or woman who comes to know how sin wrongs God, and comes to understand this, cannot but stand in amazement and wonder at God's infinite patience, that such a great God, who sees Himself so struck at, fought against, opposed and wronged by such wretched creatures, yet forbears crushing them to pieces immediately.

I beseech you, brethren, consider this. Take along with you what I have said about sin, how it is against God, and then consider how all sins that are committed are done in the presence of God. He stands and looks upon them. Do but think sometime with yourself, when you are among a great concourse of people, among a company of profane, wretched people in the market, in a fair, a tavern, inn, or alehouse, how is God's name blasphemed there? What daring of the blessed God? What scorning and condemning of His Word and Sacraments and ordinances?

Now carry that thought further. Think of how God is wronged in all these, struck at in all this, and what an infinite God this is, and then think how God stands by them, hears every oath, sees every filthy act of uncleanness, sees every drunkard, and yet, when the least word of His mouth is enough to sink them into the bottomless pit, yet God is patient the first, second, and third time. Yes, a hundred times.

Perhaps you have been a blasphemer for twenty years; forty years a swearer, and when you come in company, O the wicked oaths that come from you! The hideous uncleanness and abominable wickedness! And yet God stands by and looks upon the swearer and is patient all the while.

Certainly, brethren, there is no man in all the world who is as wronged as God is, and yet man is not able to bear wrong from his equal if he has power in his hand to prevent it. "What! Shall he wrong me? I will make him know what it is to wrong me!"

You cannot bear any wrong from your fellow creature. O consider what wrong God has born from you and others. Stand and admire the infinite patience and long-suffering of the Lord! Truly, brethren, when any man's conscience comes to be enlightened and awakened, then the greatest wonder in the world to such a conscience is the patience and long-suffering of God. "Oh! That God should be so patient and long-suffering unto me all this time of my life, that I am out of hell!"

He stands and wonders that he is out of hell, and wonders at others who are not so affected with the patience of God. Certainly, brethren, that much wrong is done unto God by sin.

If any one man had all the patience of all the men and women in the world put into his heart, all the patience and meekness that ever was in all the saints since the beginning of the world all distilled into the heart of one man or woman, and suppose that this man or woman were as wronged as God is, it would be impossible that this man or woman should not break forth with revenge against those wrongs done to him or her. It would be impossible for such a one to bear all of this. As far as he can see himself able to right himself, this far he could not bear the wrongs done to him. But now God shows Himself here to be infinite in patience and long-suffering, as well as infinite in any other attribute of His.

Brethren, it will be a special part of the glory of the great day of judgment that when all the wrong that was ever done to God by sinners from the beginning of the world shall then be opened at the day of judgment. Alas, we see but little wrong done to God now. We look upon notorious wretches and think they wrong God, but we only see a little. But, at the day of judgment, then all the secret villanies and wickednesses that ever were committed in secret places since the beginning of the world, in all the places of the world, shall all appear. And then how will it appear to men and angels how God was wronged by His creature? And then the patience of God will be seen, that He should be so patient so many thousands of years, notwithstanding that there was so much wrong done to God and never revealed to man, but God sees it all this while.

This will be a great part of the glory of this day of judgment. If our hearts were enlightened, we would begin now to give God the glory of His patience which we shall see at that day.

Chapter 19

(A Fifth Corollary) Hence see a way to break your hearts for sin, and also to keep you from temptation.

A fifth corollary, hence, is this, if sin is so much against God as you have heard, then here you may find a means and way both how to break your hearts for sin, and how to keep yourselves against temptations for the time to come. I put them both together for brevity. This is the strongest way and means I can show you to break your hearts. Would you gladly break your hearts for sin? "O" some would say, "what a hard heart I have!" Many put up papers complaining of the hardness of their hearts and desire the minister and congregation to seek God to break their hearts. Well, would you gladly have broken hearts? Would you have your hearts troubled in such a manner as you may give glory to God? This is the way.

There are two ways to humble the heart for sin. There is looking upward unto God, and seeing whom it is you have sinned against, and looking downward to thine own misery, and what you have deserved by sin. Now many pour downward and look nothing but downward to sin, and what is the desert and punishment and misery; but they are not kindly broken, though they are troubled and vexed. But now, if you would have your hearts kindly broken for sin (for this is one use of direction, that we may get our hearts broken for sin), look upwards and behold Him whom you have pierced.

That is, (1) behold God in His glory, and what an infinite, blessed Being God is, and how worthy of all the honor the creature can give. Set this before your eyes in a fixed and settled way.

(2) Look upon God, in all the relations God has to you, as your Creator from whom you had your being, as He who

preserves your being every moment. Look upon Him as your Lord, infinitely above you, at whose mercy you wholly lie. View God thusly, and see Him in His glory and the relations He has to you and, thus, by beholding God in such a manner is a special way to work strongly upon the heart. For hereby I come to see, as it were, the present evil of sin. The other is only a sight of the evil of sin to come. It is like when a man or woman looks upon sin as bringing hell. That is only to look upon the evil of sin that is to come after. But we know that present things have the most affect. For example, if any good thing is coming, it does not take the heart as much as a present good.

When the soul makes the good of the promises to be present, then they affect the soul. But, if the soul looks upon them as coming, they do not affect as much. So, if the evil of sin is looked upon as bringing hell and misery, this is looked upon as coming afterwards so that it may be avoided. But, if I look upon sin as against God, then I look upon sin as a present evil upon me that flows from the very nature of sin and cannot be avoided. And this evil is even now upon me and flows as immediately from the nature of sin as light does from the sun itself. So, then, looking thus upon sin is a mighty means to break the heart.

And then for avoiding sin for the time which is coming. When temptation comes, you say it is strong and overcomes you. Now, would you avoid sin for the time to come in temptations? We read of Joseph. You know how he beat off the strength of the temptation, and when he might have done evil in secret, see what prevailed with him, *Oh how shall I do this great wickedness and sin against God?*

Notice that it was not "How shall I do this great wickedness and bring danger and misery upon me?" but "How shall I do this and sin against God?"

So if you can have your eye upon sin and remember what special things you have heard of the evil of sin, when temptations come you can say, "How shall I do this and sin against God?" O remember this, you servants who have opportunity in secret to do evil!

Joseph was a servant, and yet this kept that temptation off of him when he was a young man. That was the honor of Joseph, a young man and a servant. When the temptation came, this broke his heart, "How shall I do this and sin against God?"

So, you young ones and you servants, go away with this lesson. When any temptations to sin come, think, "Oh! I have heard in such a point and out of such a text how sin works against God, strikes at Him, and wrongs Him. How shall I do this and sin against God? It is impossible and unreasonable that it should be done upon any terms!"

Set this one argument against the most powerful temptation and it will certainly prevail. Psalm 97:10, *Ye that love the Lord, hate evil.*

What! Do you hear how sin is against God, strokes at God, that it is evil not only against you and endangers you, but strikes against God? Oh, all you who love God, hate sin! Let your hearts be set against sin because it is so much against God.

Oh, brethren, there are many people who, indeed, avoid sin, but it is on poor, low grounds, very low, and low are the grounds of many people upon which they avoid sin. There are many who will not do such and such evils. They will resist a temptation to such and such a sin. Why? Mark the ground. According as the grounds of men and women are upon which they do or avoid doing such a thing, so judge your own hearts. If their grounds are only low and mean, then their spirits are low and mean.

For example, many abstain from such and such sins. Why? "Oh, if I do this, I will be discovered and I shall be made ashamed. Therefore, I will not do it."

It is good to resist sin for any reason, but, if this is the chief cause, it is a poor, low, base thing, and argues a great deal of lowness in the heart to resist sin only for this reason.

"Oh, if I do this, I shall be discovered and incur the displeasure of my father, my master, or my dear friend. This may incur punishment, or, it may be, that I shall be put out of my family," or other similar arguments.

I say, it is true to bring in all the arguments we can to oppose sin, but when these are the chief things, when these are the only grounds that keep you from the wickedness your heart is set upon, that is not a good thing. If you could be sure that it would not be discovered, if you could be sure that your friends would not be displeased, you could find it in your heart to meddle with it, could you not?

Oh! Know that you have a base heart, you who have no other grounds to keep you from sin. If you were a Christian, and God had rightly made sin known to you, your reasons for not sinning would rise much higher. "Oh, I am to deal with God, an infinite, glorious First Being, and if it is sin alone that strikes at this infinite, glorious, eternal First Being of all things, then I will avoid sin whatever becomes of me. Yes, whatever I suffer I will not have anything to do with sin." This is an elevated spirit. This heart is likely to stand out against sin.

Alas! Those poor, low grounds upon which many resist sin...though they may stand out against sin a little, against a weak temptation, if a strong temptation comes, it will quickly break through the hedge. All those poor, low grounds and arguments, temptations will quickly break through them. But when the heart is raised to oppose sin on such grounds as those of which we have spoken, this denotes a heart truly raised by God. And such a one is likely to stand out against temptations in a greater manner than others do.

Truly, when the heart is possessed with this thought, it cannot parley and reason with the temptation as others can. Yes, this one principle of sinning against God will so fill the heart of a man or a woman that, though it does not stand reasoning and answering everything, it will even burst out, either in tears and lamenting that it should be pestered with temptation, or burst out into resolution against it.

I remember an excellent story reported in the Book of Martyrs. You may find it in the life of King Edward, that young prince who died at some fifteen years of age. In his time there were two bishops (otherwise good and who later proved to be martyrs, and yet you may see what the best of them were in those times). They came to persuade the king to yield to a toleration of the Mass, and it was for his sister; not for the whole kingdom, but merely for his own sister that they desired him to yield to a toleration of the Mass in her chapel. He stood against it though he was young, thinking it a dishonor to God. Well, they pleaded and reasoned with him, telling him it was in the best interests of state policy, and they used other grounds as well to persuade him to tolerate popery. Thus you see what kind of men these were, but I bring this forth to show that this poor king, though young, had his heart possessed with this principle, that he would not do anything against God. He could not answer the bishops who came so subtly but, instead of answering their reasons, he burst out with tears, and then they were convinced and confessed that the king had more divinity in his little finger than they had in their whole bodies.

So I apply that to you young ones. Perhaps temptations to that which is a sin against God come subtly, strengthened with this and the other arguments. But have your hearts possessed with this truth, "It is a sin against God!" Oh, when you cannot answer the particulars of temptation, burst out and weep and cry, either for your condition (that you should be pestered with that which you know to be a sin against God) and say, "I would rather lose my life, suffer anything in the world, rather than sin against God!"

If your hearts are filled with this principle, when temptation comes, you will be ready to burst out and weep before the Lord. And this will be as strong an answer to temptation as can be, and Satan will quickly avoid you if, when you find yourselves pestered with temptation, being dogged and pursued by it, you are filled with this principle, "That sin is against God." If you can get alone and fall weeping and lamenting that your hearts are even ready to break from the consideration of this principle, this will be the strongest way and means to resist temptation that can be.

Chapter 20

(A Sixth Corollary) If sin is this sinful, it should teach us not only to be troubled for our own sins, but also for the sins of others.

Sixthly, if sin is so much against God, and wrongs God so, hence it should teach all those who know God and have any love to God, to be troubled not only for their own sins, but for the sins of others, for sin wherever they see it. Oh, I see the blessed God wronged, fought against, struck at. And this should go near the heart of all those who have any love to God at all. It was thus with David in Psalm 119:136, *Rivers of water run down mine eyes because they keep not Thy laws.*

It is true, every man and woman should especially look to themselves, and their hearts should be especially troubled for their own sins, but mark that the saints who know how sin is against God, their hearts cannot but be wonderfully troubled when they see that God, so dear and precious to them, thus wronged. *Rivers of water run down mine eyes because they keep not Thy law.* Oh, when (I put it to you in the name of the Lord) in all your life did you shed one tear for the sins of those among whom you live? For the sins of your family? Notice verse 158, *I beheld the transgressors, and was grieved.* Oh, I was grieved and pained in my heart.

Yes, thus it will be with you if you love God. When in your family you behold your father and mother acting carnally, and spending all their lives without the knowledge of God, and going on in ways of sinning against God, you should get alone and mourn and lament for it. Oh, it is that, if anything in the world would do it, that would break a parent's heart. If there is a young child, a youth or maid, to whom God begins to reveal Himself, and the parent speaks, perhaps against them or God's people, and swears, and profanes God's Day, or speaks against His ordinances, though it is not becoming for you to speak to them about it, but, if you can, before them, let tears drop from your eyes, or get alone and fall down and lament before God. If you can, by lamenting, reprove their sins so that they can see you lamenting for them, this may break their hearts. Notwithstanding, if it does not break their hearts, it has this in it. Certainly, if anything in the world will stir us and break our own hearts, this should be it, to see God dishonored in the world as He is, though our hearts are never so hardened otherwise.

There is a story of a child of Cressus who was born dumb. He saw a soldier ready to strike his father and kill him, and the affection he had for his father broke the bars of his tongue and he cried out, "Oh, why will you kill the king?" He cried out thus, though he had never spoken before; but the stroke against his father made him speak.

So you, man or woman, though you have your heart dead in other things and have no mind to speak, yet when you see wretched men and women strike at God (as they do, I have shown, in their sin), if you have any heart in the world, any life in the world, when you see this stroke at God, then speak! Oh, that should burst all bars asunder!

Though you are never so meek in your family and can bear other things, yet you should show that you cannot bear sin against God. Oh, I beseech you to consider this and see how near this comes to you. How many of you know this to be true of you? If anything is done against you, from either neighbors or family, you cannot bear it. But, you can bear that which is done against God and never be troubled for it!

There are many masters who, let the servant neglect his work and displease him, cannot bear it. But let his servant be wicked and break the Sabbath, deny God His time, let his servant swear or do such wickedness, he might only say, "Why do you do this?" Or he may say, "You should not do this." Or, it may be, he will take no notice of it at all!

Certainly, that man knows neither God nor sin, or he has little relation to God who takes such little notice of that which is done against God. Yet that which is done against himself, he cannot bear.

Take this along with you. If you have any relationship to God, your hearts will be more troubled for the wrong done to God by your children and servants than when you are wronged by your servants or children. Oh, how many men and women would go and wring their hands to their neighbors and friends saying, "Oh! There has never been a man or woman as miserable as I am! My own children out of my bowels wrong me and do what they can to hurt me!" This is accounted to be a bitter lamentation; but now, why does your heart not melt and lament when you can say, "Oh, the child out of my loins, how he wrongs the blessed God of all the world! Oh, that an enemy to God should ever come out of my loins!"

I think this should move tender-hearted mothers to see that they should bring forth such as would go on in ways of enmity against God Himself. Suppose one from your own bowels should be a traitor to the Parliament, and do mischief to the state, would this not trouble you, that one from your loins should be a traitor to the Commonwealth? This would be a grievous vexation.

Now, is it not more of a vexation if you have a wicked child, one out of your bowels who strikes at God and is a traitor to the God of heaven? These do more mischief than if they destroyed a whole nation. I say, if a man should live to destroy, to undo a whole land, there would not be as much evil in it as in one sin against God.

You would say that he was a miscreant who was born to undo a whole nation, and woe to me that I should bear one who should live to do such mischief to undo a state. Now, if you bear one who strikes against God and wrongs God in ways of sin, this should trouble you as much as the other. Therefore, never be at quiet until you see some work of grace, until you see the heart of your child called in.

I remember Augustine said this of his mother, and I propound this for mother's example, he being very wicked for awhile and his mother godly, "Oh, it grieved her heart that she should have a child go on in such wickedness against God, and she prayed and wept." Augustine said of her, after God had enlightened his eyes to consider what she had done for him, "I persuade myself, my mother did as much labor and endure as much pain for my second birth as ever for my first birth."

This is his testimony of her, that, by her prayers and tears for her child's salvation, who was so wicked, he verily believed it cost her as much labor for the second birth as for the first. Upon which, when she came and complained to Ambrose about her child, he well said, "Be of good comfort, surely a son of so many prayers and tears can hardly perish." And he, indeed, did not, for he proved a worthy instrument of God's glory afterward in the church.

Now is there any mother in this congregation who can say, "I have labored as much, and it has cost me as much pain, for the second birth of my child as ever it did for the first?"

Certainly, if you knew what sin was, and how much against God it was, it would cost you a great deal of travail when you see your children wicked. It would cost you much prayer that you might not have a child who is an enemy to God, a traitor to the crown, scepter, and dignity of Jesus Christ.

Oh, brethren! Does it not pity your souls to see that infinite, blessed, holy, dreadful God to be as wronged in the world as He is? It should move us to pity to see any saint, any man or woman of an excellent, gracious spirit, abused or wronged. As Solomon said, there was a wise man in the city who was not regarded, though he delivered the city.

To see just one man of wisdom, who has any excellency in his spirit, to be wronged should trouble any ingenious heart. But then I reason thus, if it would be, and should be, such a trouble to any ingenious heart to see any one man of a gracious spirit wronged and abused, then how should it trouble any ingenious, any gracious heart in the world to see the infinite, blessed, glorious God to be wronged in the world by sin as I have already shown that He is in every sin when I revealed to you how sin is against God. Oh, that I might possess your hearts with this principle, for I know of no principle of greater power, through the strength of Christ, that will do more good to your spirits than this one.

Chapter 21

(A Seventh Corollary) If sin has done this much against God, then all who are now converted need to do much for God.

Seventhly, another is this: if sin has done so much against God and so much wronged God, hence it follows that all those who have heretofore lived in a sinful way, and God has now been pleased to enlighten them and work upon their hearts, need now do much for God. This follows clearly. You lived heretofore in a ways of sin, and what did you do in all this? Nothing but strike at God and wrong God all the time of your natural estate until God opened your eyes and awakened your conscience.

Oh, think now, "What a deal of wrong have I done to God all my life? If I have done nothing else?"

Well, now, God opens your eyes. Oh, now, you need to do much for God. If God has showed Himself and given hopes of mercy and has pardoned you, this will certainly prevail with any heart that God has turned.

"What! Have I done so much against God heretofore? Oh, I have cause to seek the honor of God upon my hands and knees all my days! What! I am such a vile wretch and yet not in hell? Yes, and do I hope to be pardoned? Oh, anything I can do for Him, though it is to creep on my hands and knees all my days in this world, to suffer all the hardships in the world, shame, loss of estate, anything in the world. No matter how great and hard the suffering is that God calls for, there is infinite reason why I should do and suffer all for God, because I have wronged God by sin."

This is how we shall turn sin to grace, as it were, and make of poison an antidote against poison, by taking advantage of sin to be more obedient unto God.

You who have been swearers and wronged God that

way, now sanctify God's name the other way. You who
have broken so many Sabbaths, now sanctify Sabbaths. It is
true, all that you can do cannot make up the wrong, but it
will show your good will, that you will do what you can and
manifest to God and all the world that if you had ten thousand times more strength than you have, you could lay it out
for God. And certainly any man or woman who has been a
great sinner, if they have been humbled and pardoned by
God, will be great saints for the time to come.

Carry this home with you, any who have been vile.
Perhaps you think you have grace because you are not as
vile as you were before; but certainly, if you have grace,
there will be holiness proportionate to your wicked life before. You will think thusly, "I have wronged God so before,
now I must live thus and so."

It will be so between man and man. If one has wronged
you, and you have pardoned him, you expect that he should
do what he can for you. It should be thus with you and God.
You have wronged God, others have sinned as well as you,
and other's sins have been furthered by you. This now
should inflame your hearts. "I have sin enough in myself,
and I have been the cause of it in thousands and thousands
of sins in others. My sin strikes at God, yes, and I have
caused others to sin and strike against God. Now, if I could
draw some from sin, I should think it the happiest thing in
the world. I would creep upon my hands and knees to draw
others from sin to God, to be in love with the ways of God,
and of religion."

Oh, you who have been forward in sin, don't think it
enough that now you are troubled for your sins and leave
them. But know that you must do for God now as much as
you have done against Him. He requires it of you. Oh, go to
your friends, acquaintances, and relatives. Labor to draw
them off of sin. Tell your kindred, friends, and acquaintances, "Oh, brother, if you only knew what sin means. Oh,
sister, if you only understood what it is to sin against God!

God has showed me in some measure. Yes, I, who went on in such and such sins, now see how I struck at God and what an evil this is. Oh, that God would enlighten your eyes. Come and hear the Word. I thought lightly of sin before, now I have gone and heard, and God has showed me what it was. Oh, that God would make you see."

Pray for them, and do not take any "nays," but go to them again and again, that so you may do something for God as you have done an abundance of wrong against God.

Chapter 22

(The Eighth Corollary) If sin does so much against God, then see why God manifests such sore displeasure against sin as He does: (1) against the angels that sinned; (2) against all Adam's posterity; (3) see it in God's giving the Law against sin; (4) see it in God's punishing sins that are counted as small; (5) see it in God's destroying all the world for sin; and (6) see His displeasure in punishing sin eternally.

Eighth, this one consequence follows. If sin is so great an evil as you have heard, if sin is so much against God and wrongs God as it does, and strikes at God, hence, then, we see the reason why God manifests such sore displeasure against sin. We find, brethren, most dreadful manifestations of God's displeasure against sin, and the ground and bottom of them is in these things which you have heard opened to you. And, indeed, if you understand and believe what has been opened to you concerning sin's opposition of God, you could not, then, wonder at God's manifestation of His displeasure against sin. There are manifold manifestations of God's displeasure against sin which, when they are spoken of and opened unto people who do not understand the dreadful evil that is in sin, they stand and wonder at it, and think that these are hard and severe things.

When ministers reveal the threatenings of God against sin, these people say, "God forbid, we hope God is more merciful than this," and all because they do not apprehend what dreadful evil there is in sin. The soul that apprehends and believes these particulars which have been opened unto you cannot but justify God when they hear the revelation and manifestation of the displeasure of God against sin. See it in these particulars. That which has been delivered is the bottom and ground of these that we shall mention, and we see the reason of all these.

First, that dreadful manifestation of God against the angels who sinned against Him. There is that revelation of the displeasure of God against the angels that might cause all our hearts to tremble before the Lord at the very thought and hearing of it. I beseech you to consider this. You who think that God is only a God of mercy, and who think that God is not as severe against sin as many ministers would make Him out to be, do but attend to what I shall say unto you, how God has manifested His displeasure against sin in the angels. Consider these five or six particulars, I will only but mention them.

1. That God should cast so many glorious creatures as the angels are forever from Himself, considering the excellency of their nature.
2. Consider their multitude.
3. Consider that the chains of darkness that they are cast into are eternal miseries.
4. Consider that this was but for one sin.
5. And consider that this was but the first sin that they ever committed.

6. Lastly, consider that God should not now enter so much into any parley with them about any terms of peace, nor ever would, nor ever will. This is the sore displeasure of God against them, that God should not look upon the angels whom He has made glorious creatures, the most excellent of all the work of His hands. There were many thousands and millions of them (for so the Scripture speaks of legions, even in one man there were legions of devils), though there were thousands and millions of such glorious creatures which God made, and these were in heaven about His throne, beholding His glory, and when these committed but one sin against Him, never but one before their fall, and the first that was ever committed, they had no example before them of God's wrath, but upon the very first sin, though it was but one that all these glorious creatures committed, they

were immediately cast down from heaven, and of angels were made devils, and reserved in chains of eternal darkness.

And so God is set against them all for that one first sin, so that He will never enter into parley with them to be reconciled upon any terms; never to consider any terms of peace, but He will cast them away from Him unto eternal torments without any recovery. This is the dreadful displeasure of God against sin.

Now brethren, of what I am speaking there is no doubting or controversy. Anyone who knows the Scriptures knows this. In some things there may be controversy, but not among Divines who have knowledge of anything about Scripture. And if you do not know this, you certainly were never acquainted with the Scriptures. Though other points are controverted, yet no one who knows God's Word questions this; this is clearly granted by all.

And the consideration of this might strike an abundance of fear and terror into the hearts of wicked and ungodly men and women, to think "Lord, how have I thought of Thee all this while, and have looked upon God as a merciful God. Though I have sinned, I have thought things would not be with me as I have heard by such and such ministers; but this day I have heard that such was the sore displeasure of the infinite God against sin that when He had to deal with those glorious angels for one sin, He cast thousands of them into eternal misery, and upon no terms will be reconciled now or ever."

You think that if you sin against God, you will cry to God for mercy and God will pardon. True, there is a difference between mankind and the angels, because we have a Mediator and they do not; but most people who speak of crying to God for mercy look upon God's nature as nothing but mercy, and not as dealing with us through a Mediator. They do not understand the necessity of a Mediator between God and them, but they think that this God who made them will hear their cry.

Now God made the angels, and they were abundantly more noble creatures than you. Now the angels who sinned but once, for that one sin are cast out forever, and God resolves that, though they should cry and shriek and shed thousands of tears for sin, He will never hear them. God's displeasure against sin is so great. Certainly, then, sin is a dreadful evil.

Suppose a prince was so angry with a great company of his nobles that he cast a great multitude of them into a dungeon. There they endured much torment, and the king made it clear that he would not even enter into parley with them so as to be reconciled, not upon any terms. Everyone would say, "Surely it is some great matter that has provoked the king!"

If they understood this prince to be very just and yet very merciful, to be sure he would do no one wrong, but was more merciful than all the men in the world and, yet, for just one offense he would cast all his nobles into a dungeon to be tormented, with no hope of reconciliation, everyone would conclude that there was much evil in that offense if it deserved this much. Would you not make such a conclusion from this?

Then learn to make such a conclusion from God's dealings with angels, seeing God is just and can do no creature wrong. Yes, God is infinitely merciful and yet casts His noble creatures, those creatures who were the highest that He ever made, for one sin with no means of reconciliation. Certainly sin has more evil in it than men are aware of, for though God has not dealt thus with mankind, yet He might. There is so much evil in sin that God might have done this with any of us and, had it not been for the mediation of His Son, we would have been irrecoverably miserable to all eternity.

Secondly consider that for one sin in our first parents, and not in our own persons, that all the children of men by nature are put in such an estate as to be children of wrath, and liable to eternal misery, and that for the sin of our parents. That will show the wonderful justice of God. *How unsearchable are His judgments and His ways past finding out!* Romans 11. Certainly God is infinitely displeased with sin, so much so that when the first parents of mankind offended God, all of their posterity, to the end of the world, are put in a damnable condition. All of them are children of wrath, and heirs of eternal perdition. Certainly, my brethren, this is a truth, and none who understand Scripture can deny it; and if you do not understand this, you have not understood a great and necessary truth of the Word of God which is necessary to eternal life. That truth is that all mankind is, by the sin of their first parents, put into a condemned state so that they are all the children of wrath by nature, as the Scripture says. We are not only in danger of God's eternal wrath through the sin that we actually commit in our own persons, but though we had never committed any actual sin in our own persons, yet the sin of our first parents is enough to make us children of wrath and be in eternal ruin.

Certainly there is a great deal of evil in sin, much more than the world thinks, when it shall so provoke God that He shall have such displeasure so as to put all mankind in the state of children of wrath for the sin of our first parents. This is a second manifestation of God's displeasure against sin.

A third manifestation of God's displeasure against sin is in that fiery law, as Scripture calls it, that God has given for forbidding and threatening of sin. Consider the dreadful manner of God's giving the Law, that it was with fire, lightning, thunderings, earthquakes and smoke, so that, as Scripture says, Moses shook and trembled at the very sight of the dreadfulness of the Law when it was first given. That was only to set forth this much to us, that if the law that God gave is broken, then God will be very dreadful to those who break it. Therefore, He gave it at first in such a dreadful manner. It may be that many bold, presumptuous sinners think it is nothing to break the Law of the infinite, eternal God; but in that God gives the Law in such a dreadful manner as you may read in Exodus 19, how dreadfully God gave the Law, He thereby declares to all the world how dreadful sinners are to expect Him to be if they break the Law. But especially consider that dreadful curse which is annexed to the Law, *Cursed is everyone that abides not in every thing that is written in the Law;* to do that which the Law of God pronounces to be done: a curse to everyone who does anything, at any time, who shall break it. That there should be such a dreadful curse annexed manifests the sore displeasure of God against sin.

A fourth manifestation of the sore displeasure of God against sin (all this but to show you further how sin is a greater evil than affliction) is seen in that we find in God's Word that God has so severely punished some sins that appear to us to be very small, little sins. And yet God has been exceedingly severe against those sins which appear, to us, to be exceedingly small. To instance in three.

1. In I Samuel 6:19, you have the example of the men of Beth-shemesh. When the ark came to them, they only looked into the ark out of curiosity. We know of no other end but curiosity. Now because the ark was a holy thing, and none but the priests of God were to meddle with it, God immediately, in an instant, slew 50,370 of them. Upon this, the text says, these men, beheld the severity of God for this offence, all said, *Oh! Who shall stand before the holy God!* If God is so holy that He cannot bear so small a sin as this appeared to be, that but for looking into the ark so many thousand were slain immediately, who can stand before the holy Lord!

Many of you have slight thoughts of the Lord and His holiness, and think you may be bold and presumptuous. You venture upon greater offences than this was, but these men, upon the venturing of this one thing, were slain, and more than 50,000 others as well. This is the displeasure of God against sin, though the sin might be very small to our way of thinking.

2. Again, you have a second example in Uzzah, who did but touch the ark out of a good intention, as it was ready to fall; yet that not being according to the Law, God struck him with death immediately. It cost him his life; he was struck with sudden death. We are terrified when we see one fall down suddenly. Now upon that offence, though he meant well and had good intentions, yet God broke in upon him with His wrath and struck him dead immediately.

Consider this, you who think you mean well and have good intentions, yet are not acting in accordance with God's Law. The least breach of the Law, though we mean well, provokes the wrath of God, and God lets out His wrath when He pleases.

3. A third example comes from the account of the poor man, of whom we read that he did but gather sticks upon the Lord's Day, and by the command of God from heaven, this man must be stoned to death, Numbers 15:32-36. You would think that these things are little matters. Alas, the poor man might need them! How many of you venture upon other things on the Lord's Day, profaning it? And yet God speaks from heaven and gives command to have the man stoned to death.

Now brethren, though it is true that God does not always come upon men for such little sins, it may be to make known His patience and long-suffering. Perhaps the Lord lets others go on for such a long time in greater sins; but yet God, by a few such examples, declares to all the world what the evil of the least sin is and how His displeasure is out against the least sin. If He does forbear, it is to be attributed to His patience and long-suffering, but not to the littleness of the sin or the littleness of the evil that is in that sin. This is a fourth.

A fifth thing wherein God manifests His displeasure against sin is in those dreadful and hideous judgments that the Lord executes abroad in the world. We have stories of it in the Scripture and down through the ages. For example,

God drowned a whole world except 8 persons; all the rest of the world was swept away and drowned. God commanded fire and brimstone to come down from heaven to burn and consume entire cities, Sodom, Gomorrah, and the adjoining cities; yes, and all the men, women, and children except for Lot and those few people with him.

And so the fire came down upon those captains and their fifties, 2 Kings 1, and the earth swallowed up Corah, Dathan, and Abiram. There is no age that has not had some one or another dreadful example of God's judgments against sin. The wrath of God is revealed from heaven against all unrighteousness.

Now, brethren, though some people have escaped, and these manifestations of God's judgments are not so general and ordinary, yet when they are, but now and then, God manifests what His displeasure is against sin, and what might be to all that sin against Him.

A sixth manifestation of God's displeasure against sin is in those eternal torments and miseries in hell that the Scripture speaks of: the worm that never dies and the fire that never goes out. When you hear ministers speak of fire that is never quenched, of poor people lying in fire burning for thousands upon thousands of years in eternal flames scalding under the wrath of God, you stand aghast at the dreadfulness of these expressions. Certainly these are only to reveal the displeasure of God against sin, because there is no finite time sufficient to manifest fully the displeasure of God against sin. Therefore, those who perish must perish eternally.

Chapter 23

(A seventh discovery of God's displeasure against sin opened from the sufferings of Christ.) First, see the several expressions of Scripture: (1) He was sorrowful to death; (2) He began to be amazed; (3) He began to be in agony. Secondly, see the effects of Christ's being in agony: (1) He fell grovelling on the ground; (2) He sweat drops of blood; (3) He cried to God, "If it be possible, let this cup pass from Me." Thirdly, there are eight considerations of Christ's sufferings.

Seventh, and this is greater than all that has been said, put all the former six things together: His dealings with the angels, His dealings with mankind, the dreadful giving of the law, His dreadful judgments for small sins, the examples of His wrath abroad in the world, and the eternal torments of hell, and yet I say all these six things do not manifest the displeasure of God against sin as this one thing of which I shall now tell you. And if there is anything in the world that should make us see the evil of sin, it should be this. If anything should make our hearts to shake and tremble at the evil of that sin of which it is so guilty, then this that now I speak of should do it; and it is this: the dealings of God the Father with His Son when Jesus Christ, who was the Second Person of the Trinity, God blessed forever, came to be our Mediator, and to have our sins imputed unto Him, and according to the Scriptural phrase, *to be made sin.*

Do but notice how God deals with Him, how God manifests Himself to His own Son when that Son took man's sin upon Himself to answer for it. Do but then consider how God the Father dealt with Him. The Scripture says that He did not spare His own Son, but let out the vials of His wrath upon Him in a most dreadful manner.

If we do but consider first that Christ, God blessed

forever, should come and be in the form of a servant, should be a man of sorrows, as the Scripture speaks, that in the whole course of His life should live a contemptible life before men and undergo grievous sufferings. But, because I must hasten, do but look upon Christ in His agony and upon the cross at His death, and there you will see the dreadful displeasure of God against sin, and in nothing more than that.

True, there is the bright glass of the Law, wherein we may see the evil of sin; but there is the red glass of the sufferings of Christ, and in that we may see more of the evil of sin that if God should let us down to hell and there let us see all the tortures and torments of the damned in hell. If you could see those people and how they lie sweltering under God's wrath there, it would not be as much as beholding sin through the red glass of the sufferings of Jesus Christ and His agony. And give me leave a little to show you how God let Himself out against His Son when He came into the garden, and a little before when He was to die and suffer upon the cross.

And for this, consider these two things:

First, the several expressions the Holy Ghost uses in the several evangelists for the setting out of those dreadful things Christ suffered as a fruit of God's displeasure upon Him.

(1) One evangelist said that Christ was very sorrowful even to the death, Matthew 26:38. He began to be (the word in the original signifies) compassed about with sorrows. He began to have sorrows round about Him and was, as it were, beset and besieged with grief; and it was to the very death, *usque ad mortem,* sorrowful to the very death. What was it for? Upon the apprehension of the wrath of His Father which He was to endure for the sin of man. He was sorrowful to the death in the apprehension of it. It may be that you, upon the sight of sin, content yourselves with some slight little sorrow. It may be that you, when you are

told of sin, cry, "Lord, have mercy on me! I am sorry for it!" and so pass it away. But Christ, when God came to deal with Him, made His soul to be compassed about with sorrows, sorrowful to the death for our sins.

(2) Another evangelist tells us that He began to be amazed, Mark 14:33. That is, when Christ came to drink the cup of the wrath of His Father, due for our sins, He stood amazed at the sight of the dreadfulness of that cup of which He was to drink because He knew what God's wrath was. He understood what it was before He drank of it, and this made Him stand amazed at it.

Many sinners hear God's wrath, and this makes them fear, but they are not amazed at it. They can pass it off and not be affected by it afterwards because they do not understand it. They do not know what it is for a creature to stand before the wrath of an infinite Deity. *Who knows the power of Thy wrath?* says the Scripture. Therefore, they are not amazed. But Christ, who knew full well what the wrath of God was and saw clearly to the bottom of it, understood to the dregs what the cup was, and He stood amazed at the sight of it when He was to drink it.

(3) Another evangelist has this expression, from Luke 22:44, *Christ began to be in an agony.* Now the word "agony" signifies a strife, a combat. It is taken from the word that signifies a combat in battle. Christ was in agony, in a combat. Combat with what? with whom? With the wrath of God which He saw coming out upon Him to sink Him. He saw the curse of the Law come out upon Him. He saw the infinite justice of God, the justice of the infinite Deity coming out upon Him. And He was in agony, in combat with the infinite justice and wrath of God, and the dreadful curse of the Law, and so Christ came to be in agony. These are the three expressions of the evangelists.

Second, consider the effects of Christ's being in agony and apprehending the wrath of His Father for sin.

(1) One effect was this, you shall find it in the story of

the gospel, *He fell grovelling upon the ground for the apprehension of God's wrath and displeasure upon Him for sin, which He was to suffer*. He fell down grovelling upon the ground. He, who upholds the heavens and the earth by His power, now falls grovelling upon the earth, having the weight and burden of man's sin upon him. He falls upon His face; He falls to the ground. Certainly, brethren, Christ had that weight and burden upon Him that would have pressed all the angels in heaven and all the men in the world down to the bottomless gulf of despair.

If all the strength of all the men who ever lived since the beginning of the world, and all the angels in heaven, were put into one, and he had only that weight upon him that Christ had, it would have made him sink down into eternal despair; for had not Christ been God as well as man, He could never have borne it, but would have sunk down eternally. This burden and weight which was upon Christ was so great that He sank down to the ground.

(2) A second effect of Christ's bearing the wrath of God for sin is this, He sweat great drops of blood. The word in the original means "clodders" of blood, blood thickened into clods. Never was there such a sweat! It was in the winter's night, a cold night, abroad upon the ground in a cold winter's night, and He had nothing else upon Him to make Him sweat but the burden of sin and the weight of the wrath of God upon Him. He, being under that burden, sweat, and sweat such a sweat as made the very blood break through His very veins and run to clodders, and so run down upon the ground as clodders of blood. And all of this was but upon the apprehension of the wrath of God, His Father, against Him for our sin.

Now you know that when porters are under great burdens, they will sometimes sweat. But never did any sweat like Christ sweat here, being under the weight of man's sin. He sweat so that clodders of blood fell from Him. One would think fear should rather draw in the blood. Fear naturally draws in blood to the heart. That is why men and women, when they are scared and afraid, are so pale in their countenance. Fear causes paleness in the outward parts because the blood returns to the heart when they are afraid; but such was the amazement of Christ upon the apprehension of the wrath of His Father for sin that it sent out blood in clodders trickling down His sides.

(3) And then a third expression which shows the effect of God's wrath on Christ is the prayer of Christ. Christ does, as it were, shrink under this weight and burden of sin and cries to God, *If it be possible, let this cup pass from Me.* When we cry vehemently we say, "If it be possible, let it be thus or thus," but Christ cries out so three times. We may apprehend Christ taking, as it were, the cup of the wrath of His Father in His hand because He knew it was the end for which He came into the world. He must drink of it for satisfaction of man's sin, and being willing to save mankind. He knew He could not be saved, but He must drink the cup. He took it in His hand and was ready to drink it but, beholding the hideousness and dreadfulness of the cup and, knowing what was in it, He put it away and cried, *Father, if it be possible, let this cup pass from Me.* But then He saw that, if He did not drink it, all the children of men must be eternally damned.

Such was our misery. If Christ had not drunk this cup, we would all have eternally perished. Therefore, Christ put it to His mouth again, as it were, the second time; but yet, seeing what dreadfulness was in this cup, He took it away and cried again, *If it be possible, let this cup pass from Me.* But yet, having love to mankind, being loath to see so many thousands of poor creatures perish eternally, He put it to His mouth a third time. Yet, seeing the dreadfulness of it, He put it away again and said, *If it be possible, let it pass from Me.*

This might make a man tremble to think that he will drink of the wrath of God, as Job said in Job 21. Thus it was with Christ, and all this while He did not drink it. But afterwards, when He came to the cross, He drank the cup of God's wrath and there cried out with another cry more bitter than all the other, *My God, My God, why hast Thou forsaken Me?* He apprehended Himself as forsaken. Oh, the wrath of the Almighty that was then upon the Spirit of Jesus Christ at that time! What! For the Son of God, blessed for evermore, to cry out thus, *My God, My God, why hast Thou forsaken Me?*

Oh, you heavens! How could you behold such a spectacle as this was? How was the earth able to bear it? Truly, neither heaven nor earth was able, for the Scripture says that the sun withdrew its light and was darkened so many hours. It was from twelve to three that the sun withdrew its light and did not shine, but there was dismal darkness in the world for it was unable to behold such a spectacle as this was. And the earth shook and trembled, and the graves opened and the rocks split in two, the very stones themselves were affected with such a work as this, and the vale of the Temple rent asunder. These things were done upon Christ's bearing of the wrath of His Father for sin. Here you have the first fruits of God's displeasure for sin, and in this you may see, surely, that sin must be a vile thing since it causes God the Father to deal thus with His Son when He had man's sin upon Him.

Thirdly, consider yet further, for there is much in it, and if this does not show the evil of sin and cause you to fear and tremble, you who are guilty of sin and whose consciences tell you so, if your hearts do not tremble, certainly your hearts are very hard and your minds are blinded, and you have but little hope of ever having your part in these sufferings of Christ. What, shall Christ suffer such sufferings, and will you go away and have slight thoughts of sin? Shall sin be so great a burden to Christ, and will you be so merry under it? Certainly you see it is more than you were aware of. It is certainly more than just for you to say, "I trust in Jesus Christ and hope to be saved by Jesus Christ."

You see how Christ felt sin. The Scripture says that He was made a curse. Were it not for the fact that we heard that from the Holy Ghost, no man nor angel would dare to say that Christ should be made a curse; in the abstract, not cursed, but made a curse. What! He who was God and man, by the sin of man was made a curse! Oh, the displeasure of God against sin! But yet to give it to you a little more fully, see these aggravations and you will say, "Certainly the displeasure of God was great against His Son."

1. First, all that Christ suffered He knew perfectly long before He suffered, and yet it was so dreadful unto Him. Oh brethren! There are many men and women who understand nothing at all of the wrath of God against sin. These think there is no great matter in it. When all the men and women in the world come to suffer this wrath, it will be dreadful to them because it will come upon them unexpectedly. They went on merrily and cheerfully in the ways of sin, and as for the wrath of God? They never thought of it. Now, then, when the wrath of God comes on them, it will be more dangerous and intolerable.

This is the reason why many people, when their consciences are awakened on their sick beds, despair, cry, and roar under God's wrath, and rage with despair. Why? Because they never, in their lives, came to understand the danger of sin and God's wrath for sin; and because it now comes suddenly upon them, they are unable to bear it.

But it was not so with Christ. Christ understood this long before. He knew what it would be before He took our nature, and He knew what it would be when He came in human nature to undertake it. Those men and women that do not know what tempests and storms are find it grievous when they come to know them suddenly. When they are in the midst of a storm or tempest at sea, oh, they are grievous! But mariners who know beforehand what they are likely to meet with do not find it grievous. But to Christ, though He knew it beforehand, how dreadful it was when it came!

2. Consider this, Christ had no sin in Himself to weaken His strength or take away His strength, and this made the burden greater. He had no sin but by imputation. But now, when the wrath of God comes upon us, we having so much sin in our natures, this weakens us, and will, therefore, make the burden of divine wrath so much more intolerable to us.

This is as it is with a sound man. If a great weight is laid upon a man who is healthy and strong, he does not feel the burden of it. But if you lay the same weight upon a man who is very sick and weak through some distemper of the body, it is grievous to him. So it is here. If the weight of sin was so grievous to Christ, who had no distemper of weakness, how grievous will it be to a sinner who is distempered and weakened so with sin?

If the shoulders of a porter were sore, and all the skin was off, and a boil was on his shoulder, how grievous would the burden be then?

So it is with us. When God comes to lay the burden of His wrath upon us, we are but weak creatures at best, but, through the distemper of sin in our hearts, we are more weak and unable to bear, because we are sore and have boils of sin. This makes God's wrath much more dreadful, but it was not so with Christ.

3. Christ had absolute, perfect patience. There was not the least bit of impatience in Christ. Therefore, if Christ, who had perfect patience, and yet cried out and sweated and was thus sorrowful under it, surely there was some fearful burden in this. Some men and women will lie and roar out under some pains and, it may be, that pain is great; but, if they had perfect patience, they would not make such dolorous cries. It is through the weakness of their patience that they make such cries, and manifest such a sense of their affliction. But Christ did not cry out in this way due to any impatience.

4. Consider this, Christ had the strength of an infinite

Deity to support Him. He had the strength of God. He was God and man. He had the strength of the Divine nature to support the human nature, which no creature can have as Christ had; for there was a hypostatic union between the Divine and human nature at that time and, yet, notwithstanding the hypostatic union of both natures, Christ expressed Himself thus, and was sensible of the wrath upon Him for the sin of man.

5. Consider this, Christ was the Captain of all who were to suffer hereafter and, therefore, if He had had no more upon Him than that which the human nature could have borne, He would have manifested (one would think) an abundance of resolution and magnanimity and not cried out so, had there not been the suffering of the wrath of the Deity and the curse of the law in it. Certainly He, who was the Captain of all who were to suffer, would have manifested it to be a light burden He met with, for there are many martyrs who have suffered outwardly as greatly as Christ ever did, as far as regards outward torture, and borne those sufferings with joy. Therefore, see that the martyrs, many of them suffering greater tortures to their bodies, have borne their sufferings with joy; no sorrow, no crying out, *My God, My God, why hast Thou forsaken Me?* No crying out, *If it be possible, let this cup pass from Me,* but an enduring of it all with a great deal of joy. Now how does it come to pass that the martyrs bore their torture with such joy, and Christ, the Captain of them all falls to the earth and cries out so? Certainly, there was more in Christ's sufferings than in all the sufferings in the world, more of the displeasure of God.

6. Consider this, that it was through the strength of Christ that all who ever suffered were enabled to suffer what they underwent. Now if Christ had that strength, that through Him all the martyrs were able to suffer what they did, certainly Christ had an abundance of strength in Himself to suffer when He came to it. How does it come to pass, then, that the strength whereby they were enabled to suffer

being from Christ, they did not manifest that horror and trouble that Christ Himself did? Certainly, therefore, Christ suffered other manner of things than they did.

7. Consider this, Christ knew what an infinite good His sufferings would do. He knew that, by suffering, He would save so many thousands, reconcile God and man, glorify His Father, and do the greatest work for God and His Father that ever was. He knew that, by His sufferings, there should be that work done that should be a matter of eternal praise, hallelujahs of the saints and angels eternally in the heavens. And yet, though Christ knew and understood what good should come from His sufferings, see how sensible He was of the greatness of them. One would have thought the good He saw that would come would have greatly lightened His sufferings, and so certainly it did.

8. Consider this, Christ knew that His sufferings were to continue but a little while. Though they were extreme, yet they would last but a few hours and then He would be glorified. And yet, though He understood that His sufferings were to last but a few hours and then He would come to glory, yet, for all this, they were this hideous and dreadful to Him. Oh Lord, then, how hideous shall the sufferings of the damned be to them! Every damned soul who goes to hell knows certainly how he must lie to all eternity. After thousands of thousands, and ten thousand millions of years, after so many thousands of years as there are drops in those mighty waters over which you sail, yet the time is no more expired than the very first moment they entered into those miserable torments.

Consider this, you who make you way in the great sea. Consider how many drops there might be in the sea, as big as the bill of a bird could carry. And suppose that this bird were to carry away one drop every thousand years; yet this bird will sooner empty that mighty sea than the torments of the damned should be at an end. Oh, how dreadful will it be to them!

Christ's tortures, which He endured but a little while made Him cry out so. Oh, brethren, put all these together and then know the evil of sin. Oh, that we could apprehend it now before we come to feel it. For this is the end for which I speak of these things and present them before you, that you may now know them, and never come to feel experimentally what they are.

Blessed be those that, in hearing, tremble and believe, and do not come to know by experience that dreadful evil in them. If God should, in His infinite wisdom, have studied (as one may speak) from all eternity to have found out a way to have presented sin to be dreadful to the children of men, we could not conceive how infinite wisdom should, from all eternity, have found out an argument to manifest the evil of sin more as in the sufferings of Jesus Christ. So that, in them, God says, as it were, "Well, I see wretched men and women will not believe the evil of sin. Well, among other arguments, I have one that, if possible, shall convince all wicked, hard hearts in the world to make them see what sin is, and that is in My Son, in My dealings with My Son, that wrath of Mine which I shall lay upon My Son. This shall make it appear to them what sin is."

Now if God has done this on purpose to render sin odious and abominable, a most dreadful evil, oh, woe, then, to that soul which, after all this, shall go on in ways of sin pleasingly and delightfully, and easily entertains sin.

THE SECOND PART OF THIS TREATISE

Sin is most opposite to man's good, and far more opposite to the good of man than affliction.

It may be by all that has been said of sin's being against God that the hearts of some (at least) may not be so much as turned. Therefore, now, we come to show how sin is against the good of man; not only against God, but against ourselves. Certainly, brethren, sin makes the sinner to be in an evil case. From that which has been said, we may conclude that, of a truth, a sinner, a wicked man or woman, must be in an evil case. This is the subject which I am to open: what an evil case sin brings us into, and thereby we shall see that sin is a greater evil than affliction. Though we have spent divers exercises upon this, yet it is as various as if we had several texts.

Now this is the argument to demonstrate, that a sinner does not only dishonor and strike at God, but sin is against his own soul, against his own life, against his own peace and comfort, against his own happiness. He undoes himself by sin. This is that which I am now to declare to you; and, for the opening of this, divers particulars offer themselves to be handled.

Chapter 24

First, sin makes a man evil, but no affliction can make him so. (1) Those who are in affliction are not the worse; but (2) those who are wicked are vile persons, though they are the greatest princes.

First, more generally thus, sin is against man more than any affliction for, first, sin makes a man to be evil. I beseech you to observe it, a man or woman is not a worse man or woman because they are afflicted, no worse than they were before, but sin makes the man or woman to be worse, and there is a great deal in this to show the evil of sin to be beyond the evil of affliction.

Take a man who is never so sorely afflicted. Suppose the affliction is as grievous as the afflictions of Job. Suppose a man scraping off his sores upon the dunghill as Job did. This affliction does not make him a worse man than he was before, only it may occasion sin, sometimes, and so make him worse. But take Job, considered in his afflictions only. He was not a worse man than when he was in great prosperity, when the candle of the Lord shone upon him. Only it occasioned some sin in Job, otherwise he would not have been the worse. And, in conclusion, he was not the worse, for as it occasioned some sin, so it stirred up a great deal of grace, as the Apostle says in 1 Corinthians 8:8-9. *For neither if we eat, are we the better; neither if we eat not, are we the worse.* So I may say of all outward things in the world. If a man has riches, it does not make him better. If he is in poverty, it does not make him the worse. If he has honor, he is not better; if he is in disgrace, he is not worse. His condition may be worse, but he himself is not at all the worse.

Therefore, you shall observe it, when the Scriptures speak of God's people being afflicted, yet it speaks of them as most honorable, and in an excellent condition, notwithstanding their afflictions. But when it speaks of some in great prosperity but wicked, it speaks of them as most contemptible and vile. I will give you an example of each, the most remarkable in all the Book of God.

1. Those that are most sorely afflicted, yet to show that they are not the worse for their afflictions. See Hebrews 11:26-28. I suppose you who are acquainted with the Word of God know the story. The Christians went up and down in the world in sheepskins and goatskins, *persecuted and afflicted, and dwelling in the caves of the earth; they had trials*

*of cruel mockings and scourgings; yea, moreover, of bands
and imprisonment: they were stoned, they were sawn asunder, were tempted, were slain with the sword; they wan-
dered about in sheepskins and goatskins, being destitute,
afflicted, tormented.*

What more can be said of affliction? If affliction can
make a man miserable, surely these people must be miserable. They were mocked and flouted; they were made the
off-scouring of the world, driven from house and home.
They went in sheepskins and goatskins.

Many think that they are miserable if they cannot go fine
and brave. These went in sheepskins and goatskins; these
were sawn asunder, miserably tormented and afflicted. It
may be that some will say, "Certainly these were in a miserable condition."

Now mark the next words of the Holy Ghost, *of whom
the world was not worthy*. They were under such sore afflictions, and yet they were such excellent persons that the
world was not worthy of them in their worst condition. They
were so excellent that the world was not worthy of them.
They were thought to be such as were not worthy to live in
the world. That is how the evil world thought of them; but
mark the difference between the judgment of God and the
judgment of the world. The world thinks they are so vile that
they are not worthy to live in the world, and God thinks they
are so excellent that the world is not worthy that they should
live amongst them.

I remember Chrysostom said this about our passage,
"They were so excellent that all the men in the world was not
worth one of them." Put all the other men in the world together, and they are not worth as much as a few of these afflicted, persecuted, tormented Christians. It is as if he should
say, "Do you see a company of poor creatures walking in
sheepskins and goatskins, living in caves and the dens of the
earth? Look upon them and take all the men of the world,
kings, princes, monarchs, rich men, mighty captains of the

world, all the other men, and put them all together. All of them together are not worth these few poor creatures who go up and down in sheepskins and goatskins.

Thus afflictions do not make a man one whit the worse. Man is exceedingly glorious in God's eyes, notwithstanding afflictions.

2. But now, secondly, come to sin; let there be sin. Although a man has never so much outward prosperity and glory in the world, he is a most vile abominable creature when sinful. See one famous example for this parallel in the prophesy of Daniel 11:2. *And there shall stand up a vile person.* Now who is this vile person of whom the Holy Ghost speaks? It is, according to interpreters, Antiochus Epiphanus, the great King of Assyria, and his very name signifies "illustrious." So the word Epiphanus signifies illustrious, famous, glorious; so that he has these two titles, (1) the great king of Assyria, and (2) the great King, famous, illustrious, glorious.

Josephus, writing of this man, told this story. When the Samaritans saw how Antiochus Epiphanus persecuted the Jews, they sought his favor and would not own themselves as Jews. They wrote to Antiochus and called him "the mighty God." This was the title they gave him in their letter, "the mighty God." Well, now, see here is one who has outward glory enough; the great King of Assyria, Antiochus, famous, illustrious, who has the title of "the mighty God." But now, because he is a wicked man, the Scripture says that a vile person shall arise. Let him be never so glorious a king, let him be called "the mighty God," yet he is still a vile person.

I beseech you, in your thoughts, to put these two Scriptures together. These who go up and down in sheepskins and goatskins are such that the world is not worthy of them; and Antiochus, the most glorious king in the world, in God's judgment, is a vile person. Thus you see that afflictions do not make a man worse, but under them he may be as good as he was before; and prosperity does not make a man better, but he may be as vile in prosperity as he was before.

Therefore, though a man may have his estate increase and his estate bettered, still he is not the better for it. We speak of so and so saying, "Oh, he is the best man in the parish, or the best man in town." What do you mean by that? "Oh, he has so much by the year, and so great a stock at sea. He is owner of ships and has part of so many ships, and he is a great man, worth so much."

True, his estate is worth something, but he (if he is a wicked man) is worth nothing. In the meantime we hear, "Oh, he is worth so much!"

Yes, but you are deceived. His money or his land is worth so much, or his ships are worth so much, but he is worth nothing himself. Therefore, the Scripture speaks of the wicked, in Proverbs 10:20, *The heart of the wicked is little worth.* Now the heart of a man is his soul, and that is the man. The mind of a man is the man; the spirit is the man. Now the heart of the wicked is little worth. His house and his land may be worth something, but the heart of the wicked, he himself, is worth nothing.

So sin makes a man an evil man, but afflictions do not make him evil. Therefore, sin is more against the good of man than afflictions can possibly be. This is the first.

Chapter 25

Secondly, sin is more opposite to the good of man than afflictions because it is most opposite to the image of God in man. Three particulars instanced and a question resolved.

This will come more close, and particularly to demonstrate it more plainly to you how that sin is more against the good of man than afflictions and trouble can ever be because sin is most against the image of God in man. It defaces that image, therefore it must be a greater evil than afflictions. Brethren, of all the creatures in the world that God made, angels and men were the only creatures that God stamped His image upon; for, as it is with princes, they do not stamp their images upon brass, or copper, or leather, upon base metals, but upon pure metals, gold or silver. And it is a sign that the state grows low when the King's image must be stamped upon lower metals. So it is here.

God would have His image stamped upon some of His creatures. Now, He would not take the lowest, meanest creatures, but God takes the most excellent creatures, gold and silver. The angels I may compare to gold, and the children of men to silver; and God makes the same image upon man that is upon angels. The same image of God that makes the angels glorious creatures makes mankind to be glorious, too, in the same image. Our natures are capable of the very same image of God that the angels themselves have, and this is the excellency of mankind. Now it is needful to show the excellency of God's image in man so that I may show you the evil of sin, in that it defaces such an excellency of man and, therefore, it is more against the good of man than any affliction can be.

1. Now the image of God in man is a glorious excellency for it is that whereby men come to resemble God in His highest excellency. It is not a likeness unto God in some

inferior thing; for, though it is true, all in God is equally glorious, yet, to our apprehensions, some things appear more glorious than others.

Now the image of God in man is that whereby man resembles God in that which appears to be the highest excellency in God Himself. It is that way in an image or picture of a man. When I draw the image of a man, I do not draw the resemblance of a man in some inferior thing, but I labor to draw the lively countenance. In that is the excellency of a man.

So it is in the image of God. Now the image of God is the holiness of God, and so, in man's soul, the impression of God's own holiness is the image of God in man. And, by that, man comes to resemble God in the top of His glory and excellency. Now this must be glorious for the creature to come so near unto God as is possible for the creature, for there is no excellency any creature is capable of higher than the image of God, only that hypostatic union of the two natures.

2. Upon this, God must take an infinite delight in looking upon the souls of the children of men. You know that a man takes delight in looking upon his own image wherever he see is. In the same way, God takes delight in looking upon His own image. There is nothing in all the world that can take the eye of God as much as looking upon angels and the souls of men, and God sees the very same thing in the souls of men as He did in His angels. The most glorious object God has to behold is to behold Himself in the creature. The more God sees of Himself in any creature, the more delight He must take in viewing and looking upon that creature. Now, no creature in this inferior world had so much of God's work in it as mankind had, having the image of God.

3. Hence it follows that all the creatures in the world were brought under the dominion of man to be serviceable to man. Why? Because he had so much of the image of God in

Him. All creatures in the world were to lie under his feet, to be perfectly subject to the dominion of man.

Now if the image of God is such a glorious thing as it is, then what would you say of that which defaces this image? That must be an evil thing, and does much to hurt man, that defaces such an excellency as this is. Now certainly sin does so.

Sin casts dirt into this image of God and defaces it. Therefore, in Colossians 3:10, the Apostle speaks of renewing grace, sanctifying grace. He says that by it, *we come to have the image of God renewed.* Notice that it is by grace. Then it is apparent that by sin the image of God is defaced.

Now, brethren, if a man took delight in a curious piece (as there are men who will give five hundred pounds, a thousand pounds, for some curious work of art), in fact, suppose that such a one prized such a piece and there came one who defaces it. Would he not account this a great evil? Would not his heart rise against that person?

Thus it is in this case. The image of God in the soul of man is the most curious piece that was ever drawn in the world by the finger of God's Spirit. All creatures in heaven and earth could never draw such a piece, but sin has defaced it. No, such is the evil of sin that one sin is quite enough to deface and take away the image of God.

We know that Adam was made according to the image of God. One sin quite defaced the image of God. We account a house to be quite defaced and demolished though there are a few stones and rubbish left. Take your monasteries and abbeys that are demolished. Though there are a few stones and rubbish left, yet the house is demolished. So all that is left of man in God's image is but as the little rubbish of such a house left after its demolishing. Yes, that which is left, according to the opinion of many of the learned, is not a remainder of the image of God in man that he had at first creation, but rather a small pittance of some common gifts of God's Spirit. For many wise and godly men hold that the

remainders of that which we usually conceive to be the ruins
and remainders of God's image since the fall is not the remainders of what is left, but that which God (for society's
sake in the world, and that He may have a church in the
world) was pleased, by some givings out of His Spirit, to
renew somewhat in those who shall not be saved. And so
they come to have some light of knowledge even by Jesus
Christ Himself. *Christ enlivens every man who comes into
the world,* says the Scripture in John 1. That is, if a man has
common light, Christ enlightens that man. If a man has
saving light, Christ enlightens that man with saving light, so
that the image of God was quite defaced by one sin.

Oh, the evil and venom of sin, that one sin quite takes
away the image of God!

QUESTION. But you will say, "Why it is not so now,
for in the regenerate there is the image of God in part renewed in them, and yet they commit many sins? How does it
come to pass that sin does not deface the image of God in the
regenerate, who do not have it perfectly, as well as the image
of God in man that had it perfectly at first?"

ANSWER. To this I answer, this is not from any reason
of want of malignity of sin, for sin would do it; but because
of the strength that is in the covenant of grace that God has
made in Christ. Hence God preserves His image in those
who are regenerate, notwithstanding the fact that they
commit many sins. And it is a demonstration of the infinite
power of God that, notwithstanding the fact that there are so
many sins in the regenerate, yet there should be preserved
the image of God in man which was not in Adam. Because
God did not enter such a gracious covenant with Adam to
preserve him, therefore God left Adam to a common course
of Providence and dealt with him in a covenant of works.
Therefore, God leaves that for sin to do in him that which it
should not do in us.

But now there is more strength in the covenant of grace,
and therefore it is that not every sin we commit defaces the

image of God. But this is no thanks to sin, nor does it argue any less evil in sin. Instead, let it be known to you who are sanctified that, when you give liberty to sin, there is this in it; in its own nature, it would quite take away all the image of God renewed in you. And certainly those who understand what a blessing there is in this, to have God's image renewed in them, cannot but see that there is greater evil in sin than in anything in the world, that I should commit that which, in its own nature would quite deface the whole image of God in me. And this is a second argument to declare the evil of sin against man's good.

Chapter 26

A third particular to discover the evil of sin as being opposite to man's good is this, because sin is opposite to the life of God in man. Before, I showed how sin strikes at the life of God in Himself. Now I am to show you how sin strikes at the life of God in man's soul. For, brethren, certainly this is the happiness of the children of men above other creatures, that God made them to be of such a nature that they should live that life the Lord Himself lives. And so the Scripture is very plain, Ephesians 4:18, where it says that they were *alienated from the life of God through the darkness of their minds*. It was the sinfulness of their hearts that alienated them from the life of God; therefore, it is apparent that they were capable of the life of God. And the life of God is the excellency of the children of men. Now the sin of their hearts alienated them from the life of God.

QUESTION. Now you will say, "What do you mean when you speak of the life of God, and that the soul of man is capable of the life of God, and show how sin is opposite to God? Certainly, if I should come and tell you of the flames of hell, and the torments of hell due to sin, perhaps I might scare some more that way; but for those who have any understanding, and truly know the excellency of man, their hearts will rise upon the opening of this more than if I should spend many sermons to open the torments of hell to you. Well, then, what is this life of God?"

ANSWER. (1) That everlasting principle of grace in the souls of men united unto Christ by His Spirit, whereby men come to act and work as God acts, and as God works for His own glory as the utmost end. As life is a principle whereby the creature moves within himself unto perfection, unto that which tends to perfections; an active principle within itself to move towards perfections is what we account life. Now that principle whereby a man shall come to move and work just as God moves and works (still speaking after the manner of man), that is, to have the likeness of God; not in the very same thing, but in the same proportion of likeness of which the creature is capable.

"How is that?" you will say.

It is this. This is the life of God (so far as we can conceive of Him), that God is a continual act always working for Himself and willing Himself as the last end of all. The very life of God consists in that, and in that consists the nature of holiness.

Now, then, when a man has such a principle within him so that he can work unto God as his last and highest end, so that he can obey God as his chief good, he works as God Himself does. Now, brethren, this is the life of God that the children of men are capable of above all other creatures, and it is this that makes them fit to converse with God Himself.

I say, it is that which makes the children of men to be fit to converse with that infinite, glorious, eternal First-Being of all things, and here is the happiness of man, that he is of that nature so that he is capable of this excellency: to have to do with the infinite, eternal First-Being. For many know no more excellency than to converse with meat and drink. Swine, dogs, and other beasts do that. But know, you are of more noble natures than this. God has made the meanest and poorest in this congregation of so noble a nature that you may come to converse with the infinite, glorious First-Being of all things.

That which puts a difference between one man and another man is this: the lowness of a man who lives in a mean condition consists in the fact that they spend all their days conversing with brute beasts and turning the clods of the earth; but noble and great men are busied in state affairs. They are raised higher because they converse with princes about great affairs of state. The things they converse about are higher, and therefore they are more noble and higher than other men.

Some children of men know of no other excellency than to eat, and drink, and play, and be filthy, and have nothing but that which beasts have. There are others, however, to whom God has revealed Himself and has made of a noble nature. While others are in base acts of uncleanness, and know no other way of rejoicing in time of joy but laughing, eating and drinking, and filthiness, these can get alone and contemplate the glory of the great God. Their souls are opened to God and He lets in beams of Himself to them. They, in return, let out beams of their love to God and their desires also. There is an intercourse between heaven and them. God opens Himself to them and they open their souls to God, and so enjoy communion from God. And they, because they have the life of God in them, are fit to converse with God.

Mark it, those things that converse one with another are such things that must live the same life. For example, man can converse with man. Why? Because he lives the same life that man lives. But man is not fit to converse with beasts, because they do not live the same life, though some men live the life of beasts. A man cannot converse with plants (but only devour them) because they do not live the same life; but those who live the same life are most fit to converse. So if man did not live the same life God does, he could not converse with God.

Hence, wicked and ungodly men cannot converse with God because they do not live the same life as God. When you talk of conversing with God, it is a riddle to many men. Why? Because they are strangers to the life of God. They have nothing of the life of God in them; it is strange to them. Therefore, they cannot converse with God. But now, that which strikes at this life, and is the death of the soul, is sin (for sin is the death of the soul). Therefore, Ephesians 2:1 begins this way, *You being dead in trespasses and sins.* Sin brings death. He does not mean a bodily death, though that is a truth, but there is this death: the life of God is gone. All men, by nature, have the life of God gone, and if ever it is renewed, it is by a mighty work of God's Spirit. But sin strikes at the life of God in us, at this candle of the Lord in this earthen pitcher.

(2) Again, the excellency of the life of God will consist in this: to make a man converse with Him. It is also in this: that God must take infinite delight in the souls of those that live His life, as before in looking upon His image, now much more when He can see His creatures work as He Himself works. This is the delight of God, to see His creatures work just as Himself. A man takes delight to see his picture, but abundantly more to look upon himself in his child, and to see his life in his child that comes to him, to see that child able to work as he works.

Suppose someone skilled in navigation sees a picture drawn like a navigator would draw. He takes delight in it because there is something of himself in it; but now suppose he has a child, and he puts skill into him, and he sees him work as he works and discourse about naval affairs as he himself would do. This is wonderfully delightful to him.

So when God sees the same life in His creature that is in Himself, that he works and wills as He does, this takes the very heart of God, and this shows the excellency of grace.

But sin is that which strikes at this life of God and brings death to the soul, wholly takes away this life, and were it not for the covenant of grace, even one sin would take away this image of God; for sin did it in Adam, and so would in the regenerate, if it were not for the covenant of grace.

My brethren, life is the most excellent of anything. As Augustine said, "The life of a fly is more excellent than the sun" (it is his expression, not mine) because the sun, though an excellent creature, has no life, but a fly, though small, has life. Though we know little of it, yet it shows the excellency of God to make a living creature; but if the life of a fly or a beast is so excellent, how much more the life of man? Now, then, what is the life of God!

Now if that is evil which strikes at the natural life of the body, the life of man.... We account those diseases most grievous that are mortal. If a man has a disease that only causes pain but was not mortal, it is not as bad as if he had a disease that caused pain and was mortal. If a physician came and told you that you must endure pain, but be of good cheer, your life is safe, this would comfort you. But take a disease that does not cause pain. It may be that the sense of pain is gone, but if the physician tells you, "Oh, you are dangerously ill because your disease is likely to prove mortal," we account that which takes a life but does not cause pain to be worse than that which causes a great deal of pain but does not strike at a life! *Skin for skin, and all that a man hath will he give for his life.*

Now that which strikes at the highest life, even the life of God, and makes the creature appear so vile before God is sin. And certainly sin makes the creature more vile than any dead carrion that lies stinking in a ditch. Sin is more vile in God's eyes than any dead dog on the dunghill is in your eyes.

This is the third particular, how sin is most opposite to man's good, even more so than affliction. Therefore, it would be better for a man to bear the greatest affliction than to commit the least sin, because affliction never strikes at the life of God. No, many do not live the life of God so gloriously as they do in affliction. Many seem to have their hearts dead in times of prosperity but, when afflictions come, then they manifest a glorious life of God.

Chapter 27

Fourthly, sin is most opposite to man's good, because it is most opposite to the last end for which man was made.

A fourth thing wherein the evil of sin consists as most opposite to man's good is this, because it lies most opposite to the last end for which man was made. In that other passage I opened before, I showed how sin opposes God in His own end, and therefore there was a great deal of evil in sin.

But now I must show how sin opposes man in that end for which God made man. I am afraid some of these things are such that some cannot go along with me in them. It is my endeavor to make things (though spiritual and above our natural reach) as low as I can; but, if there are some who do not understand, I hope others do, and such (I hope) will make use of what I speak. For certainly these things I speak of declare the evil of sin more, and will keep an ingenuous spirit from sin more, than all the evils and torments of hell. It is more against man's last end.

Now we used to say the end and the good of a thing are the same. That which is the last end is better than the thing itself. Therefore, whatever strikes at the last end is the greatest evil of all. The happiness of any creature is to enjoy its last end. For example, the greatest good or the last end of a plant or tree is to flourish and bear fruit, and to be fitted for the service of man. This is its end. And what is the evil of a tree? When it comes to flourish, and when fruit hangs full upon it, if it is blasted and never attains its utmost end; it is never serviceable for that for which it was appointed. That is the evil of it. And we account it a great evil if we see this flourishing tree, when it is full of fruit, be blasted before it comes to maturity. So look upon man's end and, if that is blasted, that is his greatest evil.

Now the end of man is this, to live to the eternal praise

of God, in the eternal enjoyment of Him. God made the children of men for this end, that they might eternally live to His praise in the eternal enjoyment of Himself. Now if man is blasted in this, there is his great evil; to blast man in this end for which he was made.

Now, no affliction does it; all the afflictions in the world do not hinder man from attaining to his end. But sin comes and directly opposes that end for which man was made. Sin crosses him in this excellency of his, in living to the praise of the eternal First-Being of all things.

Now before, I could not show you the evil of sin except by showing you the excellency of the image and life of God. So here, I cannot show you the evil of sin, being opposed to man's last end, except by showing you the excellency of man's last end. Now the excellency of man's last end, I mean the good God has made man for, appears in this.

1. It is such a kind of excellency as is worthy of all the good there is in man's nature, or that man's nature is capable of. For the end and happiness of anything must be that it must have as much excellency in it so that all in that thing must tend to making him happy. Man's nature is capable of the image and life of God. Now that which must be the happiness of such a creature must be worthy of such an excellency as the image of God and the life of God in man. Therefore, it must be a very high and glorious excellency.

2. That which is man's happiness and end is that which is worthy of all the ways of God toward mankind. Now I beseech you, observe this thing. The ways of God towards the children of men, in bringing them to His last end, are the most glorious of all God's ways to any creature. God never manifested as much glory in the world, nor will He ever manifest as much glory to all eternity in anything, as He has manifested in these ways of bringing mankind to the attaining of the end for which He made him. Now, if God is so glorious in that way of His, concerning His working, in bringing man to his last end, then, certainly, that end of

man, that happiness for which man was made must be very glorious, because it must have so much glory and excellency in it as must be worthy of all the glorious ways of God's working towards Him.

It is thus with man. There is not a wise man who does any greater work, manifests any greater skill, or lays out great cost but will do it for such an end as that end, if it ever attained, shall be worth all his cost, skill, and pains. For a wise man to bestow such cost, skill, and pains upon a mean thing is absurd and ridiculous. And no wise man but if he bestows much cost and pains, and manifests much skill, but he will be sure it shall be for that which, if he attains to that he aims at, it shall be worth all.

If a man has a great investment in a voyage, he aims at such an end as may be worth his investment. So when God above all things lays out His wisdom, power, mercy, goodness, and faithfulness, and sets at work all His counsels to be laid out upon such a business as to get man to attain to His last end, then, certainly, man's end and happiness must be worth it all. And it must be a glorious thing God intends for the children of men, to make them happy, when the great counsels of God, and the ways of God's wisdom and power, are so about this business of bringing man to happiness.

Now, if there is such a glorious happiness for mankind, then that which is most opposed to this great happiness must be very evil. Now sin directly opposes man's happiness, the end for which man was made. And thus you see the evil of sin.

When God comes to awaken man's conscience, and enlightens man's soul to see how sin crosses their happiness more than any affliction, they will choose, rather, to be under the greatest affliction than the least sin.

OBJECTION. "Aye, but it may be," you will say, "it does not cross man's happiness, but that he may come to be happy for all sin?"

ANSWER. I answer, of its own nature it directly crosses man's happiness; it quite undoes man. And if God, by His power, fetches it about another way, this is not thanks to sin, but to God.

Chapter 28

Fifthly, sin is more opposite to man's good than affliction, because it is a defilement of the soul. (1) It defiles all a man meddles with. (2) Sin is the matter the worm shall gnaw on to all eternity.

The evil of sin against a man's good appears in this, it is the defilement and corruption of the soul, a rottenness in the soul. Affliction is not the filth and corruption of the soul. The soul may be as clear from filth and corruption, notwithstanding affliction, as it was before man sinned. Sin is the rottenness of the soul, and therefore such a kind of defilement as (1) it defiles all things a man meddles with, and all his actions. It makes a man vile, and defiles everything that comes from him.

To the unclean, all things are unclean and impure, Titus 1:15. It defiles the creature and everything he has to do with, and everything he meddles with.

(2) It especially appears in this, that it is no other than the matter for the worm to breed in that shall gnaw upon the soul of the wicked to all eternity. You read in Scripture that the damned shall be punished with fire that shall never go out, and the worm shall never die. What is that worm that shall never die? The worm of conscience that shall gnaw upon their spirits to all eternity.

Now, what breeds this worm and supplies it with matter? No other but the corruption of sin in the soul. For, as with worms (as the Holy Ghost makes use of that metaphor) that breed in the corruption and filth of a man's body, there are some worms that breed in the body that are deadly. But out of what do these worms breed? Out of the filth and corruption of the body, and the corruption of the body supplies matter for the worm to gnaw upon.

Worms breed in timber and trees. Upon what do they

breed but the corruption of the timber when it begins to rot. So, then, worms breed out of corruption and live upon corruption.

So that worm of conscience that shall lie gnawing upon the souls of those that perish to all eternity is nothing else but that which breeds from the filth of their hearts. While they live here, the worm breeds. Therefore, you who live a long time in sin, old sinners, grey-headed sinners, though you do not feel the worm gnaw for the present, yet ever since you were born, the worm was breeding, and it will be a great and dreadful worm hereafter. Know this, you supply an abundance of corruption for that worm to feed upon another day. You do not feel it now, but the longer you live before you feel it, the more dreadful it will be then. All those who have corrupt hearts and have this worm breeding in them, if God would make the worm gnaw now, it would be well for them, for there are ways to kill it here, to kill the worm of conscience.

If it gnaws, there is a sovereign medicine, the blood of Christ. And, certainly, there is no medicine in the world to kill this worm but the blood of Christ. And those that God intends to kill this worm in, and those who shall not have it gnaw to all eternity, God lets it gnaw now. The ministry of the Word makes it gnaw and pain them, and they feel such pain that, wherever they go or whatever they do, the worm lies gnawing upon their hearts. They cannot sleep, they cannot eat their meat.

"Alas! What, should I eat and have my worm gnaw there!"

And they can never be at rest until God applies the blood of Christ, and then they void the worm, as it were. How will you rejoice when in your children the worms are great and put them to pain, if the physician gives them that which makes them void them, how do you rejoice to see the worm that would have been the death of your child? It might have grown bigger and bigger if it had not been taken away.

So I dare say, there is never a soul here before the Lord but has, or had, a worm in your breasts that, unless it was cured, would lie gnawing to all eternity. It is that which breeds in the filth and corruption of your hearts.

Suppose a man had a little dirt on his face. This would not endanger the life of the body. But, when there is corruption within and defilement of the body within, that breeds diseases, and will breed worms. It may be that it will breed the wolf that lies gnawing at their breasts.

Many women have had it in their breasts that lies gnawing upon their flesh; but know, your sin breeds another manner of worm or wolf that will gnaw worse than it ever did.

And this is the evil of sin. It is not only the defilement of the soul, but such a defilement that breeds such a worm that will gnaw upon conscience to all eternity.

Chapter 29

Sixth, sin is more opposed to man's good than affliction, because sin is the object of God's hatred; but God does not hate anyone because of affliction.

Sin is the only object of the hatred of God; nothing is the object of God's hatred but sin. God does not hate a man or a woman because they are poor. God may love them as well as any monarch or prince in the world, even though they are poor. God does not hate a man because he is sick. You do not hate your children because they are sick or weak. All the afflictions in the world do not make a man an object of God's hatred, but sin does.

Mark that expression in Scripture, Psalm 5:5, *The fool shall not stand in Thy sight, Thou hatest all workers of iniquity.* So that sin makes the creature the object of God's hatred. God does not say, mark it, that He hates the work of iniquity only, but the *worker* of iniquity.

God does not hate the creature as He made him, but, through sin, the creature comes to be hated; even the workers of iniquity. Now observe the strength of the reason, that which makes a man the object of God's hatred must be a greater evil than that which can stand with God's everlasting love; for afflictions, though they are strong and bitter, may stand with God's eternal love. Nay, observe, they may stand with the same love with which God the Father loved His Son, Jesus Christ. You can read this in John 17, the latter part. There Christ prays to the Father, "that Thou mayest love them with the very same love with which Thou lovest Me."

Now God the Father loved Christ and yet God the Father afflicted Christ. Christ was under sore afflictions, and yet at that very time God the Father loved Him.

So a man or woman, notwithstanding all their afflictions,

may have the very same love of God the Father that Jesus Christ Himself had, in a manner the very same. And I think this might be a mighty encouragement to afflicted souls.

Are you afflicted with poverty, bodily sickness, persecution, anything? Know, for all this affliction, God may love you with the same love He loved His Son. But sin makes the creature the object of God's hatred.

"But," you will say, "God's children have sin."

Of its own nature, it would make them objects of God's hatred, but then comes the blood of Christ, and the purchase of His blood procures peace between God and man. But I speak of it in its own nature, and those who God looks upon in a sinful condition, He cannot look upon them without hating them.

Now that which makes a man the object of God's hatred must be very evil. For example, when any affection runs in one current, it must run very strong. It is this way with the sea. Suppose there were many arms and rivers to break the strength of the current; it would not run so powerfully. But when there is one current, the current of the ocean runs very strongly.

So it is with the affections. When the affections are only set upon one object, then they are strong. When love is scattered upon this and the other thing, then it is not strong, but when it is upon one thing only, then it is strong. When parents have many children, they may not love any strongly, but when there is only one, then their love for that one is great.

So it is in hatred. Where there is hatred of many, there is not as much hatred against one. But where it runs in one current only, there it is strong. So here, there is no object that God's hatred runs out against but sin alone. Therefore, the hatred of sin must be very powerful.

Oh, for a man or woman to live to be the object of the hatred of the eternal God, how dreadful an evil is this! We desire to be beloved where we are of every one. What a sad thing it is to live in a family or town where no one loves you. Men desire to be loved even though it is only by a dog! They will boast, sometimes, that such a dog or a horse loved his master. When he comes home, they will leap and skip and fawn on him.

Do we take delight to have our neighbors or family love us? To have the dog love us? Oh, what is the love of an infinite, eternal, glorious God!

A man accounts it an evil if the dog only snarls and barks at him; this we account an evil. Oh, what an evil is it, then, to have the infinite, eternal, only-wise God to be an enemy, and for me to be the object of His hatred! Oh, think of these things!

And brethren, in these times, it is to be feared you contract an abundance of sin. You will have more to answer for before these next days are gone than you had before. Oh, let this stop the course of some sin that otherwise might be committed in these times of sensuality. Therefore, when you see some go on in sinful ways, do you stop and say, "God forbid that I should do as they do. I have been in such a place and heard what sin is. I have heard how it is against God, and this might stop me. But this day I have heard how it is against me and my own soul, and how it destroys my own soul. Therefore, I will hate sin everlastingly."

Chapter 30

Seventhly, sin is more opposed to man's good than affliction because sin brings guilt upon the soul.

There is more evil in sin than in affliction, because sin is more opposed to our own good than affliction, and that in this seventh respect. Sin brings guilt upon the soul; it makes the creature stand guilty in the presence of God. Now guilt upon the soul is a greater evil than any affliction can be. That is the thing I am now to open.

Guilt, what is that? It is the binding over of the sinner to God's justice and to the Law; to answer and be liable to what the Law requires as punishment due to the sinner so that, then, for a creature to stand bound over to God's infinite justice and the Law has more evil in it against man's good than all the afflictions and miseries in the world. This is the thing I am to make good.

A sinner goes up and down with the chains of guilt upon him. Iron chains grating upon the sore flesh of a man is not as tedious and grievous as the chains of guilt upon conscience. Certainly, this is one special reason why many wicked men and women are as froward as they are, because they have much guilt upon their spirits. As iron chains would grate raw flesh, so does that guilt lie upon conscience, and that makes them as froward and peevish as they are: froward against God and against man.

There are many men you will deal with whom you shall find against the Word, extremely froward and perverse against their acquaintances, neighbors, family, and closest friends. And we cannot imagine, sometimes, what the reason might be. Certainly, this is one special reason. There is so much guilt upon their consciences and spirits, and this so disquiets and vexes them that they fling out at God and His Word, and everyone else as well. They can have no quiet since they are so vexed and galled with the guilt upon their spirits.

There is plenty of reason to suspect much guilt to be upon those that are so outrageous and can bear nothing; who have their hearts rise against the Word especially.

Brethren, if you see anyone who has any light of conscience, and has made profession heretofore, if such a one shall frowardly fly out against the Word and those who are godly, you may conclude that there is some woeful guilt upon that person's spirit. That is why he is as froward, peevish, and disquieted as he is.

So we find it in Saul. He was a man, at first, of a very quiet spirit, very moderate; but afterwards, Saul, being a man who was very enlightened, but who had forsaken God and had contracted an abundance of guilt upon his soul, was a most froward, perverse spirit - as much so as any we read of in the Book of God. How froward was he with David. How froward was he with the priests of God? So outrageous that he slew them all; a bloody man after he had contracted much guilt.

Do you see men so froward, outrageous, and bloody? Oh, there is much guilt within them upon their spirits; great breeches between God and their souls, and the guilt of sin within grates upon their hearts, and that makes them as outrageous as they are!

If guilt is upon the soul, it takes away all the comfort of everything. That man or woman who has an enlightened conscience, and has guilt upon themselves, can take little comfort in anything they enjoy.

No affliction in the world can take away the comfort of what we enjoy like guilt can do. If you have afflictions one way, you have comfort another.

If a man goes abroad and meets with hard dealings, he can come home and find comfort, perhaps, in his wife. A close friend may rejoice him or, it may be, he has comfort in his children. But now, let a man or woman have a guilty conscience, he has no comfort abroad, no comfort at home. Yes, the more comfortable the things are he enjoys, the more trouble there is in his spirit.

For example, take a man with a guilty conscience. When he looks upon comfortable families, comfortable estates, money coming in, or a close friend, he will likely say, "Oh, but if I did not have some guilt upon my soul, I could rejoice in these," but that guilt which lies upon his conscience takes away all the comfort of these. And if he sees others who do enjoy these things he says, "Oh, this man may have comfort in a close friend, his children, or a good estate, but he does not have guilt upon his spirit, and he does not have that breach between himself and God like I have."

It may be that the world does not know where his shoe pinches him and what saddens his spirit. Many men have comforts about them (though they cannot be said to enjoy them), yet their hearts are troubled and disquieted, and nobody knows the reason. Oh, there is guilt upon their spirits. They think within themselves, "Oh, if it were with me as it is with other men, it would be well. Surely they do not have the guilt I have. If they did, they could not but be disquieted as I am."

Again, guilt brings woeful fear upon the conscience. No affliction can bring such fear upon the conscience. Though there should be never such troubles and fears and confusions in the world, alas, this is not as terrible and fearful as the fear the guilty conscience has.

Take a man or woman whose conscience is delivered from the guilt of sin. Such a one, though heaven and earth should meet, is not greatly troubled. Certainly, brethren, in these great fears among us, so that you are scared by everything, it is partly because you have not thoroughly made peace between God and your souls. Some guilt lies upon your spirits and consciences and, this indeed, will make everything terrible to you if it lies there.

Guilt upon the conscience makes thoughts of God seem

terrible. Now, it is a greater evil for the creature not to be able to look upon God, and to have thoughts of God, without being pierced with terror than it is to be under any affliction in the world. Sorrows, fears, disgrace, and persecutions are not as terrible as being in such a condition that I cannot look up to God, nor think of God, without having the thoughts of His majesty be terrible to me.

A guilty conscience cannot endure to have thoughts of God. It is terrible to him and, therefore, he labors to take his thoughts off from God by being with people, by sports, by business in the world, because the thoughts of God pierce his heart. And so the presence of God is very terrible where guilt is upon the conscience, and the conscience of such a one cannot endure to come into God's presence, nor into the communion of saints where God's presence is.

He cannot endure to pray; the thoughts of that strike his heart. To go alone to pray, to go into the presence of God alone, is extremely terrible. And this is a sadder condition than to be under any affliction. It is better to be under any affliction than to be in such a case where the presence of God is terrible, whether it be the presence of God in prayer or the presence of God in His Word.

Oh, the Word is terrible to such a one! The Word of God speaks nothing but terror as long as guilt remains upon the conscience. This is worse than affliction, that the Word, which is a treasure of sweetness, goodness, and comfort to those who are gracious and godly, should be filled with terror to the soul of one who is full of guilt. Yes, to such a one, all the ways of God's providence are full of terror. If there is any judgment of God abroad, oh, the terror that this brings upon his soul.

Brethren, sin is committed quickly. You have a temptation come, and you fall upon the sin and act upon it. The sin, the act of it, is transient and quickly gone. The guilt is that which sticks to you.

When a man or woman has satisfied their lust in a sinful

way, the guilt sticks behind. Perhaps the time is gone, as far as the pleasure of it. Perhaps it was yesterday, or such a night or time when you had the pleasure of it, but now the sin is gone (the pleasure of it) but the guilt sticks, and that abides upon your spirit to all eternity, if you do not tend to it.

No, certainly, it must stick upon the spirit. It is not in the power of any creature in heaven or in earth to deliver you from it. The guilt so remains that, though you do not feel it now for the present, it may stick terribly for many years afterwards. But affliction is terrible only for the present, not for afterwards. Guilt and sin lay a foundation for misery for many years after. No, many times it is grievously painful to them long after it is committed, as it was in the case of Joseph's brothers.

We read of them that they committed that great sin against their brother, and it did not trouble them for long. But twenty-two years after, when they were in affliction, the guilt of their sin came to them afresh when they were in prison. Now it was twenty-two years from the time they committed that sin to the time when they were in trouble there!

So you who have committed sin and think some slight sorrow may wash it away, know that the guilt may abide upon your spirits perhaps twenty, perhaps forty years after. And you who are young, take heed and know that sin is more evil than any affliction, for the sin that you commit when you are young may abide upon you, and youthful sins may prove to be ages of terror.

It may be with you as with a man who gets a bruise. When he is young, he does not feel it, but when he is old, it aches in his bones and puts him in terrible pain many times. So many young people do not feel sin when their blood is hot, but afterwards, the guilt of sin abides upon them, and it is the torment of their souls when their blood is cold.

Now what evil is there in sin that may do him mischief

perhaps twenty or forty years later. Think of poison. There are some poisons men may have skill in. They can give poisons that will not work for three, four, perhaps even seven years later, and yet they know certainly that, if the man is not cut off before (unless God works extraordinarily), he shall die at the end of seven years from that poison he took seven years before. So sin is such a thing that it will do a man mischief for many years afterwards.

Again, the guilt of sin has this evil in it, which appears in that difference between men who come to suffer with guilt and men who come to suffer without guilt. Take those who have come to the most grievous sufferings in the world, who do not have the guilt of sin upon their consciences, who have all clear between God and their souls. Their sufferings are joyful, and they can rejoice in tribulation and troubles.

For example, think of the martyrs in persecution. How did they rejoice and glory in their sufferings? With what a spirit of magnanimity did they come through their sufferings? But take those who suffer through guilt, like malefactors. When they come to suffer, what shame and confusion is upon them!

Thus, affliction is nothing to them who have no guilt, but those who have the guilt of sin upon them, when they come to suffer, their guilt is a thousand times more than their affliction. There is a great deal of difference between a man who is guilty of treason and a man who is only accused of treason. When a man who is guilty of treason comes to suffer for it, there is shame and confusion, and dismal darkness in the spirit where there is guilt. But let one be accused for treason, or any such horrible crime, and has no guilt upon his spirit. Such a one can go on with joy, comfort, and peace. Whatever can be done to him is very little or nothing when guilt is removed.

The truth is, there is no suffering that can equal the suffering that guilt brings. The guilt makes the suffering evil, otherwise not. If one man comes upon another man who is suffering, it is nothing without guilt.

So it is true, when God comes, it is nothing if we are at peace with God. But now, when God comes with any such affliction, and the affliction has the mark of sin upon it and stirs up your conscience to accuse you for it, then the heart is ready to sink when the affliction bears the name of the sin together with it.

I remember the difference of David's spirit at various times. One time it was, *though an host encamp about me, yet will I not fear,* and *though I walk in the valley of the shadow of death, I will fear no evil,* Psalm 23. Another time, he was afraid when he fled from Absalom. And, when there was a breach between God and his soul, when he had brought guilt upon his spirit, then David was quickly cooled. And, upon any occasion of trouble, David was quickly frightened.

This is a seventh thing wherein sin appears to be a greater and more evil thing than affliction, because it makes the soul guilty before God.

Chapter 31

Eighthly, sin is a greater evil to man than affliction because it is that which put the creature under the sentence of condemnation.

Sin is that which puts the creature under the sentence of condemnation, and so makes more against the good of man than any affliction can do. To have a poor creature to see himself stand before the great Judge of all the world and have the sentence of condemnation come out against him is a greater evil than to have any affliction that all the creatures of heaven and earth could bring against him.

For example, take a malefactor who is to stand before man's judgment seat and is to receive the sentence of condemnation. Is this not a greater evil to him than if he should lose his estate, than if he had some sickness in his body or pain in his limbs? To stand thus and receive a sentence, he looks upon as a greater evil than could possibly befall him in this world. But then, when the soul shall see itself stand before the infinite, glorious, eternal First-Being of all things, and when the soul looks upon God sitting upon His tribunal, passing the sentence of eternal death upon him, this is another manner of evil, much more grievous than any affliction or suffering that could befall him.

But now, know that there is not any one sin that you commit (but if you look upon it as in itself) but that God sits, I say, upon His throne and passes the sentence of death upon you as really as ever He will do at the great day of judgment. It is done now as really and as truly in this world as ever it shall be at the day of judgment. There is but one difference; then it is irrecoverable. No, let me say it this way, it cannot be recalled here. No, certainly, it shall not be recalled. It may, however, be transmitted to Christ. He must bear it, he must have the sentence. It is not properly recalled.

God is not like a judge who passes down a sentence and, then, afterwards, annuls it. No, but God passes the sentence down and condemns the sinner. Christ comes in, though, and He puts the sentence of condemnation that is passed upon you on Himself. So that the sentence is not properly nullified, but transferred to Christ.

Ecclesiastes 8:11 says, *Because sentence against an evil work is not speedily executed, therefore the heart of the sons of men are fully set in them to do evil.* Mark it. The sentence against an evil work is not speedily executed. It appears from this that there is a sentence against every evil work.

The sentence is out, brethren. You go and get drunk, or you go and commit some sin, I say, immediately the sentence of death is clapt upon you. The sentence is out against all sinners.

You see men go on and live in prosperity a great while in the world, but they are under the sentence of death all the while sin is not removed by the blood of Christ; and all the comforts that any man or woman have in the world who are in their natural condition, and are not delivered from condemnation by Jesus Christ are all as meat, drink, and refreshments granted to a condemned malefactor before his execution.

Suppose a malefactor is condemned, but his execution is not until two or three days later. In that space of time, he has granted to him liberty to have meat and drink, company, and he may refresh himself in those two or three days; but he has forfeited all his estate, and the tenure now upon which he holds any comfort is not the same as that which he had before, but it is only through the bounty of the prince that he has comforts.

So it is here. Wicked men have committed sin, and the sentence of death is out against them, and they have forfeited all the comforts of their estates and their lives; but God, in His patience, grants to them some outward comforts for a few days before their execution and, upon this tenure, do all wicked men hold their estates. I will not say that every wicked man is a usurper of his estate, as some, perhaps, have held, that they have no right at all before God. He has some right to meat and drink before execution. He has a right to what is given to him by donation and bounty, but not that right which he had before.

So I say, for wicked men who have estates in this world, they have a kind of right to that which they have, but how? Just that right that a condemned man has to his dinner or supper before execution. This is the right of wicked men to their estates. That is, God, of His bounty, grants a little while before execution that they shall have a few comforts to them in this world. And this is the evil of sin, and the least sin; there is not any one sin but the fruit of it is condemnation. And, brethren, you must not mistake here, to think that wicked men are never condemned until they come before God in the day of judgment. They are condemned here. Mark what it says in John 3:18, *He that believes not is condemned already*. Condemned now, not hereafter, but a condemned man already. This is a sad condition, indeed.

If a man had the sentence of death so passed that the whole Parliament could not help him, you would think that this man was in a sad condition. Now let me speak it, and God speaks it to the conscience of every sinner. I say, you who stand before God in any one sin, and are not delivered through the blood of His Son, Jesus Christ, you stand so under the sentence of condemnation that all the creatures in heaven and earth cannot help and deliver you. You must have some help beyond the help of all the creatures in heaven and earth to deliver you.

When Paul would comfort the saints against all the troubles and afflictions they meet with, Romans 8, he began with these words, *There is no condemnation to them in Christ Jesus*. It is as if he should say, "This is the comfort - no condemnation."

If I know I am delivered from the sentence of condemnation, let fall what will, I am well enough; but this be sure of, there is condemnation to those who are not in Christ.

I remember that Luther had this speech when he had received assurance of pardon of sin, that he was freed and absolved by God. He cried out, "Lord, strike. Lord, now strike, for I am absolved from my sins. Thou hast delivered me from sin; now strike. Now, let any affliction befall that possibly can. Let never so much trouble attend, I am absolved from sin. Now, Lord, strike."

This is the eighth: sin is more opposed to the good of man than affliction, for it brings them under the sentence of condemnation.

Chapter 32

Ninthly, sin is a greater evil to man than affliction, because it breaks the union between God and the soul.

Sin is a greater evil in this: it is the very thing that breaks the union between God and the soul. It is that which does it, and no affliction does that. Now, brethren, this, I confess, might seem to be less than that of hatred, and might have come before it, but now I bring it in here, that it breaks the union between God and the soul. Isaiah 59:2 says, *Your sins have separated between you and your God!*

We are to know, the souls of men are capable of a very near and high union between God and them. The more spiritual anything is, the more power it has to unite, and the more near the union.

For example, the beams of the sun, because they are very spiritual, can unite a thousand of them into one point, as it were; but grosser things cannot so unite themselves together. So, brethren, God, being a Spirit, and our souls, being spirits, come to be capable of a most near communion with one another. And the souls of men are nearer a glorious union with God, in this regard, than any creature but the angels.

Because the object of man's understanding is not any particular truth, but *veritas,* truth in general, truth itself in the whole latitude is the object of man's understanding. So the object of man's will is not this good or that good in particular, but *bonitas,* good in general in the full latitude of it.

It is not so with other creatures. They have their objects in some particular thing, in such a limit and compass, and they can work no further nor higher. But it is otherwise with man's soul. God has made man in such a kind that the object of his soul should be truth and goodness in the full latitude, in the infiniteness of it. Take it in the utmost extent that can be, yet still it is the object of the soul of man.

Now hence it is that the soul of man is of such a wonderful, large extent, even capable of God Himself, of enjoyment of union and communion with God Himself, which otherwise could not be. No other creature has to do with infiniteness, nor can have to do with it but men and angels, and upon that ground, because God has made them of so large a nature that their faculties should be of so large a nature. Now hence it is that man is capable of the enjoyment of God in such a glorious manner.

We have these expressions in Scripture, *He that is joined to the Lord, is one Spirit,* I Corinthians 6:17. He is made one spirit with God. A most strange expression that the soul of a poor creature should be made one spirit with God, and yet so it is. And so John 17:21 gives us two or three notable expressions, *That they may be all one, as Thou Father art in me, and I in Thee, and that they may be one in Us.* Christ prays that the saints may be one in Him and in the Father, as the Father is in Him and He is in the Father; so they may be one in Him. And verse 22 says, *And the glory which Thou gavest Me, I have given them: that they may be one, even as we are one.* Christ has given the saints the same glory God the Father gave Him. And to what end? What was the effect of that glory Christ gave to the saints? It was *that they may be one with the Father and with the Son.*

So you see, mankind is capable of a wonderful, near union with God. Oh, consider this to raise your spirits. You who look after such low things, and think there is no higher good than to eat, and drink, and have your pleasures in the flesh. Know that the meanest and poorest in the congregation are capable to receive that glory God gave His Son, Jesus Christ; that you may be one with God the Father and the Son, as God the Father and the Son are one. Not every way, but know there is a likeness. Christ Himself has expressed it.

Therefore, you who have your hearts so low, who mind

nothing but these things below, know that you have noble things to mind if your hearts consider it. But here is the evil of sin, sin breaks the union between God and the soul. It separates God from the soul. It keeps off from God, that infinite, eternal, glorious fountain of all good. It keeps Him off from you. It makes you lose God and all the good in God.

By sin you depart from God, which is the curse of the damned at the day of judgment. *Depart from Me, you cursed,* Matthew 25. You here, for the present, in every sin, begin to have that dreadful sentence executed on you.

Depart from Me, you cursed. You do it yourselves while you are in sinful ways. There is a real, actual departing from God, and an executing of that sentence, *Depart from Me, you cursed.* You think there is little evil in sin; but if you knew that God is an infinite God, and then knew the union you are capable of with God, and then saw sin break this union, this would make you see sin to be the greatest evil in the world.

Chapter 33

Tenthly, sin is more against man's good than affliction, for it
stirs up all in God to come against a sinner in way of enmity.

The evil of sin as being against our good consists in
this, it stirs up all in God to come in way of enmity against a
sinner. And this is another manner of business than to suffer
affliction. A most dreadful place of Scripture for this is in
Leviticus 26:24 & 28, *If you walk contrary to Me, I will*
walk contrary unto you. What is that? "All My glorious attributes shall work against you." It is as if God should say,
"Is there anything in Me that can make you miserable? You
shall have it. If all My power or wisdom can bring evil upon
you, you shall have it. I will walk contrary in all the working
of My attributes, and in all the ways of My providence."

And a most dreadful place we have in Psalm 34:16.
There God says, *The face of the Lord is against them that do*
evil. Mark it, the face of the Lord. What is God's face? It is
the manifestation of Himself and His glorious attributes. The
face of the Lord is against them that do evil. Oh, that you
would consider this, you who do evil, whose conscience
cannot but tell you that you do evil. Know that the face of
God is against you, and is this nothing to have the face of
God against you? The face of God is terrible in the world
when He meets with a sinner. One sight of the face of God
against a soul cannot but overwhelm the soul and sink it
down to the bottomless gulf of eternal despair, if God does
not hold him by His mighty hand. There is much terror in it.

Another remarkable text is 2 Samuel 22:27, *With the*
pure Thou wilt show Thyself pure, and with the froward
Thou wilt show Thyself froward, or "unsavory." But it may
be translated, "With the perverse, Thou wilt wrestle." So
that those who are froward and perverse, and walk in a sinful way, God wrestles it out with them. God puts forth His

power to wrestle and, certainly, if God wrestles with you, He will lay you on your back.

It is a dreadful thing that God should use such speech, that He will wrestle with man, for all men in sin, as I showed before, wrestle with God as if they would have the day. God will have His will, and you shall have the fall. You wrestle and God wrestles. You know wrestlers put all their strength forth against one another. Know, then, that God puts forth all His strength against every sinner.

And, that I may bring it more fully to your senses, consider this. Where does any creature get the power to bring evil upon you or to torment you? Surely it has something of God in it. For example, fire has power to torment the body, and it is only one spark of God let out through the power of that creature, otherwise it has no power. And again, another "creature," swords and weapons; they have power to gash and wound the body. From where do these instruments get their power? It is but some drop of God's power through these instruments.

So one disease has power to torment one way, and another disease has power to torment another way. Where does any disease get power to torment? Only from this, there is some little bit of God's power let out through that disease. Now, if the tormenting power of all "creatures" is only from God letting out His power through them, what a dreadful thing it will be, then, when God's power shall be infinitely let out against the creature?

Take all creatures in their various powers to torment, put them all together, one creature in one kind and another creature in another kind, and this would be great torture. Now, all the power of God is the various powers of all the creatures put together in one, and infinitely more. And when that comes against the creature, it must make them miserable. It is another manner of matter than afflictions when all in God comes out against the soul, and there is not any one sin that does not put a person in danger of this.

Chapter 34

Sin is more opposed to man's good than affliction, for sin makes all the creatures of God at enmity with a sinner.

Eleventh, in the next place, the evil that sin has beyond all the evil of affliction is this, sin makes all the creatures of God to be at enmity with a sinner. I say, sin puts a sinner in this condition, that all the creatures of God are enemies unto the sinner. They are all as the host of God that comes out against a sinner, ready, armed with God's wrath, ready and bent to execute the wrath of God against a sinner. The creatures of God are called God's host, not only because they are armed with God's wrath, but because there is in them a propensity to destroy those sinners who sin against the God of their being.

Every creature is ready and cries, as it were, to God, "Oh, Lord, when wilt Thou give me commission to take away such a wretch? Lord, such a one is a filthy, wretched blasphemer, a Sabbath-breaker, a drunkard." You live all this while and have been at peace, and yet they are still crying, "Lord, shall I go and take him away, and send him to his own place?"

If you could hear it, all the creatures in the world cry like this, and they are all desirous to send you to your own place and take you away.

I think, sometimes when I see a sinner, that I hear all the creatures cry as did Abishai, the son of Zerviah, in 2 Samuel 16:9. Abishai was one of David's soldiers and, when Shimei cursed David, he said, *Let me go over I pray thee, and take off his head; why should this dead dog curse my Lord?* So when you are blaspheming God, the creatures look upon you with disdain, and they rise against you, and all the creatures say, "Oh, this dead dog, this wretched creature, how long shall he live to blaspheme God? Shall I cut off his head? Shall I go and send him down to his own place?"

It would terrify your heart if you could hear every creature crying to God to be your executioner. And certainly, when God gives commission, and God falls upon you, every creature will fall upon you. You read this in 2 Samuel 18. When Joab fell upon Absalom, immediately the ten men fell upon him and slew him too, as soon as Joab gave the stroke. So, as soon as God gives the stroke against the sinner, certainly all other creatures are ready to fall upon the sinner also.

So you see, then, that sin brings a man to such a condition where all creatures are at enmity with him. When once the soul is reconciled to God and his sin is pardoned, all creatures are at peace with you. You are then in league with all the creatures. We should account it an evil condition to be in such a place where all the men in the nation are our enemies and stand ready to murder us. Certainly, all the sinners in the world are in the midst of the creatures of God that stand ready armed with God's wrath against them.

Hence it is then once God enlightens the conscience of a sinner, he fears everything. Proverbs says, *The wicked flee when none pursueth them.* It is very observable that Cain, after he had committed that sin of slaying his brother, said, *Every one that meets me will slay me.* Who was there, then, in the world? Nobody but his father and mother, and yet everyone that meets him will slay him. He was afraid of everything and everyone because he had sinned against the Lord. So every enlightened conscience that knows what sin means, when he comes to have conscience awakened, is afraid of everything. If there are thunderings, lightnings, storms, tempests, it sees the wrath of God in this storm and tempest, in this thunder and lightning. "Any stirs abroad in the world are but messengers of God's wrath against me," says the awakened conscience.

This is the misery of a sinner, and then how much greater is the evil of sin than affliction!

Chapter 35

Twelfth, sin is a greater evil to man than affliction because it puts a man under the curse of God.

No, further, it puts the creature under the curse of God. It separates the creature for evil, Psalm 4:2. It is said, *God separates the righteous man for himself.* So sin separates the creature for evil and makes him "anathema," accursed. God says in Deuteronomy 27:26, "Cursed is every one that abides not in every thing that is written in the Law to do it." He is accursed in all that he has and does. The curse of God is against him. And here observe, sin not only deserves a curse, that the creature should be accursed, but of its own nature it is a curse and makes the creature accursed in its own nature.

Thus you may see the evil of sin by the excellency of grace. Grace not only brings excellency upon the creature and brings a blessing, but of itself it separates the creature for a blessing. For what is holiness but grace? They are usually expressed for one and the same. Now what is holiness but the consecration of a thing for God? So that when holiness comes into the heart, that is nothing else but that gracious principle whereby the soul of a man or woman, before common to lust and sin, comes to be separated from all these things and to be consecrated and given up to God Himself. That's holiness!

Now sin must be contrary to holiness. As holiness is a separation of the creature from other things, and a consecration of it unto God, so sin is a separation of the creature from God and all good, and a devoting of it unto wrath and misery and a curse, and all evil whatsoever in its own nature. It is not in the desert only.

Many men think sin, in its desert deserves a curse, but they do not understand how sin, in its own nature, separates the heart from God and so gives it up to all evil, all misery, as grace does to all good. This is the evil of sin and, therefore, there is more evil in sin than there is in affliction.

Chapter 36

Thirteen, sin is the seed of eternal evil. Therefore, it is more harmful to man than affliction. A use, thereof, is this: see that those men are deceived who think to provide well for themselves by sin. Use 2. The ministry of the Word is for our good, as well as God's glory.

Further, sin is a principal evil, so I call it, because it is a principal of eternal evil to the creature. I do not mean that it deserves eternal evil only, but of itself it is eternal evil. For example, grace does not only deserve eternal happiness, but it is the seed of eternal happiness. It is that principle which, if left alone, will grow to eternal happiness.

So sin not only deserves eternal misery, but it is the seed of eternal evil; and sin itself will be the executioner of your soul and will prove an intolerable misery to the soul. Though sin is the very element in which many men and women live and delight themselves, yet let it be known that this sin not only deserves that God should bring His wrath upon you for it, but that sin will prove eternal torment to you.

For example, take the fish that plays and leaps in the water. The water is the element that the fish delights in, but, if you put fire under this water, that water which was the element in which the fish skipped, played, and delighted itself, will be torture and torment to the fish as it becomes boiling hot.

So sin is the element where men play and delight in their sinful ways as the fish does in its water. But when God comes and mingles wrath with sin, that very sin, which was your delight, shall be torture and torment, and a principle of eternal evil to you. Thus sin is a greater evil than affliction.

For example, afflictions (in the form of diseases) bring pains and sorrows to the body; but they will wear themselves out in time and the disease will go away. But sin is such a principal evil, and such a misery to the creature, that it will never go out, but continue a principal of eternal misery. Thus you have seen how sin is against our own good.

There are some things to say by way of application in this work.

Use 1. Sin is against our own good. Hence, all those promises that any sinful way makes to you to provide for your own selves in, and your own good, are all deceitful and will deceive you. The way of the wicked deceives them. Certainly you are mistaken if you think to make any provision for yourself in sinful ways. And the best way for any man or woman to provide for themselves is to abandon sin. Would you provide for yourself and your own good? Would you be a true self-love? Abandon sin, for sin is against your own good.

Use 2. Again, hence, you see that the ministry of the Word is that which is for our good, and that which makes for your good as well as for God's glory. God, in sending the ministry of the Word, sends it for your own good as well as for His own glory. Why? What does it do? It only seeks to get away your sins and make them bitter and grievous unto you.

I have, in many particulars, opened the nature of sin and how grievous and evil it is to you. Now, what is the intent of this but to get the serpent out of your bosoms, that which will do you mischief, and all this is for your own good.

Certainly, if God were ever to open your eyes, you would then desire, with your faces upon the ground, to bless God that ever He sent His ministers to show you what sin is. Many times men's spirits rise against the Word and look upon God's ministers as enemies. "Oh, he is speaking against me!"

No, it is not against any one's person, but against your sin, man or woman, against that which will do you mischief and undo you.

Again, many cry out against the minister as did that man

against Christ, "He comes to torment us before the time." No, it is against your sin, man! It is against that which will undo you.

Many are ready to say of the minister as was said to the prophet Elijah, *What, hast thou met me, oh, my enemy!* But, as the prophet said, "Do not my words do you good?"

Certainly, that which makes sin grievous to you does you as much good as creatures can be done to. Many have sin in their stomachs, who rise against the minister and the Word like the sick man's stomach rises against the glass or the pot in which the medicine is. But when, for that evil grief within, he vomits, it makes him sick for awhile, and the man throws up many filthy things, much noisesome stuff, then he cries out, "Oh, blessed be God! Though I had pain, yet this takes away a great deal of that bad stuff that would have bred diseases."

So, though our ministry may put you to pain, yet you will bless God when that is cast out which it has to deal with. Many people, when they hear the Word, have their spirits rise up against it; but, when it has pleased God to get away their sins, though upon hard terms, they have blessed God that they ever heard the Word that troubled them or ever saw such a man's face.

I remember something that was said to me. A man, when he sat and heard me, was persuaded that everything I spoke was against him personally, though he was a stranger I had never met. He professed that his spirit rose against both the Word and the speaker. He went home, and the Word worked on him and worked out sin, and he came, not long after, and blessed God that he ever heard that sermon. And so certainly it will be.

I have shown you in these thirteen particulars how evil sin is against your own souls. Know, then, if the minister, by the Word, can but get away your sin, you will see it higher than the greatest good and happiness that you ever had in all your lives; that ever you understood that which

would do you so much hurt. "Alas," you will say, "I did not
see sin would do me so much hurt. Woe to me if I had not
heard the evil of sin. If I had known the evil of sin by feeling, what would have become of me?"

You have heard and read much of the evil of sin. Now
think, if these things are so grievous in hearing and reading
them, what a woeful condition will that soul be in that must
feel it, that must have every one of these particulars made
good to the full? Certainly such a soul must be in a woeful
condition.

Now the Lord so sanctify and bless unto you the reading
or hearing of all these evils, that none of your souls may
ever come to feel them.

Chapter 37

Fourteenth, sin is worse than affliction because it hardens the heart against God and the means of grace.

The opposition sin has to our own good is such that it has more evil against ourselves than any affliction, and for the manifestation of that we have opened thirteen particulars. Thus far we have gone. There are two more particulars to discover the evil of sin as against our good more than afflictions.

Sin is worse than affliction as it is against ourselves, for it is that which hardens the heart against God and the means of grace more than any affliction. I do not speak now of hardening the heart against God in opposition to him, but as in opposition to our own good that we should receive from God in the use of the means of grace. And so sin is more opposite to our good than afflictions.

Affliction usually furthers the means of grace and prepares the heart for entertaining the means of grace. That is what affliction does, but sin hardens the heart against it, and hinders the ecstasy of the means of grace upon the souls of men and women. In Hosea 5:15 we read, *in their afflictions they will seek Me early.* Then the more afflictions are upon them, the more ready they are to seek Him. Isaiah 26:16 says, *When thy chastening was upon them, they poured forth their prayer.*

Many men and women who never knew how to pray, who would say that they could not pray in their families, that they could not pray in secret, that they only had learned to say words as children, would not otherwise pray; but, when afflictions are upon them, their hearts could be driven to God, and they could find how to pray otherwise.

There is a saying about mariners, "He that knows not how to pray, let him go to sea." This notes that, when a man comes into the waves, tempests, and storms, this will teach him how to pray. You mariners, consider if it ever taught you how to pray. I would think that, of any sort of men in the world, mariners would have the gift of prayer because they are so often in affliction and so often in danger of their lives. Many times they find that, though they do not know how to use their mouths, to fashion their tongues to anything but oaths at other times, yet, when they are in danger of their lives, they can fall to prayer and pour forth their prayer. *When Thy chastening is upon them, they pour forth their prayer,* and that word translated "prayer" there, in the original is a word that signifies "to enchant." The reason comes from this, because enchanters put a great deal of efficacy in a few words, closed their sentences in a few words, and thought there was much efficacy in them. So the prayers that come from men and women in affliction have much efficacy in them. They are not vain, light words, but have an abundance of efficacy.

So, then, afflictions further the means of grace in the hearts of men and women. They bring them to the Word and furthers that also. They are as the rain that softens the earth and fits it for the plow. *Plow up the fallow ground of your hearts, saith the Lord.* The Word of God is as the plow to plow up the fallow ground of your hearts.

Now husbandmen know that when the earth is dry and hard, they cannot plow. Their plows are kept out; but when rain comes and softens the earth, then their plows can go. Many times it is so with the hearts of many men and women when they are in prosperity. The sunshine of prosperity being upon them, the plow of the Word cannot get into their hearts; but when afflictions or sickness comes, then the plow of the Word can get in and cast up the fallow ground of their hearts. Times of afflictions bring men and women to the Word.

I remember reading a sermon of Chrysostom to the people of Antioch where he told them that when they were in trouble, then their congregations were thrust and filled. It was at such a time when Theodocius the Emperor, by the instigation of the Empress, his wife, was angry with the city and threatened to come against it and destroy it in a warlike manner. Then all the people got together and the congregations were thrust, and then they prayed and sighed, and there was great and much prayer when they were afraid the King would come in anger against the city to destroy it.

So afflictions, troubles, and fears, bring men and women to the means of grace, and make the means to be profitable many times. As it is with the seed that is sown, if there is a dry, hot time after the sowing, it lies under the clods and does not come up; but if rain comes, than that which was sown several weeks before springs up. So we sow the Word of God in your hearts, but the seed lies under the clods as long as there is the hot sunshine of prosperity until afflictions come and the rain of affliction brings the Word out and then something appears.

We have known men who never seemed to be worked upon by the Word, yet when God has laid His hand upon them in some affliction, then there has been brought to their remembrance such a truth that they heard such a time, and then they have acknowledged the power of the Word, and conscience has then been awakened, and not before.

It is reported of Beza, that famous instrument of God in the church, that he was a Papist, and lived in Paris in great honor. He was a man of great esteem and good birth, and had preferments there; yet he often had misgiving thoughts that he was not right and that the Protestants were in the right because he had read the Scriptures and compared the controversy. Yet, because of his great honors and preferments in Paris, all went away and could not prevail; but God laid a great sickness upon him, great afflictions, and then that which was only on his spirit now sunk into his heart more deeply. So, then, as soon as he began to recover, he left Paris and all his preferments and went to Geneva. It was there he made public profession of the truth.

Thus, afflictions further the means of grace, but it is otherwise with sin. Sin, if left alone, hardens the heart desperately against all the means of grace. It is true, though, that God may sometimes put forth His almighty power and, notwithstanding all the sin in the soul of a man or woman, may make the means of grace effectual though man's heart is never so stout and stubborn in their ways of sin. Yet God may be pleased to come, by His almighty power, and overpower the heart, as He does many times.

Yes, God sometimes lets men go on in horrible wickedness to manifest His power all the more. When the prophet Elijah would have fire come to devour the sacrifice, he poured much water upon it so that the power of God might be more manifest. So God suffers deluges of sin to be in men and women sometimes that He might magnify His power so much more in the efficacy of the means of grace.

But yet we are to know that sin, and every sin of its own nature, hardens the heart against God in the use of all the means of grace. Yes, and so hardens the heart that, if men and women live any long time under the means of grace and continue in the ways of sin, it is a thousand to one whether they are ever worked upon afterwards.

Usually we find that where the means of grace comes to any place, it works mostly at first. I do not, nor will I, limit God, but for the most part, at first it works upon men and women before they have, by sin, hardened themselves against it. If once they have continued some little time under it, and their hearts have followed their sin and so come to be hardened, it is a most dangerous thing, and many times God leaves them forever to their hardness.

Yes, such evil there may be in sin. If a man or woman has an enlightened conscience, and goes against the light of their conscience when they live under the means of grace, any one sin against the light of conscience may forever harden them.

You who have come to the Word and have heard, these things have come near to your soul; and yet there has been that violence of corruption to go against the light of your conscience, and that particular truth that has been made known unto you from God, that one sin may be enough evil to harden your heart so that the means shall never do you good. Therefore, there is a great deal more evil in sin than in any affliction.

I beseech you to consider this one note further in it. God comes many times, yes, usually with an abundance of grace to the souls of men and women in their afflictions, and that is the continuance of their afflictions and in the increase of their afflictions. Yet the means of grace work. But God can never come with grace while they sin unless sin is decreased.

I say, God never comes to make any means of grace effectual unless there is the decrease and taking away of sin. The means of grace may be effectual with the increase of affliction, but the means of grace can never be effectual without the decrease of sin. Therefore, there is more evil in sin against ourselves than in affliction.

Chapter 38

Fifteen, sin is worse to us than affliction, because sin brings more shame than affliction.

There is more evil in sin than in affliction, as being against ourselves, in regard of the shame that it brings. Sin brings more shame than any afflictions brings. Romans 6:20, *What profit, or what fruit had you in those things whereof you are now ashamed?* Sin is that which brings shame, not only to a man or woman in particular, but likewise to a whole nation when sin prevails. Proverbs 13:34, *Righteousness exalteth a nation, but sin is a reproach to any people.*

Afflictions are not a reproach any further than they are the fruit of sin, and then there is shame in them (but we will speak of this afterward). But sin is the proper cause of reproach and shame, and certainly this Scripture has been fulfilled concerning us. Our sin has been a reproach to this nation. There was a time when this nation was honored among other nations, and was a terror to them; but of late, since we have sinned and grown superstitious, coming nearer unto popery, there has been more wickedness among us.

This nation has been an exceeding reproach. We may apply for that to Hosea 13:1 where, according to the interpretation of most, *when Ephraim spoke, trembling, he exalted himself in Israel; but when he offended in Baal, he died.* That is how interpreters carry it. There was a time when Ephraim spoke and all the nations around him trembled, and he exalted himself above other nations; but when he sinned in Baal, then he died. His honor died, he was a dead notion, and nobody regarded him.

True, time was when England spoke there was trembling, and England exalted himself above other nations; but since we have sinned in Baal, and there has been so much idolatry and superstition, we have been a dead nation in respect of what we had been before. Sin is a reproach to any nation, a shame. There is no such shame in affliction as there is in sin. Sin brings shame.

That which argues worthlessness in any, that which argues that there is little good or worth in any, brings shame. Or if anyone should do anything unbeseeming either his own excellency or that which is supposed to be in him (as to lie in the more, or to go naked, to behave themselves in some manner that belies the excellency that is in them), this brings shame. See Job 30:7. It was contemptible and a shame for those who went up and down, braying among the bushes.

So for any man to do anything beneath the excellency of a man is a shame. Now there is nothing so beneath the excellency of a man as sin. No affliction brings a man under his excellency as sin does. Therefore, no affliction can be such a shame to man as sin.

Now the rational creature that is guided by counsel in his actions is the proper subject of shame. Brute beasts cannot be capable of shame, because they have no counsel to be the cause of their actions, but the reasonable creature, failing in that which is his aim, coming short of the rule of his work, through his unskillfulness, does feel shame. For example, take any workman. If he does any work beneath the standard of that work through unskillfulness, it causes shame. He comes to be ashamed of it.

Now sin must bring shame, because it comes beneath the standard, the rule, of eternal life. Therefore, it must cause shame. It is true that it is a greater shame to fail in natural things through ignorance than to fail through willfulness; but in spiritual things, the greater shame is to fail through willfulness. And the greater the art, the greater shame it is to come short of the standard of that art.

Take, for example, a general. It is a greater shame for him to fail and come short of the rules of military art than for a country-man to come short of the rules for husbandry, because one is more noble than the other.

Now, brethren, the art of divinity, the guide to eternal life, is the most noble of any art, and for any creature to fail and come short of this art is the greatest shame that can be. Though men are ashamed of anything else, whether they are a painter, a workman, or a husbandman, if they come short of the standard, they are ashamed. But if men fail in the rule of eternal life, they are not ashamed then!

I remember that Augustine had this expression, "A scholar, if he fails in pronouncing a word, and pronounces it amiss, if he pronounces *Omer* for *Homer*, he is ashamed of that; but men are not ashamed of breaking the rules of divinity," and there are more failings in the breach of the rule of divinity, and in failing there, than in any art whatsoever.

Now sin is the greatest shame, and the reason why sinners are not ashamed is because they do not know the excellency of man. They do not know wherein the excellency of the rational creature consists, and therefore they are not ashamed of that which brings them beneath the excellency of the rational creature.

Besides, they do not know God's infinite holiness, therefore they are not ashamed. They are now among other sinners, and they think that, though some seem to be religious, yet others are as bad as themselves in their hearts at least, though not in practice.

Nero, because he was bad, thought others were as bad as he was. So a wicked man, when he cannot see others break out in such great sins as he does, yet he thinks they are as bad some other way, and have sins equally as great. And because they live among them that are as bad as themselves, and live in the same sins, therefore they are not ashamed.

A coal miner living among other coal miners is not ashamed but, if he lived among princes and noblemen, he would be ashamed. So wicked men in this world, because they live in this world among sinners, conceive them to be sinners like themselves and are not ashamed. But when God shall come to open what sin means, and what the holiness of God means, and when they see themselves stand in the presence of a holy God, then they will be ashamed.

But certainly sin is a greater shame than affliction. None need be ashamed of affliction any further than it has a connection to some great sin, but sin in the greatest prosperity has shame with it.

Chapter 39

*He who sins wrongs, despises, and hates his own soul.
Use 1. Then see the maliciousness that is in sin. Use 2. To
pity those who go on in sinful ways. Use 3. Let sin be dealt
harshly with.*

Thus we have discovered how sin is more against our
good than affliction is. Now there are divers things which
follow hence as consequences. I spoke of one or two before
and will name them no more. But only this far, hence we see
that sin is more against ourselves than anything else.
Therefore, it is the worst way for any to provide for themselves by giving way to live in any sinful course. And for
this I shall add two or three Scriptures I did not speak of before to show how men go against themselves. Those men
who think to provide best for themselves, the truth is that by
going the way of sin they go most against themselves. You
have these three notable expressions for this in Scripture.

First, men by sin wrong their own souls.

Second, that they despise their own souls.

Third, they hate their own souls.

If I should charge these three things upon the most vile
sinner at this present moment before the Lord, "Oh, you
wrong your own soul. You despise your own soul. You
hate your own soul!" he would be loath to yield to it. And
yet the Scripture charges this upon sinners, Proverbs 8:36,
He that sins against Me wrongs his own soul. He not only
wrongs God, that was in the first thing we opened, but by
sin he wrongs his own soul.

You will say, "I do nobody wrong. I thank God that nobody can say I wrong them." But you wrong your own
soul, and certainly it is as great an evil to wrong your own
soul as to wrong the body of another, and a great deal more.

Nay, further, mark, *All them that hate Me* (that is,

wisdom and instruction, the rule of life) *they love death*. It is a strange expression. If any of us ministers should say to you, "You love death," you would think it a rash speech from us. The Holy Ghost says this of all who hate instruction.

If there is any truth of God revealed against sin, and your heart rises against it, you love death, you love ruin, and you love your own destruction. And what pity is it for men and women to die? Who can pity them that die eternally when they love death? If they love death, they must have it. So the Holy Ghost says that they wrong their souls and they love death. Proverbs 15:32 says, *He that refuseth instruction despiseth his own soul*.

When you come and hear any instruction against any sinful way and refuse it, you despise your own souls, as if your own souls were worth very little. Hence it is that men and women, though they hear that sin tends to the death of their souls to their eternal ruin, yet if they have any temptation they will venture upon it. What is this but to despise your soul? Though your soul is worth a whole world, this is to despise it and to account it of little worth.

There is none so poor in this place, the meanest boy, servant, or girl but who has a soul worth more than heaven and earth. But, though the meanest here has a soul worth more than the world, we see it everyday that, to get twopence or fourpence, they will venture the ruin of their souls. Is not this to despise their souls? It is as if their souls were not worth twopence or fourpence; and they will lie or steal to get that which is less!

No, not only so, but they are haters of their own souls, and this you have in Proverbs 29:24, *He that is partner with a thief, hates his own soul*. There is an instance in that one sin, but it is true of every sin, for this must be taken as a rule to help you to understand the evil of sin. Know that what is said of any one sin is virtually true of all. That evil which is in any one sin is virtually in any sin. He hates his own soul who goes on in any one sin. Therefore, if you will provide for your own good, you must abandon sin.

OBJECTION. But, it may be said, "Is that lawful for a man to abstain from sin out of self-respect? I am showing how sin is against ourselves, therefore, I am urging you to abandon and take heed of sin since it is against ourselves. Then this question arises, "What, should we abstain from sin out of self-respect? What good is in this? Is that from grace?"

To that I answer three things.

ANSWER 1. At first, when God begins to work upon the soul, God usually moves us from self most. And these self grounds work most to take men and women off from the acts of their sin (from outward acts at least) and to stop them from the commission of sin and bring them to the means of grace. God makes use of self motives at first. But yet the work is not done until the soul goes beyond these. It is good for men and women to abstain from sin upon *any* grounds. There is so much evil in sin that is is well, upon any grounds, that men and women abstain from sin; unless the ground itself is a greater sin than the sin I am abstaining from. But yet the work is not done, therefore:

ANSWER 2. Know that, when grace is come into the soul, God uses self arguments and self motives to further the abstaining from sin (and it is lawful to do so), yet self motives and self arguments are not the chief and highest of all. But:

ANSWER 3. That which most pitches upon and most fully answers this question is this. If we only knew wherein our self good consists, which is certainly to live to God. Our self good is in this, not only the glory of God, but our own good and happiness. Our self good is in our living to God, that infinite First Being of all things. Now, if we understand this, we may make to be our highest aim in abstaining from sin and in doing any good that which is our self good. But we must not make it our highest aim *because* it is our self good. We must look to God above ourselves, but the same thing that is our self good, our own good, may be made our highest aim of all, which is our living to God and His praise. Thus, God has connected our good and His glory together. So, then, the same thing which is the highest end of all is that at which I must aim, God's glory and His praise, and it is also our highest good. So we may aim at it in our chief aims.

Secondly, if sin is so against us, I shall give you three uses of it.

USE 1. We see from this the desperate maliciousness that is in sin. It follows thus: for a creature to sin against the blessed God and to get no good to himself either, yes, to do harm to himself is a horrible mischief and malice. Certainly, if there is this maliciousness against man, then there is certainly malice against God in sin.

Suppose that you should get ever so much good; suppose that you, by sin, could get the greatest good that any creature ever had. You must not commit that sin, it would be wickedness to do it!

When you sin against God, you do mischief to yourself. Not only do you not get any good, but you do that which is the greatest wrong and evil to yourself, and yet will you go on in sin against God? Oh, what do you think of God? And what hurt has God done to you that you should be so malicious against Him, that you should dishonor Him and strike at Him? Not only do you get nothing for yourself by sin, you undo yourself by sin. Men will rather go on in that way that is dishonorable to God though they venture their own damnation to do it.

It's one of the highest expressions we can have against our enemies, "I will get even with him. I will get my revenge on him though it costs me my last coin." We account this as desperate malice in a man, but we do more against God. Though we may not use this language, yet God sees this language in our sins. "Well, I will do that which the Word forbids though I undo myself. I will venture my own perishing, my own eternal destruction. I would rather that be done than do that which God would have done."

There is this in every sin. Brethren, because we do not examine what is in sin, we think it only a little. We only see the outside, but when God comes to unravel out sin and to pick out all that His omniscient eye sees in sin, then it will appear to be evil, transcendently evil.

USE 2. If sin has so much evil in it, if it is more against us than affliction, then it should teach us to look with pity and an abundance of consideration on men and women who go on in ways of sin. Ah, poor creatures, they undo themselves. Their ways are against themselves, and they will work their own ruin and misery by these ways of theirs. You who are tradesmen, if you see a man going on in ways of trading so that you know he will certainly undo himself, you look upon him with pity. Poor, young man, he goes on in such a way as he will undo himself. The more a man has a hand in doing himself hurt, the more he is to be pitied.

You mariners, if you see one at sea do things from ignorance so that he, by and by, will be thrown into the sea or find himself upon the rocks, and his is willful in his way, you pity him. He is an object of your pity. Do you see any man or woman, your father or mother, brother or sister, husband or wife, or any whom you love dearly, going on in ways of sin? Oh, pity them! Let your heart bleed over them, poor wretches; they will undo themselves eternally.

Suppose you saw a group of men stab and murder themselves and lie dead in the streets, and it should be asked of you how they came to die. If your answer was that every one of them murdered himself, would it not be an object of pity? If you see men and women go on in sin, every one of them stabs and murders and does mischief to himself. They cut their own throats, this is the way of sin. Though they do not see it themselves, if God opens their eyes they will see it; and, certainly, they shall see it before long and they will be forced to cry out in the bitterness of their souls, "Woe to me, woe to me, I am lost and undone, and I have undone myself!"

Therefore, brethren, we should not look upon sinners as they are in the height of their prosperity and the ruse of their pride, but look upon them as what they will be within a short time. Look upon them in their end and then learn to pity them.

Although sinners go on conceitedly and boast of their evil ways for the present, pity them so much the more, for the more any sinner is conceited and boasts in his way, the more dangerous is his condition; the more dangerous sign the seal of God is upon him to seal him in his destruction. The more conceited any man is in anything that will ruin him, the more lamentable is the object therefore. Many times, when we see men under grievous afflictions, we go to our neighbors and see them lie under God's hand, in grievous pains and tortures of body, crying out dolefully. It makes your heart bleed and draws tears from your eyes and you say, "Oh, the lamentable condition this man or woman is in!" You pity them in affliction because they are in such grievous pain.

But now you have another neighbor, and you hear him swearing. Certainly, though you pity the other neighbor under affliction, yet to hear him swear is more pitiful than to hear the other roar out in the most grievous torture any man or woman was ever in. When we hear them in torture, we have our hearts bleed and are not affected with their sinning. This is a sign that we do not know the evil of sin.

Further, if you should hear one in the anguish of conscience crying out, "I am undone, I am damned, I am damned," in the anguish of his conscience crying out, you look upon such with pity.

Now this I say, those that are in the greatest torment of conscience for their sin are in a better case than those who go on most conceitedly and boast in their sin. Do you see one who is your neighbor, or in your family, or who is a friend who, when he is rebuked or reproved for any sin, is careless or hardened in sin? I say, this man or woman, servant or child, is in a worse condition and is a more lamentable object than if you should see another in the greatest horror, anguish, and trouble of conscience, crying out most bitterly because of sin, for there is a great deal more hope for this man or woman who cries out in anguish of conscience for sin. He may be saved and not eternally ruined by sin. There is a great deal more hope. Therefore, learn who is to be pitied, for sin is more against our own good than any affliction.

USE 3. If sin is so much against ourselves, then learn to deal harshly with sin. For thus it follows, that which we look upon as our own enemy we are willing should be harshly dealt with. Now, nothing is such an enemy to our good as sin is.

If you apprehend that anyone has done you hurt, or intends to do you hurt, you think you may take liberty to let yourself out to the utmost to revenge yourself. But this is sinful, and it is a distemper in your heart to do so. But you men and women who have your hearts filled with revenge, because you conceive that others have done you harm, here is an object God gives you permission to let out your revenge to the full upon - sin! Other men do you harm, therefore you think you may let out revenge. That is your wickedness, for vengeance belongs to God. But sin does you more harm than any man can, and in this God gives you permission to revenge yourselves upon sin.

Revenge yourself as much as you can. Look upon it as most mischievous. There are some spiteful and vengeful men who have it lie smoldering in their hearts because they cannot let it out upon objects as much as they would.

Now here is an object you may let it out as much as you can, to revenge yourself and to seek the ruin and destruction of sin, and to labor to use it as harshly as possibly you can.

In 2 Corinthians 7:11, when they had committed sin, the Apostle said, *what revenge was there*. They manifested their repentance by revenge upon sin. Follow your sin with a deadly hatred if you will. You have a hateful disposition against others, follow sin with as deadly a hatred as you can.

It was an argument of David's heart, cleaving to Absalom when Joab was to go against him, *Use the young man kindly for my sake*. This was an argument David's heart had with him. So when you would fain have sin used kindly, gently, it is an argument that your hearts are not set against sin as much as they should be. No, you should not say, "Use sin kindly," but roughly and harshly.

As the prophet said of one who came to destroy him, "Use him roughly when he comes to the door." So when sin comes to the door, when temptations are seeking to have entrance, use them roughly at the door and say, "Let the righteous smite me. Oh, that the Word might come as a two-edged sword to stab and slay my sin. Oh, that when I go to hear the Word, I might meet with some hard thing against sin."

That is how we should think when we come to the Word. When sin has got a blow from the Word of God, bless God and say, "Blessed be God, my sins this day have got a blow. This sin of mine that has done me so much harm, and has so pestered me and hindered my peace and comfort, blessed be God that this day it has received a blow."

This is how we should do because sin makes so much against ourselves. And thus we have finished the two first heads of sin being against God and against ourselves. Now there are four more.

THE THIRD PART OF THIS TREATISE

Chapter 40

Sin is opposite to all good, and therefore a greater evil than any affliction opened in five things. (1) Sin takes away the excellency of all things. (2) It brings a curse upon all. (3) Sin is a burden to heaven and earth, and all creatures. (4) Sin turns the greatest good into the greatest evil. (5) Sin, if left alone, would bring all things to confusion.

Thirdly, sin is opposite to all good in general. Sin is opposite to God and to ourselves and, I say, in the third place, it's against all kind of good and therefore a greater evil than any affliction. Now for that, there are five things to be opened. Only in the general, take this sure rule. There must be more evil in sin than in any affliction, because there is no other evil that is not opposed to some particular good. An affliction is opposite to the particular good contrary to that affliction; but sin is opposed to every good. Not only is sin opposed to the contrary virtue, but it is opposed to every good. That is what divinity teaches us. Though heathens in morality teach that one sin is opposite to the contrary virtue, divinity teaches that one sin is opposed to every virtue and every good, which appears in five things.

First, sin spoils all good, takes away the beauty and excellency of all good whatsoever. It may be said of anything that has an excellency when sin comes, as it is said of Reuben in Genesis 49:4, *His excellency is gone, is departed, he shall not excel.* Therefore, Romans 8:20 says, (through the sin of man) *all creatures are subject to vanity.* The whole world is put under vanity through man's sin.

Now, then, it appears by that that the luster and beauty and excellency of glory of all things in this world are spoiled by the sin of man, for all it put under vanity by sin. And sin not only makes the heart vain, and so is against ourselves, but all things in the world are put under vanity by sin. The excellency of your estate, of your parts, the excellency of any creature you enjoy, all is spoiled through sin. Therefore, in Titus 1:15, it is said, *All things are unclean to the sinner*. He says, *To him that is unclean, all things are unclean*. This is the first, your sin is opposed to all good and spoils all good.

Secondly, sin brings a curse upon all. I opened before how it puts man under a curse, but now I am to show how it brings a curse upon the whole world, Genesis 3, *Cursed shall the earth be for thy sake,* and so by the same reason upon the whole world that you have to do with. Not only the sinner but, through man's sin, the whole world is under a curse, and therefore it is a most dangerous thing for any man or woman to seek after happiness in the things of the world when the whole world is under a curse, and will you seek your happiness in that which is under a curse? No marvel, then, that the devil himself is called the god of this world. Why? Because the world is accursed through the sin of man. Sin brings a curse upon the whole world.

Thirdly, sin is a burden to heaven and earth, to all creatures. Romans 8:22, *The whole creation groans and travails in pain to be delivered,* and that through the sin of man. Now what is the evil of sin? When it is so weighty that it makes the whole frame of heaven and earth groan to bear the burden of it. It may be that your sin is light to your soul. You carry it lightly, but as light as it is to you, it is such a heavy burden to heaven and earth and the whole frame of the creation that, if God did not hold it by His mighty power, it would shake it. Not only shake, but fall down.

Fourthly, sin turns the greatest good into the greatest evil. Therefore, it is opposed to all good. For example, take the greatest good of man in prosperity. The more prosperity you have, though a fruit of God's bounty, yet your sin turns it into the greatest evil to you. If poison gets into wine, it works more strongly than in water. So sin, in a prosperous estate, usually works more strongly to turn it to a greater evil than sin in a weak estate. Poor men, by sin, have their water poisoned, and rich men, by sin, have their wine poisoned. Now poisoned wine has more strength than poisoned water. And it turns not only prosperity, but the best means; not only the means of grace, but the better any means is you enjoy, the more evil it is turned into to you unless the means take away the sinfulness of your heart. If you retain the sinfulness of your heart, the more powerful sermons you hear and the more glorious truths that are laid open, the worse will be your condition and you will one day curse the time that ever you had such means.

Yes, sin turns God to be the greatest evil, and makes Him the greatest evil in His attributes. And Christ Himself (though infinitely good) is made to be the greatest evil. Christ is a stumbling stone to wicked men, and laid by God to be a stumbling stone. What! Christ, the precious corner-stone, who has infinite treasures of all excellency, in whom the fulness of the God-head dwells bodily, yet this Christ is a stumbling stone, and the greatest evil through sin to wicked men. So, then, one day they will curse the time that ever they heard of Christ. So sin is opposed to all good because it turns the greatest good into the greatest evil.

Fifthly, and lastly, sin is the greatest evil because, if it is let alone, it would bring all things to confusion. Therefore it is said, "by Christ all things subsist." Were it not for Christ, who sets Himself against the evil of sin, all things would be brought to confusion. 1 John 5;19, *The whole world lies in wickedness*. Just as carrion lies in slime and filth, and there rots, so the whole world would be in the same case that the carrion is that lies in filth and brought to confusion were it not that God has His number of elect, and they keep the world from confusion.

Now, put all these together. Sin spoils all, brings a curse upon all, is a burden to heaven and earth, turns the greatest good to the greatest evil, and would bring all things to confusion if let alone. This is the evil of sin in opposition to all good.

There are but three more: 1. To show how sin is the evil of all evils whatsoever; 2. It has a kind of infiniteness in it; 3. It has reference to the devil. But these I cannot come to in this chapter, but shall in the following to conclude all.

You have read much of the evil of sin and how it is above all afflictions. Afflictions are of a lower nature. Oh, brethren, this is what we should seek for and prize, to enjoy those means that may lessen sin and oppose wickedness among us. And of all others these are the two great means to crush sin and bring it down, or make it less in all places: the great ordinance of the magistracy and the great ordinance of the ministry.

Now (as I told you before), reproach has come to our nation through sin, and where is it that sin has grown to the height that it has but because there has been corruption in both; great corruption in the magistracy and great corruption in the ministry among us.

We read of Dan and Bethel, two calves set up there. Dan signifies judgment and Bethel signifies the house of God. So there was great corruption in Dan and Bethel, places of judgment (magistracy) and Bethel, the house of God (ministry).

Now it has pleased God of late to begin to be merciful to us this way, through that great ordinance of God. He has appointed for us the Assembly of Parliament, to purge both Dan and Bethel, magistracy and ministry, to cast out corruption from places of judgment and the house of God. And as we are able to bless God for this, so we are to further this work of theirs, and stand by them to the utmost that we are able in all good ways, those worthies of God in that great assembly, for the finishing of that work which they have begun that our sins and wickedness may be done away with from among us.

And for that which has been done, certainly God has received much praise, and we have cause to bless God for it. Those who have gone on in a good way, according to what the Law permits them, are to be encouraged; and in a more special manner, you who are the special means of good to this land, I mean in regard of safety and your employment; the mariners, in whom much of the strength of this nation consists, for our walls are water and wooden walls. Seas and ships are the walls of this land and, therefore, much of the good, safety, and prosperity of this state depends on those men.

And if God stirs up their hearts to the maintenance of their protestation, and Parliament, and liberties, and to set themselves up against popery and superstition, and to encourage the Parliament in their good way, this is what we are to bless God for and encourage you in.

We read in Judges 5 that several tribes, when the people of God were in straits, would not go up but had many excuses. Others went to help in the cause of God, Judges 5:14. See how many excuse themselves, but especially in the 16th verse, *Why abodest thou among the sheep-folds to hear the bleatings of the flocks?* "Oh," Reuben said, "we must not leave house and cattle; we must not go out." And Giliad abode beyond Jordan, and Dan abode in ships. Some think Dan did not live near the sea, but thought they ran to ships and abode there. And Ashor continued by the seashore and abode in his breaches. He pleaded thusly, "We must continue our business in making fences against the sea. We have many breaches, and we must continue there and look to our business." But Zebulon and Naphtali placed their lives in jeopardy in the high places of the field! Who are those two, Zebulon and Naphtali, who were full of courage and zeal when others were full of pleas and would not venture their lives? Who are those that ventured their lives? These two were the special tribes of mariners who were forward rather than the others. That these were mariners appears in

Matthew 4:15, *The land of Zebulon and Naphtali by the way of the sea beyond Jordan,* these that lived by the sea. Others would not stir that lived by the sea, but Zebulon and Naphtali placed their lives in jeopardy.

Now mark it, God seems to remember this. They did not places themselves in jeopardy in a good cause in vain. God remembers it many hundreds of years of later. When Christ comes, the first tribes that seem to be enlightened were these. The people that sat in darkness saw a great light, and to them who sat in the region and shadow of death, light is sprung up. They sat in darkness, a company of poor mariners, exceedingly ignorant of the ways of God, and Christ comes first to them and brings light to them.

It may be that God might aim to show mercy to these tribes rather for this which they did in appearing in as good a cause, though it was with jeopardy to themselves. So go on, and in a good cause appear and venture yourselves to assist these worthies of our in whom so much of our good consists, and God will remember this in spiritual mercies.

Would you have the means of grace continued, and the means of light come to them that sit in darkness? If you would have the blessings of Zebulon and Naphtali, then be Zebulons and Naphtalies to go out, whatever excuses others have, and place yourselves in jeopardy for the good of this Commonwealth.

THE FOURTH PART OF THIS TREATISE

Chapter 41

That sin is the evil and poison of all other evils, showed in several particulars. First, it's the strength of all evils. Second, it's the sting of affliction. Third, it's the curse of all evils opened in five particulars. Fourth, sin is the shame of all evils. Fifth, the eternity of all evil comes from sin.

There are four things which, unless we are well-instructed in and know, we will know nothing to any purpose. The things which we must know are God, sin, Christ, and eternity. These are the four great things that you need to be well-instructed in. The knowledge of sin I have endeavored to set before you. In this argument I have showed you the evil of sin above all affliction. The next thing I am to open to you is the fourth general head, propounded in the fifth chapter, and that is that sin is the evil of all other evils.

It is the very core, the essential part, of all other evils. There's nothing that would scarcely worthy of the name of evil if sin were not in it. That it is the evil of all other evils will appear in these particulars.

First, it is the strength of all other evils. The strength, the prevailing strength that any evil has against man is from sin. There is no evil that would have any prevailing strength to do us any harm if there were not sin in it. That is certain. Nothing in heaven, earth, or hell would do any of the children of men harm were it not for sin, if there were no sin to give it strength. The strength of any evil that can do us any harm is from sin.

Let the evil be never so small, yet if it comes armed with the guilt of sin it is enough to undo any man or woman in the world. This is the reason for the difference in the power, the prevailing power, of any cross and affliction in some more than others. You shall have some that, let them have but the smallest cross and affliction upon them, have their hearts sink. They are not able to stand up under it. Others who have a hundred times more upon them go under it with joy. This is the special difference, one has the guilt of sin in the evil, and the other is delivered from it.

One learned man used this comparison, I remember, to express the difference in afflictions. Afflictions are like water, and a little water upon a man's shoulder in a lead vessel is a great deal heavier than much more water in a vessel of leather or wood. Take a leather bucket filled with water; it is not as heavy as a little water in a lead vessel. So a little affliction, where there is much guilt of sin, is abundantly more heavy than a great deal of affliction where there is not the guilt of sin.

Haman could not stand before such a petty cross as to have Mordecai refuse to bow his knee. Being a wicked man, that cross being with sin, troubled him sorely. And Achitaphel, when he was crossed in his way, could not bear it.

Therefore, brethren, if you would bear afflictions, this is your way. Your wisdom is to labor to know where the strength of an affliction lies if you would overcome it. As you know, the great care of the Philistines who desired to overcome Sampson was to know where his strength lay. If they could, by Delilah's means, find out the strength of Sampson, they thought they might easily overcome him. So, certainly, if you could but find out where the strength of your afflictions lie, it is easy, then, for you to have fears and disquiets taken away. The reason why fears and disquiets overcome you as they do is because you do not find out the strength of them. If that were found out and gotten away, you might quickly overcome afflictions, and they would be light to you. The prevailing strength of all afflictions is from sin. This is the first thing to show that sin is the evil of all evils.

Secondly, not only the prevailing strength, but the bitterness, the sting of affliction, that which makes it bitter to the spirit, is sin. Sin makes it come like an armed man with power. And besides, sin makes it inwardly gall at the very heart, sting like a serpent, as the Apostle says of death, I Corinthians 15:56, *The sting of death is sin.* So that which he says of death is true of all evils, of all afflictions, that are but makers of way to death. The sting of a sickness, the sting of the loss of your estates, the sting of discredit, the sting of imprisonment, the sting of all afflictions and that which makes them bitter to the soul is sin. You have a notable place, Jeremiah 4:18, *Thy ways, and thy doings have procured these things unto thee, this is thy wickedness, because it is bitter, because it reacheth unto thy heart.* In the Greek it is, "This is thy wickedness, and because it is bitter it reaches unto thy heart." That interprets the word. He is saying this, your wickedness has procured this, and the punishment to your wickedness is bitter and reaches to your heart because it comes as a punishment of your wickedness. So it comes to be bitter and reaches to your very heart.

Oh, when sin is affliction, it comes to the heart and is very bitter. Were the guilt of sin taken away in any affliction, the soul might be able to make use of that expression of Agag in a better way than he did, and come joyfully and cheerfully to look upon any affliction and say, *The bitterness of death is past.* So, if God lays any affliction upon me or my family, the bitterness of death is gone. The bitterness is gone because my sin is gone.

Sin is, as it were, the rotten core in an apple or fruit. It will make all the fruit to be bitter and rotten. And so take away the rotten core, and you will not taste so much bitterness in the fruit. So if sin, the rotten core, is cut out, affliction will not be so bitter. This is the second, all the prevailing strength of affliction is from sin, and the bitterness and anguish of spirit in affliction is from sin.

Thirdly, the curse of all evil is from sin (the strength of

all evil, the bitterness of all evil, and the curse of all evil). I have shown before that sin brings a curse upon ourselves, yes, how it brings a curse upon all good. Now I am to show you how sin brings a curse upon all evil. It is that which makes the affliction to be accursed.

We have a most excellent Scripture for this to show the difference between God's afflicting His people whom He has pardoned, when sin is pardoned and removed, and God's afflicting the wicked and ungodly, whose sin is yet upon them. A most admirable text for this, and the difference between these two, that you may see what a difference sin puts upon affliction when it is upon us, is Jeremiah 24:5 compared with verse 9. We have before us God's expression of the differing estate of His people by the basket of good figs and evil figs. Those that were godly were like good figs and those who were wicked were like evil figs. Mark the different dealing of God with both. Both were in captivity, both good and evil, they must both be delivered in to the hand of their enemies; but see the difference, verse 5, *So I will acknowledge them whom I have carried away captive into the land of the Chaldeans for their good.* Mark it, they must go into the land of the Chaldeans, but it must be for their good. God says, "Though I afflict them, yet because I have pardoned them, let them know I aim at nothing but their good."

Then he speaks of the bad figs, the wicked men in captivity, verse 9, *I do deliver them to be removed into all kingdoms of the earth for their hurt.* I will send them, they shall go into captivity, but I intend them no good. It shall be for their hurt; to be a reproach and a proverb, a taint and a curse in all places where I shall deliver them.

I beseech you, keep this text by you. That which is said of this particular affliction is true of every affliction. When God brings any evil upon any wicked man or woman, such as are in their sins, God certainly intends their hurt. He brings it for their hurt, even the same affliction that befalls one whose sin is pardoned, and God intends it for their good. So the privilege of godly men who have their sins pardoned through Christ, how different that is from the estate of wicked men who have the guilt of their sin upon them.

Sin is the curse of all evils. It will deliver them for their hurt that it may be a curse to them. Now this argument would enlarge itself to show how sin brings a curse upon every affliction and what it is. And that thereby we shall make it appear that sin is a greater evil than affliction, I will but briefly name what might more largely be insisted upon.

1. When there is sin and affliction, affliction comes out of God's revenge for sin. God looks upon the guilty creature with indignation and wrath. "Here's a wretch that has been bold to sin against me, and now My hand shall be upon him." And so, when the sinner is under God's hand, God is so far from looking upon him with pity and compassion that He looks upon him with indignation and wrath as an enemy. And this is a sore evil, that when God, who is the God of all mercy and infinite compassion, gets a wretched sinner under Him, He looks upon Him in the depths of His affliction with indignation and wrath as a loathsome creature. He shall be cast out in His wrath. God casts out a sinner and curses him when He looks upon him in such a manner.

2. The curse of afflictions, when it comes in such a manner in way of sin is in this, God regards neither the time, nor the manner, nor the measure of the affliction. Whether it is a time seasonable for the sinner or not, whether the manner is acceptable, whether the measure is such that the sinner can bear; no, let that go, God does not mind that.

Indeed, when God comes with His afflicting hand upon those to whom sin is pardoned, whom He looks upon in Christ, He weighs out their afflictions. God comes and with His wisdom orders it for the due time, and weighs it out for the due proportion, that there shall not be one dram put into it any further than their strength can bear. He does not tempt us beyond our strength. He does not lay upon us what we are not able to bear. This is true of His people. But when God comes upon those who have the guilt of sin lying upon them, He will come at the time that is most unseasonable for them, at the worst time that can be.

For example, when a husband-man wants to cut a tree to make it fruitful, he will observe his time and lop his tree in its season, perhaps about this time of year (this sermon was preached on the 23rd of January), and then it will grow up. But, if he means to have it die, he lops it about midsummer when the tree has sent forth its sap, and then the tree dies.

So God, when He comes to His children with afflictions, will come in a seasonable time, such a time to lop when lopping may make them more fruitful. But when He afflicts wicked men, He comes to them as to a tree at midsummer, when they are flourishing, and then cuts them down and they perish. God does not regard the time or season for their good when He comes in a way of a curse for sin.

And so for the manner and measure of affliction; when God comes to His children when sin is pardoned, God weighs it out. As a skillful physician weighs out medicine, though that which the patient takes may be poison in itself, yet the physician will be sure there shall not be one dram too much, and that there shall be enough mixed with it which shall be proportionable to weaken the strength of that poison so that it shall not do harm but good. But now, if he gives poison to vermin, he gives it without mixture or weight. He never weighs it for them, he lets them eat and burst themselves. He will give no help there. When he gives poison to vermin, it is to destroy them.

So it is with all afflictions that come to wicked men. When God comes upon them in a way of curse for sin, God gives it to them as we give poison to vermin to destroy them; but the afflictions that God gives to saints, when their sin has been pardoned, may indeed by poison in their nature, but they are so weighed out that there is not one dram too much. They are so mixed with the ingredients of the mercy and goodness of God that they only work good to the people of God to work out corruption and do them no harm at all.

Here's the difference between afflictions upon those whose sins are pardoned and those who have their guilt still upon them. Hearken to this, you who have the guilt of sin. When any evil comes to you, for all you know it comes to you as poison to vermin to kill you. Whereas, if your hearts were humbled for sin and your sin was pardoned, though you are under never so much affliction, it comes as that does from a skillful, loving Physician who weighs out the medicine to do the patient good. This is the second thing wherein the curse of affliction consists when it comes for sin.

3. The curse of afflictions, when they come for sin, is in this: all afflictions that come merely for sin are but forerunners of the miseries of hell itself. I say, they are the forerunners of the very torments of hell. Let the affliction be never so little in itself, yet it is the harbinger and forerunner of those dreadful, eternal torments that you must bear. It is but a messenger from the Lord, whatever they are. What, do you feel them to be grievous and tedious for the present; some grievous, tedious distempers, some trouble or disease you have? They are but a taste of that bitter cup full of wrath, and they only give you notice of what dreadful things you are to endure when time shall be no more.

4. No, they are not only forerunners to give notice of what it will be like, but they are the very beginnings of the miseries of hell. Every evil a wicked man suffers he may look upon as the beginnings of everlasting torments if he dies in this condition, if he is not delivered from the guilt of sin. And this is what makes it grievous. It is not so much the pain that lies upon a man for the present so that he, by this pain, is told what he will have forever. It is like a summons to him to bear the wrath of God eternally, and this is that

which is the beginning of that everlasting torment he shall endure. Suppose there was a man about to be executed, and he was to die some grievous and fearful death. And suppose that the executioner inflicted a little pain upon him when he tied his wrists together and the man cried out at the pain in his wrist. Alas! What is this? Does he cry for this? What is this but a preparation for those dreadful torments that are now about to be executed upon him?

So all men and women who are in the guilt of sin, when they have any affliction, sickness, or trouble, as long as they are in that state, they may look upon it as merely the girding of their hands with the cords. A little pain they are put to by the strictness of the cords that bind them, but this is only to the body, and so prepares them to be cast out into utter darkness. You know the phrase from Matthew 22:4, take him who came without the wedding garment, and *bind him hand and foot and cast him into outer darkness.*

Your afflictions are merely as bindings to you. They are only the beginnings of those everlasting pains you are likely to have. And that should make the least affliction of any ungodly man or woman in the world exceedingly dreadful to them. Now I feel pain, but what is this but the beginning of sorrows? I am now sinking, but how far I shall sink, I do not know.

5. Again, all afflictions, when they come in a way of curse for sin, are sent to ripen men and women for destruction and, therefore, they harden their hearts and make them often fly out against God. There is no affliction sent in a way of a curse that does not ripen any man or woman for eternal misery. Oh, consider this, you who have been under great afflictions. It may be that you are delivered from pain and think yourselves safe. Examine this. How is it? Are not your hearts more hard than before? Are you not more greedy upon sin than before? Know, then, that this is a dangerous sign. That affliction was only sent to ripen you for destruction and eternal misery. Though you have escaped for a time, yet they

only were ripeners to hasten you to everlasting destruction. And in these things consists the curse of sin in all evils that befall us. This is the third.

Fourthly, sin is the evil of all evils for it is the shame of all evils. It is that which makes any affliction to be a shame to us. I remember before, in opening the nature of sin as being against our good, that I showed sin was a shame to the soul whether there was affliction or not. But now I am to show you how sin puts shame into other evils; not only brings shame to ourselves, but puts a shame upon the evils and afflictions that are or shall be upon us.

For example, a malefactor is stigmatized, is branded. Well, there is pain to his body in the branding, and then there is the shame that is in the brand that goes along with the pain. And therefore it is that it might be a note of perpetual shame and reproach. So, in afflictions, there is the pain of the affliction, and then there is the shame that is upon men through the affliction. Let men be branded and, if it is not for their sin, if it is for righteousness, then their brands are honorable. Let them be stigmatized never so much. Let their ears be cut off and branded with an "s" or any other brand in the cheeks or foreheads. If it is for righteousness, this is their honor and glory. As the Apostle speaks in a triumphant way, *I bear about with me the marks of the Lord Jesus.* And he glories in it.

So, for any man to be branded for Christ, he bears the marks of Jesus Christ. Though there are marks, there is no shame. So in any affliction God sends, if there is no sin, there may be pain but no shame; but when God comes upon men for sin, by the very affliction God points out, as it were, the sin of man. Oh! Then it is not only painful, but an abundance of shame and confusion goes along with it. Therefore, in Jeremiah 24:9, God says, *He would cast them out for a reproach, and a taunt, and a byword.* For a reproach as well as trouble. The shame of affliction comes from sin. This is the fourth thing.

Fifthly, the eternity of all evil comes from sin. I remember showing before how sin was a principle of eternal evil, but this is in another regard. I am not speaking of sin now as I was then. That was as it is in its own nature. Sin itself was a principal evil and brought an eternal evil. But this I say here: sin puts an eternity upon that present evil you suffer if the guilt is not taken away.

No creatures but the reasonable creatures are subject to any eternity of evil. Whatever evil is upon any other creature, it cannot have that denomination of eternity; but the evils upon a sinner may have a denomination of eternity upon them. For this, observe this one note. There is in grace (that is, in itself) an eternal good, and it brought eternal good. But further, grace is not only in itself a principle of eternal good and brings eternal good, but grace makes that very good that we have now to have an eternity upon it. It not only procures that hereafter it shall have eternity, but makes our present good to be eternal, though it is conveyed in another way.

For example, we have an abundance of comforts from creatures and God's ordinances. It is true, we shall not have our comforts conveyed to us from creatures and ordinances, but those who have grace shall have the same comforts they how have from the creature and the ordinances conveyed immediately from God as the Fountain. That which you now have from cisterns and conduits of conveyance, you shall come to enjoy the same from God immediately, and really, another way. So that no man or woman in affliction (if gracious) needs to be troubled for anything. This is a true maxim in Divinity, "A Christian may have many crosses, but no losses." A Christian never lost anything.

How can that be, you say? A Christian receives good, in husband, in wife, in children, in estate, and they have losses in these as well as others.

No, they are crossed for the present, but never did any Christian have any loss. We may assent to this as a certain truth. No godly man or woman, who has had sin pardoned, has ever had any loss since that time. Grace, I think, should be very precious in your thoughts if this is true, if I can make this good.

If I were to come and tell you mariners, you merchant-adventurers in dangerous seas, what course you should take so as never to have any more losses, you would think this is good news, if it was not a fancy and a deceit. If you found it to be true, you would account your time well-spent, though you heard nothing but this. Certainly, I can tell you a way where you shall never have loss in the world, the way of godliness. Get sin once pardoned in Christ and you shall never have any loss.

Suppose that I had a pipe laid into a fountain of water which would bring that water to me. Later, the water stops coming through the pipe. Yet, if I come to enjoy the very fountain and have no loss of water (for I get it from the fountain), though the pipe is stopped, I have the same water I had before.

So it is with a Christian who has any loss from the creature. For thus we are to know, all creatures are but as so many pipes of conveyance of comfort and good from God, the Fountain of all good in the creature, and He is pleased with one kind of pipe to convey comfort from one creature, and from another in another way. Some have greater, and some have smaller pipes, as God shall minister in His wisdom and providence to His servants.

But, now, one who is godly, though they are the poorest man or woman in the world, has an interest in God Himself, the Fountain of all good. And, therefore, if any pipe is cut off and stopped (as perhaps at such a time you lost a thousand pounds, or three or four thousand pounds), you still have a God and an interest in Him, and there all is made up. And there is this art in godliness, and the skill, that still you may come and enjoy that immediately from God, and suck that from the Fountain that you did from the pipes. So that a

Christian may lose much of his estate, or comfort in friends, so that he shall never receive it from them anymore, but he goes to God and enjoys it in God. So that present good which he had here, he makes it all up in God.

Thus, grace makes that good and comfort you have here now to be an eternal good, only the conveyance is in another way, more immediately from God and, therefore, is the sweeter and the fuller.

So sin puts an eternity into every evil. Observe that sin does not only deserve that you should have eternal evil befall you hereafter, but whatever evil you have now, sorrows, distresses, anguish, or troubles upon you, sin will make that sorrow, anguish, or distress to be eternal. Though not, perhaps, conveyed that way, by that channel, yet you shall have that to be immediately let out through God's wrath and justice. All the evil that you ever bore here from any creature (here, perhaps, you have a grievous disease. Oh! It greatly afflicts and torments you; perhaps you die), the strength of that evil is gone, but the torment upon you by the disease was nothing else but the wrath of God working through that channel and let out through that. Though now you die, and the manner of the disease is gone, yet when you come to hell, there you shall meet with the same grievous pain, only in another way. That is, the wrath of God shall let out this evil immediately through His wrath, which was mediated through the creature before, and now it is immediately from Himself.

And this meditation, rightly considered, is enough to bring the proudest, stoutest sinner on the earth to consider how the wrath of God is all that evil to a sinner that all the creatures in heaven and earth are able to convey, and much more.

And thus you have this opened, how sin is the evil of all evils.

THE FIFTH PART OF THIS TREATISE

Chapter 42

Sin has a kind of infiniteness in it, opened in seven particulars. First, because nothing but an infinite power can overcome it. Second, sin has a kind of infiniteness because it has an infinite desert in it, expressed in three particulars: (1) the desert of the loss of an infinite good; (2) it deserves to put an infinite distance between God and you; (3) it deserves infinite misery. Third, sin has a kind of infinite evil because an infinite price is required to make an atonement between God and man. Fourth, there is a kind of infinite evil in sin because we must hate it infinitely. Fifth, sin is an infinite evil because it is the universal cause of all evil. Sixth, the Scripture makes use of evil things to set out the evil of sin. Seventh, there's an infiniteness in sin because the Scripture sets out sin by sin itself.

A fifth general head that was propounded in the beginning was this: sin has a kind of infiniteness of evil in it.

It is true, we must acknowledge that nothing but God can properly be said to be infinite. There is not an infiniteness in a strict sense in sin, for then, certainly, all the mercy of God and all the power of God could never overcome it. Therefore I do not say it is properly infinite. Well, but there is a kind of infiniteness. It comes very near to infiniteness if we may so speak, though it is somewhat improper to say it comes near, but we must speak so that we understand. You will see in the opening what I mean.

For example, there is a kind of infiniteness of evil in sin beyond all bounds. First, because nothing but infinite power can overcome it. Take the least sin that any man or woman lies under the power of. Nothing but the infinite power of God can overcome that sin. And this is the reason why man who have had many convictions of conscience of the evil of sin, many resolutions against sin, many vows, covenants, and promises against sin have failed. Oh, when they are sick, then they see the evil of sin. They promise that, if God will restore them, they will never do the like again, and they speak from their hearts. They do not only dally, but they truly think they will never come in company again and commit sin any more because it is so evil.

But when they are well, they are under the power of sin as before, and all their resolutions and experiences, and all their own strength and power, and all the means they have are nothing. Though sin is opened to be never so vile, and they are convinced of that, it all comes to nothing. Certainly, there is more dreadful evil in sin than we are aware of, and all the pleasure and profit we have by sin can never equal the evil that is in sin. And this they see, and therefore promise and hope they shall never commit such sins again.

Perhaps there has been such a thought in your heart. It may be that God has had some beginnings to come in by His power into your souls. This is the way of God's coming into the hearts of men and women, when He comes to convince and give them such resolutions. But know, all your resolutions cannot overcome sin. Perhaps you may forbear for the present. The acts of sin for awhile may be restrained; but nothing but the infinite power of an infinite God can overcome any one sin, any one lust. *Sin shall not have dominion over you,* Romans 6:14, *for you are not under the Law, but under grace,* says the Holy Ghost.

It is as if He had said, "If you are not now under the grace of the gospel, in which the infinite power of God comes upon the soul to deliver it from the dominion of sin, sin would forever have dominion over you. But sin shall not have dominion over you because you are not under the law but under grace."

It is the grace of the gospel, through which this infinite power of God comes upon your hearts, that keeps sin from having dominion over you.

This is the first. There is a kind of infiniteness in it, because nothing but the infinite power of God can overcome it.

Secondly, there is a kind of infiniteness in it because it has an infinite desert. It deserves that which is infinite. There is an infinite desert in it, therefore a kind of infiniteness in it. For example, the infinite desert of sin may be set out in these three particulars:

1. The desert of the loss of an infinite good, all the good in God. By every sin, you deserve to be deprived of that good there is in God. That desert comes upon you to lose all the good that is in the infinite God, not in this or that particular good, but in the infinite God, and all the good in Him.

2. Every sin makes an infinite breach between God and you. Not only do you deserve to lose all the good in God, but it puts an infinite distance between God and you. Abraham could say to Dives, when Lazarus was in his bosom, "There is a great gulf between you and us." There is a great gulf between the sinner and those that are godly; but what a gulf is there between God Himself and the sinner? If there is such a gulf between Abraham and Dives, surely there is a greater gulf between God Himself and a sinner.

3. The desert of sin is infinite in regard of the infiniteness of misery, pain, and torture that sin deserves. They cannot possibly be infinite in degree, for it is impossible for a finite creature to bear any one moment pains that are infinite in degree. But because it deserves infinite torment, it must therefore be infinite in time; because it cannot be infinite in degree, and so it is infinite this way, in duration. Thus sin is infinite. Certainly, that which makes such an infinite loss and such an infinite breach, and brings such infinite tortures, must be infinitely evil in kind.

Thirdly, sin is a kind of infinite evil because there is required an infinite price to make an atonement. Nothing can make an atonement between God and a sinner but an infinite price paid. You may think, when you have sinned, that it may quickly be made up again. Every fool can sin, can be drunk, can be unclean and wicked; but when you have sinned, how will you get it away? All the angels in heaven and men in the world cannot do it. All the creatures in heaven and earth cannot get away one sin.

You let out your thoughts idly. Take the guilt of one sin, that of an idle thought. I say, it is beyond the power of all the angels in heaven and creatures in the world to get away that sin. It must be an infinite price. There must be more done to get away the guilt of this sin than if God should say, "Here is a poor creature who has sinned and is guilty. I will make ten thousand worlds for his or her sake, and they shall all be given that I may manifest My mercy towards them." Now if God only delivers you from one sin, He does more for you than if you should hear Him speak from heaven and say that He would do all that for you.

You know what the Apostle said, I Peter 1:18, *For as much as you know that you were not redeemed with corruptible things, as silver and gold, from your vain conversation, received by tradition from your fathers, but with the precious blood of Jesus Christ, as of a lamb without spot or blemish.* Not with gold and silver. If it were gold and silver, all the gold and silver in the world would not redeem one person; but it was with an infinite price with which you were redeemed. And mark this, *from your vain conversation.* He does not say "your vain, wicked, notorious idolatry," but *your vain conversation.* Yes, and that vain conversation which you might have some plea for, received from the tradition of your fathers. You will keep your old customs you received from your fathers, received a great while ago. You cry out about new things, new kinds of ways.

"Now I am sure," you will say, "I have lived this thirty or forty years, and I never knew such things, and heard of such things," and so you will rest on the tradition of your forefathers. Mark what the Scripture says, speaking of those who were delivered from their vain conversations, and the vanities received by tradition. These were redeemed by the precious blood of Jesus Christ, not with gold and silver. Though you stick to them as being such as you received from your fathers, yet know that all the world cannot deliver you from the guilt of one of these vain conversations.

If you knew all, you would see that there is so much evil in one sin as required a price to ransom you from it worth more than heaven and earth, yes, worth more than ten thousand heavens and earths. There must be a price laid down of infinite worth.

And observe this before you go away. There may be a price laid down to ransom a captive, and this price may note not so much the greatness of the deliverance as it does the worth of the person for whom the price is laid down. The person is worthy not from the miserableness of the bondage, but from the greatness of the person.

But it is not so here. The reason for the greatness of the price of your ransom is not from the worthiness of the person. We are poor, vile, dirt, dross, and filthy before God.

What, if you were all buried to all eternity, what great matter would it be? But God has paid a great price to note the greatness of your misery and the evil you have brought upon yourselves by reason of sin, and therefore this is the price of our ransom. This is the third thing wherein the infiniteness of sin appears.

A fourth thing to discover a kind of infiniteness of evil in sin is this. Sin is so evil that, let there never be so much hatred against it in your soul, let there be as much hatred against it as possibly can be, yet there is enough evil in sin to raise the hatred higher and higher, if it were possible, to an infinite hatred. Therefore, there is a kind of infiniteness in sin.

If sin were but a mere infinite evil, then there might be some bounds and limits set to the hatred of our sin, but that cannot be. There can be no bounds or limits set to the hatred of our sin, but we are to hate it more and more still and, if we could, let it grow to an infinite hatred. Therefore, there must be some kind of infinite evil in it.

Other things are not so. We may set bounds to our hatred in other things but, when it comes to sin, there are no limits to be set to the hatred of it.

For example, it notes the infiniteness of goodness that there is in God. Why? Because we are to love God, and our love to God must be without any bounds at all. We love Him this much, and still our love is to go further and higher and higher and, if possible, we are to raise our love to be infinite, because He is an infinite good who is the object of our loves.

So it is with hatred on the other side. We are to hate sin. We are to hate it more and more, and still grow in hatred, and never set bounds to our hatred. Why does this not argue a kind of infiniteness in sin as well?

And here, brethren, by the way, you may have a note of your true love to God and true hatred against sin as to whether it is right or not. If you would know if you love God truly, then set no bounds to your love; not only to your love to Him, but to your love to His ways, and your love to grace and Christ and the like. Set no bounds.

That man or woman who would be religious, but only so far, and says, "Why are you so strict and so hot?" who sets bounds to the working of their hearts in religious ways, let such men and women know that their religion is in vain. It is merely a natural religion.

I remember a speech made by Seneca, the heathen. Though he applied it another way, yet he made it appear that he had some understanding of this truth. He said, "Would you know when desires are natural, and when they are not natural? If they are natural, then they are in bounds and you set limits upon them. But when they break bounds, then they are no longer natural." But he applies it to sinful desires (for he knew no better than desires at their highest, as they had some naturalness in them), and he says, speaking of sinful desires, "As long as you keep your desires in certain bounds, they are natural and good; but when once you let them out beyond bounds, they are no longer natural."

We may very well apply it to speak of the work of nature and the work of grace. Would you know whether the ground of your desires or work are natural or supernatural? You may know them by this: if you propound limits and say, "thus far you will go," this certainly is a natural work. But when the heart lets out itself to God without any limits or bounds, this is a supernatural work.

So, you dislike sin and would not commit it? But this is the question, is your dislike or hatred natural or supernatural? If it is natural, then there are some limits and bounds you propound, that is, you will not commit such gross sins and live in such opens sins; and upon such and such grounds, you will abstain from such and such sins. But if there is a supernatural work, your hearts are set against all sins with a kind of infiniteness without any bounds or terms. You will set no bounds to your hatred of any sin.

That man or woman who hates sin so much that they will set no bounds at all unto their hatred, and will admit it upon no terms, this is a supernatural hatred.

Many are against sin naturally; but in that true hatred it is so boundless that there must be no bounds set to your hatred. It evidently shows sin to have a kind of infiniteness of evil in it.

Fifthly, sin has a kind of infiniteness in it in that it is the universal cause of all evil. As God appears to be an infinite good, because He is the universal cause of all good, this sets out the infiniteness of God's goodness in that He is the universal cause of all good. So it sets out the infiniteness of sin in that sin is the universal cause of all evil. All evil flows from it. That is the fifth thing.

Sixthly, there is an infiniteness of evil in sin. It appears thus, that as the infiniteness of good in God is shadowed out unto us by all good things, and in us as much as we and the

Scripture makes use of all good things to shadow out the goodness of God, this manifests an infiniteness of good in Him. So in as much as the Scripture makes use of all kinds of evil things, only to set and shadow out the evil in sin. This makes it appear there is a kind of infiniteness of evil in it.

For example, think of all the deadly creatures the Scripture makes use of to shadow out the evil in sin: vipers, serpents, dogs, cockatrices, dragons, and wolves. It is as if the Holy Ghost should say, "Do you see any evil in such creatures whom you account the worst? Put them all together and that is in sin and more."

So, take all kinds of uncleanness, the vomit of a dog, menstrual cloths, all this only shadows out the evil in sin. Look at leprosy, plague, darkness, even death itself, any hideous evil. All these only shadow out the evil of sin. We might mention many more to show you the evil of sin. And, in that, the Scripture makes use of so many evil things to show the evil of sin. This shows sin has a kind of infiniteness in it.

Seventh, as God's infinite goodness is set out thusly, that He is His own happiness and blessedness, in this God appears to be infinitely good because His is His own good and happiness. There is no higher good than the goodness of God; no higher blessedness than the blessedness of God Himself because He is infinitely good and blessed.

So the Scripture sets out to us the evil of sin by itself, because there is no greater evil to set out sin by than itself. Therefore, this shows that there is a kind of infiniteness of evil in sin. And, therefore, you have that verse in Romans 7:13, *Was that then that was good made death to me? God forbid, but sin that it might appear sin working death in me by that which was good: that sin by the commandment might become EXCEEDING SINFUL.* He does not say that sin might appear to be exceedingly miserable, but that it might become exceedingly sinful.

So the sinfulness of sin is that which lets out the evil of sin more than another other thing does. It was the speech of the heathen, Seneca, "It is the punishment of sin to *have* sin. So it is the reward of virtues to have them. Godliness, in itself, is the excellency of a man, and sin, in itself, is the misery of a man, and this is a proof of this, that there is a kind of infiniteness of evil in sin.

Now, then, by all these seven discourses of the evil of sin, having a kind of infiniteness in it, this one thing comes fully and powerfully from them.

"Oh," you say, "to fall into sin again and to be prevailed upon by any such temptation as this is no great matter. If I do no worse than this, I hope it is well with me. Besides, others do worse."

I say, to yield again to the commission of any sin upon such a temptation is a great wickedness. What, do you make comparison of sins and use any such words when you have heard or read it, and it has been proven to you that sin has a kind of infiniteness of evil in it?

No, that which I thought to have finished here, but cannot now come to, but shall in the next chapter show the reference sin has to the devil, shows the greatness of sin above all evils. Sin is that which makes the soul conformable to the devil. Afflictions do not; they make the soul conformable to Jesus Christ.

I suppose you know the place in Philippians 3:10. Mark the difference there between sin and affliction. Paul there *accounted all things dung and dross for the excellency of the knowledge of Christ.* And what more? *That he might be found in Him, and that he might know Him, and the power of His resurrection, and the fellowship of His sufferings, being made conformable unto His death.*

He desires, above all things, to have the fellowship of His sufferings, and to be conformable to Christ by afflictions or sufferings. It is true, it may be that many account all the world to be nothing so as to be conformable to Christ in glory in heaven. But here is the work of grace (and I beseech you to observe this in the conclusion and carry it away): a gracious heart accounts all the world dung and dross to be conformable to Christ in His sufferings. There is that much excellency and glory in the sufferings of Jesus Christ.

Now you see the wide difference between afflictions and sin. Sin makes a man conformable to the devil; afflictions make a man conformable to Jesus Christ.

I would like to have showed, in several particulars, how sin makes us conformable to the devil. I will only name this one now, and it is that which might be enough to make every soul fall out of love with sin. By sin, you join with the devil and conspire with the devil against God Himself. There is no creature who is against God other than men and devils.

The devil was God's first enemy, and now man comes in and conspires with the devil. Now we would account it a great evil if we had a child who joined with a traitor against the Commonwealth. We would moan, "Oh, my child is joined with this traitor, and conspires against me and the state."

Before sinful man, there was only one sort of sinful creature in the world, the devils. Now by sin, man comes in and joins in conspiracy against the blessed God, and so one generation after another. Perhaps the father comes and conspires with the devil, and then the child, and so on in succession. And this should come near our hearts to humble us for our sins and wickedness that, in this, we are those who, of all creatures that ever God made, conspire with the devil against the blessed God, the Fountain of all good.

THE SIXTH PART OF THIS TREATISE

Chapter 43

Sin makes a man conformable to the devil, opened in six particulars. First, sin is of the same nature as the devil. Second, sin is from the devil. Third, sin is a furtherance of the devil's kingdom in the world for (1) by sin we oppose Christ's destroying the devil's kingdom in the world; (2) by sin you oppose your prayers when you pray "Thy Kingdom come"; (3) by going on in a way of sin, you become guilty of all the sin in the world. Fourth, sinning is fulfilling the will of the devil. Fifth, sin sells the soul to the devil. Sixth, sin turns the soul into a devil.

The sixth and last demonstration of the evil of sin is from that reference which sin has to the devil.

The Scripture speaks of afflictions, that they make us conformable to Christ; but sin makes us conformable to the devil. There are six things to be opened about this. I have mentioned the first, which was this, that sin was of the same nature as the devil. Every sin has the same kind of malignity in it that the devil has.

But, secondly, all sin is from the devil, either originally or, at least by way of a cause, helping it go forward. Sin is the work of the devil, not only joining with him, but his work. Therefore, Christ is said to come to dissolve the works of the devil. Sin is from the devil. Therefore, it is said in 1 John 3:8, *He that commits sin is of the devil, for the devil sinneth from the beginning; and to this purpose the Son of man was manifest, that He might destroy the works of the devil.*

He who commits sin is of the devil, for sin comes from the devil. And so we have John 8:44. Brethren, these things which I speak concerning the reference sin has to the devil, though they may seem hard and harsh, yet it is to be observed that no one speaks as much of sin as coming from the devil as John, who was of the most loving, sweet nature of any of the disciples; and yet, when he comes to speak of sin, he speaks of it in the most harsh terms that possibly can be. So that it does not come from harshness, but may stand with a loving and sweet nature to speak of sin in the harshest terms we can, for John, the most loving and beloved disciple of Christ, so full of love, spoke more harshly of sin than anyone, especially in its reference to the devil. He said in John 8:44, *You are of the devil, and his lust you will do.*

Thus it is with sin. The lusts of sin come from the devil, and it makes a man or woman to be the child of the devil. So the Scripture is clear that it comes from him originally. All sin that is in you is originally the spawn of the very devil himself in your souls, and originally it comes from him. As all sin originally comes from his temptations and suggestions, so also the devil helps forward and further all sin that is in your souls. This is the evil of it.

But here understand this rightly. The devil is not the cause of all sin in the same way that God is the cause of all grace. It is true, the devil has a hand in every sin, but not such a hand in sin as God has in grace; for God has such a hand in the work of grace that He not only gives a principle of grace, but all the operation of grace is so from Him that it would never stir but *by* Him. He gives the will to work and do all. The will and the deed are from Him. But all sin is not so from the devil, though originally it is. Yet we are to know that, though the devil should tempt us no more, there is enough in the hearts of men and women to sin against God all manner of sin, even from the innate corruption now in them. If the devil were destroyed, sin would not be destroyed.

In grace, there is no power to work but by God's working together with it; but in sin there is a power to work without the devil's working. Though the devil is forward enough

to work with our corruption, yet I say there is enough corruption in our hearts to work all kind of sin, even though the
devil should not tempt us anymore. Therefore, we must not
lay all upon the devil, as many do. When they fall into any
wickedness, they will say, "This is the devil," and they will
lay all the fault upon the devil and think to take it off themselves by doing so. No, know this. Though the devil labors
to further it however he can, yet there is such corruption in
you that it would stream forth from you, though the devil did
not stir it at all. Therefore, charge your own hearts as well as
the devil.

In the work of grace, we must give all glory to God; but
in the work of sin, we cannot allot all the fault to the devil.
We are not to take any of the glory of the work of grace to
ourselves, but we are to take a great part, yes, sometimes the
greatest part of sin to our selves. However, the devil is the
cause of sin originally and helps forward it.

Thirdly, all sin is the furtherance of the kingdom of the
devil in the world. You know that the Scriptures say that the
devil is the prince who rules in the air, and is called the god
of this world because he rules in the children of disobedience. There is a kingdom of the devil set up by sin in the
world and maintained by sin in the world. It has a succession in the world by sin. So that all sinners who continue in
ways of sin do, what in them lies, to uphold the kingdom of
the devil in the world, and the rule of the devil in the world.

1. Therefore, men in sin are exceedingly opposed to the
end of Christ's coming in the world; for it is Christ's end in
coming in to the world to dissolve the kingdom of the devil,
as you had it before in I John 3:8. It is a special end why
Christ came in to the world to bring down the kingdom of
the devil, and yet you, by sinning, uphold the kingdom of
the devil. So you do what in you lies to oppose and resist the
very end of Christ's coming into the world.

There is much in this consideration to humble the hearts
of all wicked men for sin. You have lived in a course of sin,

it may be, for many years. Now, brethren, know that the Lord charges you with this, this day, that all this time you have lived in a course of sin, you have done what lies within you to oppose the end of Christ's coming into the world. If you could, you would hinder the end of the death of Christ and all that He has done, for the special end why Christ came into the world was to dissolve the work of the devil, and you keep up the work of the devil.

2. Again, it follows from this that you directly contradict your own prayers. When you pray *Thy kingdom come* in the Lord's Prayer, you pray there that the kingdom of Christ might come but, in every way of sin that you take liberty in, you oppose the kingdom of Christ. How can you take the name of God in vain and mock God in this prayer? Every wicked man and woman in the world mocks God in praying the Lord's Prayer when they say *Thy kingdom come,* and yet live in such ways as upholds the kingdom of the devil instead of the kingdom of Christ.

3. Yea, further this follows, that by going on in ways of sin, you come to be guilty, and stand charged for all the sins that were ever committed in the world. This may seem to be a hard thing, to charge any man or woman who now lives in ways of sin that, by that sin of yours in which you now live, you come to be guilty of all the sins that were ever done in the world since the beginning of the world. I will undertake to prove that here.

You know the Scripture charges those who persecuted the prophets as being guilty of all the persecution of the prophets who ever were. "All the blood that was shed from Abel to Zacharias shall come upon this generation," said Christ, Matthew 23:35-36. Why so? Why should all the blood shed from Abel to that time come upon that generation? The reason is this, because they continued the succession of that sin of persecuting the prophets. As there was persecution of the prophets before, so they go on and uphold this succession of that sin.

Now, by holding the succession of a way of sin, we come to be guilty of all that sin that went before.

For example, suppose there should be treason against a king or state by some vile, treasonous act. Now the father commits the first act, the son later goes on in the same way, and his children come after him and go on in the same way. Now, I say, the children, the grand-children, and the great-grand-children are guilty of the first treasonous act that was committed. Why? Because they uphold the succession of the treasonous act.

So now, sin that was in the beginning of the world, was to bring in the kingdom of Satan, and the next generation upheld it, and the next generation went on in the same way, so that every generation is not only guilty of those particular sins which they commit, but they are guilty of all that went before, because they uphold the succession of the kingdom of the devil and the opposition of the kingdom of Jesus Christ.

For instance, take one who scorns religion. That is one sin (we cannot open things except by instancing them in particulars). If you are a scorner of religion, know that you are not guilty of these acts of scorning only in yourself, but you are guilty of all the scorning of godliness since the beginning of the world. Why? Because you hold a succession of that way of scorning religion. So a blasphemer may be said to be guilty of all the blasphemies in the world. Why? Because he upholds the succession of that way of sinning against God, and so opposing the kingdom of Christ and upholding the kingdom of the devil. This is the third thing, sin is the upholding of the kingdom of the devil in the world.

Fourthly, sin is a fulfilling of the will of the devil. That is another distinct consideration, and you shall see that, in the opening of it, it will be of distinct use to you. I say, it is a fulfilling of the will of the devil. That place is very famous in 2 Timothy 2:26, *That they may recover themselves out of the snare of the devil who are taken captive of him at his WILL.*

There wicked men are taken captive by the devil at his will, or, to do his will. So you may read it. Some are ensnared by Satan to do his will. His lusts you do, as Christ speaks. You may think you do your own will in sinning, but certainly you do the will of the devil as well as your own.

For instance, that passage in Ephesians 4:26, *Be angry, but sin not; let not the sun go down on your wrath; neither give place to the Devil.* You think you give place to your own passion, but you give place to the devil and fulfill the will of the devil. You come by sin to do the devil's drudgery and slavery. You do the work he sets you on, and his will you fulfill.

Now for such a noble creature as man is to come to be a slave of the devil is the lowest of all creatures. It must be a very dreadful thing. It is an evil to be in slavery to anything vile or base.

I remember reading a story of Gunno, King of the Danes. Having overcome a people, he set a dog over them to be their governor. That is, he wanted all the commands to go out in the name of the dog, and the people were to be under the government of the dog. He did this in disdain and indignation against those people he overcame. But now, as he would show the baseness of that people whom he designed to be under a dog, much more debasing is it for an immortal soul to be under the command of the devil, and all wicked man are under the command of the devil himself.

You will not fulfill the will of God when it is opened to you out of His Word and His will, though that is what you ought to do. You stand out against the will of God. But now, you who think it is such a bondage to be obedient to the will of God are brought under a worse bondage. You are fain to be obedient to the will of the devil! And certainly, those men and women who think they are most at liberty when they are free from obedience to the will of God, by that liberty come to be under bondage and slavery to the devil.

All wicked men who think it is much to obey God must be obedient one way or the other. We must all be servants, obedient either to the will of God or to the will of the devil. Which is best, then?

Wicked men think it is a brave life that they may have their own will. True, if they might have their own will they might think it a brave life. But know, you have the will of the devil rather than your own will. In that you do his will, you fulfill the will of the devil.

To be in slavery, not only to the devil but to any man, is a great evil. To be at the will of man, yes, to be at the will of a good man is an evil. I should be loath to live in any such Commonwealth as that I should be under the will of man in it, any further than might be revealed and bounded by some set law. This difference between a slave and a subject is this: a slave is such a one as lives under an arbitrary government. That is, the will of such as are in authority is their law, and they are ruled by no other law but by the will of those who govern them. There is no law set to know when they shall offend and when not. When their rulers say, "This is an offence," they are punished simply because the ruler's will is crossed.

But now subjects are not bound to obey any man any further than some set law requires their obedience. That is what it means to be a subject, and that is the very difference between a subject and a slave. If men in authority should command anything (though it is good), yet I am not bound in conscience to obey at all *because* they command, unless it is by a law, unless they command it by a law. If the authority commands it merely at his will and says, "I will it, therefore you must do it," there is no tie upon the conscience.

It is ordinary for men to think, "If men in authority command, they want to have such a thing done." They say, "Oh, authority commands!"

We deny that! Authority commands nothing but what it commands by law, and then we are bound to obey or to suffer, if it is a law. But if it is not a law, though it should be the will of men in authority, it does not bind us at all until it comes to be a law any further than there is equity itself in the thing in its own nature; for then people come to be in slavery when they come to be subject to the will of men without a law.

Now, brethren, this: if it is slavery, and a great evil to be subject to men, though good men, subject to their will and nothing else, without a law, then what an evil is it to be in subjection and slavery to the will of the devil? Merely at his will? And yet every wicked man is so.

We should account it a very sore thing if we should come under arbitrary government, to be subject to the will of men. Now as long as you remain under the power of sin, you remain under the government of the devil himself. This is a sorer evil than affliction.

It would be better for a man to live in any country, though not as fruitful as England, and suffer hardship in his estate, so that he might live like a free man, than to live here, or in any other fruitful country, and live under arbitrary government. This we hope for, not to be under the wills of men, but the laws made by them. Then it would be better to endure hardship and any affliction than to bear this, to be at the will of the devil and to fulfill his will.

Fifthly, in reference to the devil, sin has this evil in it. If it grows to a height, it sells the soul to the devil. When Elijah met Ahab, I Kings 21:20, Ahab said, *Hast thou found me, O my enemy? And he* (Elijah) *answered, I have found thee, because thou hast SOLD thyself to work evil in the sight of the Lord.*

Now if he sells himself, he must sell himself to somebody, to something. We cannot sell a thing unless to sell it to somebody or something. Now to what must Ahab sell himself? Certainly to no one but the devil. He sold himself to work iniquity and wickedness, and wickedness, when it comes to the height, is a selling of ourselves to the very devil himself.

We cry out for those poor, miserable creatures who sell themselves to the devil. We say, "Oh, how they are deluded and dulled who sell themselves to the devil!" Certainly, every wicked man and woman in the world, when sin grows to the height, sells themselves to the devil.

Sixthly, and lastly, when sin grows to height, it turns the soul into a devil. It makes men and women to become devils when once it grows to a height. The Scripture is very clear in that. You know what is said concerning Judas, John 6:70, *Have not I chosen you twelve, and one of you is a devil?* And so ordinarily the Scriptures speaks in this kind of a phrase, Revelation 2:10, *Fear none of these things you shall suffer, behold the devil shall cast some of you into prison.* Why? Is the devil come to be a warrant officer, or to give warrants to cast into prison? No, but it is spoken of wicked persecutors whom the devil sets on to work, that they are called by the name of the devil.

When sin comes to a height, it makes the sinners to be such that they are pronounced to be devils. The devil shall cast some of you into prison, and one of you is a devil. That is a strange metamorphosis.

We read strange fiction, of some creatures turned into other creatures, but this, for the creature to be turned into a devil, is the strangest metamorphosis that can be.

Brethren, what made the devil a devil? They were once glorious angels, more glorious creatures than men or women, but what is it that should make them devils now? Nothing but sin. It is sin that made angels to be devils and, therefore, do not wonder so much that sin should make men and women to be devils incarnate. Do not wonder at the phrase of Scripture seeing that angels, by sin, yes, the sin that the angels committed, immediately turned them into devils.

Therefore, do not wonder that the continuing in acts of sin should turn men and women into devils, when it grows to the height.

These are the six particulars in this head, of sin's reference to the devil. (1) It is of the same nature with the devil, and joins with him against God. (2) It is the work of the devil, that is, he is the original and helping cause of it. (3) It furthers the kingdom of the devil. (4) It fulfills the will of the devil. (5) When it grows to a height, it sells the creature to the devil. (6) It turns them into devils.

From these six, follow these notable corollaries and consequences to show the dreadful evil in sin beyond all affliction.

COROLLARIES AND CONSEQUENCES FROM ALL THE FORMER PARTICULARS

Chapter 44

The Frst Corollary. It is worse for a man to be sinful than to be turned into a beast.

First, then, it is worse for a man to be sinful and wicked than if he were turned into a beast. It is worse to be like the devil, to fulfill his will, to be a servant to him, to be turned into a devil, than to be turned into a beast. And yet we should account it a great misery if God should put any one under such a punishment to turn your bodies into beasts. I remember reading of Lactantius, where he quotes Tully, "Who would not rather die than have his body, the body of a man, turned the shape of a beast, though he should retain the mind of a man, under this condition?" It was as if God, by His power, should turn the shape of a man's body, to be just like a dog or a swine, and yet he should have the mind of a man. The soul should be kept within such a body, the form of a dog or a man, and he should go up and down in the world as a dog or a swine, yet he would have the mind of a man.

Now, this heathen said, a man would rather die than be so. Then how great an evil, said he, is it for a man to have the soul of a man turned into the fashion of a beast, though his body continues still in the form of a man. A heathen could say this!

By this it appears that, though we do not see God work such miracles, as to turn the bodies of men and women, by His judgments, into the shapes of swine or dogs, or such creatures as He might do if He pleased, but we see this ordinarily, that the souls of men and women are turned just into the very fashion and shape (as I may so speak) of the sensitive souls of brute beasts. A drunkard or a glutton? His soul is just like the sensitive soul of a barking dog, and they bark like (no, a great deal worse than) a dog. And those who are wickedly subtle are like foxes. And the Scripture speaks of cruel men like they are wolves. Their sins turn their souls to be like the very spirit and sensitive souls of the brute beasts. So that they are in a worse condition than if their bodies were turned into the shape of brute beasts. But when their souls are turned to be like the devil, this is a great deal worse than if they were like brute beasts. This is the first corollary.

Chapter 45

The Second Corollary. It is worse to be sinful than to be afflicted with temptation from the devil.

Secondly, from the reference sin has to the devil, it follows that for any man or woman to be wicked is a great deal worse than to have the greatest trouble and affliction by any temptation from the devil.

There are many men and women who are exceedingly pestered with hideous and horrible temptations by the devil, and who are so troubled with them that they are even weary of their lives and do not know what to do. Many send up papers to the minister in public, desiring to be prayed for, because of that sore affliction upon them, those dreadful temptations of the devil. Wherever they go, wherever they are, whatever they are doing, when they are hearing a sermon, reading, if they go to prayer, still hideous temptations of the devil come upon them, and this wearies their lives. They would rather endure any misery in the world.

I dare appeal to you who are troubled with these hideous temptations of the devil which dog and follow you. Would you not rather endure loss of estate, sickness, poverty and shame, disgrace, rather than have these hideous temptations follow you? Oh, you should have many quickly make their choice! "Rather let any thing befall me than have such hideous temptations pursue and pester me."

Now if such hideous temptations are a greater evil in your account than all afflictions that can befall your body, then much more evil are your sins than all afflictions; for sin has greater reference to the devil than temptations, and they make you more like the devil than temptations do. Temptations may be nothing more than those which befell the Son of God Himself.

Christ was pestered with temptations, hideous temptations, temptations to deny God, to tempt God, and to worship the devil himself. Temptations befell Christ, as hideous as could befall anyone, and He was the Son of God, beloved of God. Therefore, your temptations are no other, no greater than what might have befallen Christ, and therefore not as great an evil as sin. They do not make you like the devil like sin does.

If temptations come from the devil, and are not entertained, though they are afflictions they are not sin. Now in that sin has such reference to the devil, it appears that sin is worse than all the annoyance you can have by any temptation.

Chapter 46

The Third Corollary. It's worse to be under sin than to be haunted by the devil.

Thirdly, hence it follows that sin is worse than to be continually in the presence of the devil. It is worse for a man or woman to be under the power of any sin than to be continually haunted by devils, and to have the sight of devils before their eyes and be in company with them. If God should lay such a judgment upon a man or woman that wherever they might be they should see devils before them, it is still worse to be under the power of any one sin.

Many are mightily terrified in the dark. "Oh! There is the devil in the room," and they think he comes to them, and there are apparitions of devils. They are troubled with this. Oh! These men and women are haunted by devils and there are houses haunted by devils. This is a miserable condition.

Now are you haunted by any wicked lust and sin. Certainly you are in a worse condition than any man or woman haunted by devils, or any house haunted by the devil. Is there any house in your parish where there is blaspheming, oaths, railing at goodness, Sabbath-breaking, and such things? This house is worse than any house haunted by devils, for sin is a great deal worse than the mere presence of the devil.

I remember reading of a tyrant, a man named Maxensius, in Hetrusia. He invented this torment to put men to death. He would have a dead man's carcass tied about their bodies and so let them go wherever they would. But he still carried the dead carcass about him and, at length, the stench put him to death. This was his tyranny.

If you should have a dead man or woman tied about your body, maybe the face of a dead man if hideous to you, but if they should be tied around you so that when you lie in bed, and when you rise, when you sit to eat meat, it should always be with you and you should endure the stink and putrefaction, what a sore evil would this be?

Now if, in the presence of a dead carcass, there is so much evil, then in the presence of the devil there is much more. Now sin, any one sin tied close to your hearts, that you carry about with you wherever you go, know there is in that sin a greater evil upon you than if a dead carcass should be tied to you, yes, than if the devil should haunt you wherever you go; because the presence of the devil is not as much as turning the souls of men and women into the nature of the devil and making the souls of men and women so like to him.

Chapter 47

The Fourth Corollary. It's worse to be given up to any way of sin than to be given up to the devil. QUESTION. How can the delivering up to Satan be for the saving of the soul?

A fourth corollary, then, is this, that for any man or woman to be left to one sin is worse than to be given up to the devil. I say, it is a greater evil, a greater judgment, for any man or woman to be left to any way of sin than to be given up to Satan. Is your soul given up to the power of any one sin? I dare here, as I stand in the presence of God, to avow that you are in a worse condition than if you should be given up to the devil.

I make good on that by using I Corinthians 5:5. We have an example there of one who was given up to the devil, and that in a right way. There is an incestuous person who committed that horrible wickedness not named among the Gentiles, who had his father's wife and committed incest with her. The Apostle commanded him *to be delivered to Satan for the destruction of the flesh, that his spirit might be saved in the day of the Lord Jesus.* He was delivered to Satan for the destruction of his flesh, but to the end that he might have his spirit saved in the day of the Lord Jesus. So that delivering this person up to Satan was a means appointed by God to save his soul.

But to deliver anyone up to the power of sin is no means to save the soul, that is a means to damn the soul, not to save it. So then, you see the reason clearly grounded in Scripture. It is worse to be delivered up to any sin than to be delivered to the devil, for he who was delivered to Satan was done so for the saving of his soul; but he who is delivered to sin is done so for the damning of his soul. This requires a little opening.

QUESTION. You will say, "How can the delivering up to Satan be for the saving of the soul?"

ANSWER. It will be necessary, in order to clear this, to tell you what this delivering up to Satan was; and the truth is, this delivering up to Satan, or excommunication from the church, was a most dreadful thing when done in a right way. It was done when the church was gathered together by the power of Jesus Christ. As certainly, where there are a company of saints who at least outwardly so appear, a church is gathered together in a solemn manner through the power of Jesus Christ, having their Elder going before them, the Officer of the Church.

When they, in a solemn manner, in the power of Christ, shall cast out any one deservedly from church communion, this is delivering a man or woman to Satan. This is another manner of business than we ordinarily are used to having by the Ordinary, or the Commissary, and Dean in the Prelate Courts. Certainly, they were but wooden daggers in comparison to this dreadful sword, to cut off from the commission of the church.

It was when the church was assembled, not the Commissary and Officers, but when the church was gathered together, to cut such a one from the church of Christ for some vile act. Not for neglecting to pay their fees or the like, these things only scared people. But if this censure of excommunication were properly executed, it would be the most dreadful thing in the world. It is that which has awed and terrified the most proud and stout sinners. The very sight of another's excommunication has terrified the conscience of those who have been by. It is delivering them to Satan and putting them out from under the protection of God, giving them up to the devil to take power over them unless they come in and repent.

And this is the way to save the soul, because if there is any way in the world to cause men to see their sin and repent, to be humbled and come in, this is it. And when no other way would do it, this many times has done it.

And, therefore, those people who live in such a condition, who want this ordinance of excommunication in the
right way, want a special means to keep off sin; both to keep
them from sin before they are fallen, and to deliver them
from sin when they have fallen into it. But to be given over
to the power of sin is a greater evil than to be delivered to
Satan.

Chapter 48

The Fifth Corollary. It's worse to be given up to one sin than to be actually possessed by the devil.

Fifthly, shall I say further (and this will make it plainly appear what an abundance of evil there is in sin, more than in affliction), though we have spoken much of it, yet all this only draws the point higher and higher, and drives the nail deeper and deeper that this truth of God might settle upon your spirits. And, therefore, a fifth corollary is this, which follows from this reference sin has to the devil, it is worse to be given up to any one sin than to be actually possessed by the devil, than for the devil to come and actually possess us as those poor creatures were in the gospel. And this is worse than to be given up to Satan.

There is a spiritual possession of Satan, as in Judas, and that is a spiritual possession of their hearts to rule them; but there is a temporal possession spoken of in the gospel, and that is of their bodies. The devil possesses them and causes them to rage and foam at the mouth, to rend and tear. The men we read of in the gospel, who lived among the graves and dead people, cut themselves with knives and stones. This was a grievous thing to see men thus possessed. Many man have extraordinary fits of convulsions and the like, and other men think they are possessed. We ordinarily make that mistake when it is nothing but a fit of convulsion. But if we knew they were really possessed, we would be terrified.

Oh, such a friend, such a neighbor lived wickedly before, and now the devil has possessed him. We thought it was a disease until now. We thought it was a convulsion, but now we see it is from the devil's possession of them.

Would you not rather endure any affliction in the world than have God say of you that the next time you swear, when you open your mouth to swear, the devil will come in and take possession of your body? Or the next evil language you speak, the devil shall come in and possess you? This would be a fearful thing, and you would take heed of this.

But I am to make this good. When you go on in sin, in any one sin, it is a greater evil than if never so many devils possessed you, than if there should be legions that possessed you. When asked by Christ his name, the demon said "Legion," because there were many. It is not as great an evil as if God should give your body up to be possessed by legions of devils.

You will say, "Surely that is a great evil," but not as great as being under the power of one sin.

"How will you make that appear?" you will say.

By this, possession does not make you hateful to God, guilty before God, and loathsome to God. Nor is it that which God hates, but it is an object of pity. Christ pitied them when He saw them thus. But sin makes a man odious and hateful to God.

I remember an excellent observation Gregory had on the book of Job. When God gave Job up to the devil and bid him do what he would, only spare his life, what is the reason the devil did not possess him? The words are so, *He is in thy hands, only spare his life.* It appears that he was in his power to possess him, but yet he did not. What is the reason? This is the answer the Ancient gives. Because if he had possessed him, then, though Job had fretted, frowned, and torn himself, it would not have been his sin, his impatience. It *was* his sin when he was not possessed.

Now because the devil envied Job, the devil would bring that upon Job which he knew to be the greatest evil as much as he could; for so all envy does. One who envies another labors to bring the greatest evil on him that he can.

So certainly the devil envied Job and, therefore, he labored to bring the greatest evil on him that he could.

Now it seems that possession was not the greatest evil; but the devil went to work to see if he could possibly get Job to be impatient and make Job curse God and sin against God. If Job should have cursed God in word while possessed by the devil, then it would have been the devil cursing God. It would not have been Job's sin as much as if he had gotten him to curse God otherwise.

Now the devil would have him to curse God so that it would be a sin in Job and, therefore, the devil would not possess him because that would have been a lesser evil. So that to be given up to sin is a greater evil than to be possessed.

Therefore, all you who have friends and children whom you see being wicked and licentious, and you have cause to fear that they are given up to the power of sin for the present, it should cause fathers and mothers to come to Christ as earnestly as ever those poor creatures did who had children possessed with the devil in the gospel. Poor women had children possessed and so did men. Fathers who had children possessed with the devil, who rent and tore themselves in the presence of Christ, cried out mightily to Christ to come and help them. The woman of Canaan cried after Christ to help her daughter, for she was miserably vexed with an unclean spirit.

So you should go and cry to God, "Lord, help if possible and have mercy upon my son, upon my daughter, for they have unclean spirits. Yea, they are in a worse condition than if possessed by the devil. I have a son, a swearing young man; a daughter who is vain and profane, wicked and licentious, stubborn and unruly. Oh, if it is possible, help me."

If you could be as sensible of the sins and wickedness of your children as, in the time of the Gospels, fathers and mothers were of the possession of their children, much might then be done.

Chapter 49

The Sixth Corollary. Sin brings to wicked men the same portion the devils have.

Sixthly, then, it follows that if sin has such reference to the devil, it must follow that the same portion the devils have must be at last the portion of wicked men. The Scripture expresses it in Matthew 25:41, *Go you wicked into the portion prepared for the devil.* And we read in Timothy that the same portion the devil has shall be the portion of wicked and ungodly men. We read in the book of Revelation of fearful judgments that shall befall such as have the mark of Antichrist on them, Revelation 14:10, *An angel followed, saying with a loud voice, If any man worship the beast, and his image, and receive his mark in their foreheads, or in their hands, the same shall drink of the wine of the wrath of God poured out without mixture, and shall be tormented with fire and brimstone in the presence of God, and His holy angels, and of the Lamb.*

Mark the dreadful judgments upon those who have the mark of Antichrist, either openly in their foreheads, in profession, or more privately in their hands. He shall drink of the wrath of God, etc. Now if such as have only the mark of Antichrist upon them shall have such dreadful punishment, what shall those have who have such a likeness unto the devil himself? The mark of the devil, who are even turned into the very nature of the devil, who are children of the devil, what shall the end of such wicked and ungodly men and women be?

And now, brethren, we have finished all these six particulars in opening the evil of sin; and therein showed that there is more evil in sin than there is in any affliction. And now I had thought to have made some good entrance into the application of this, for though all this while in the explanation, I have mingled some application, yet there remains many excellent, useful considerations which flow from all that has been said of the evil of sin, that, if possible, it may be brought to your hearts, that all may not vanish and come to nothing in the conclusion.

Now this one use I had verily thought to have gone through. I shall only name it, and show what I intend in it, and I shall finish it in the following discourse.

Chapter 50

Use 1. To show that trouble of conscience for sin is another manner of business than melancholy or timidity.

Hence, it follows plainly from all that has been spoken, if sin is worse than affliction and is not to be chosen rather than affliction, then that trouble of conscience for sin certainly is another manner of business than merely melancholy distemper. It does not come from melancholy or foolish timorousness and the like.

There is another manner of business in trouble of conscience for sin than the world thinks of. This is the first use that follows from all that has been delivered. I think all of you should yield to the strength of this consequence. If you have heard or read what I have opened, it should take this effect in you all: "Well, then, by what I have heard now, I come to understand what the meaning of trouble of conscience for sin is."

I have heard, heretofore, of many men and women who are troubled for sin, and I wondered what it meant. I wondered what it was that troubled them. Many young people may be heirs of great estates and and excellent good friends, of healthy bodies and good jobs. All is well for them, and yet they may be mightily troubled for sin. Yes, perhaps there are some who, in the view of the world, lived very civilly but in the secret have been guilty of some notorious, profane course. Yet when God shall but settle any one sin upon their hearts, and trouble their conscience for any one sin, they could not bear the horror of their conscience for this one sin.

Well, I have heard this of the evil of sin, and it tells me that I have had mistaken thoughts about it. I thought all was just melancholiness, and even madness, and the physician must be sent for, and merry company sent for, because men and women have such poor and mean apprehensions of the evil of sin. Therefore, when many are troubled in conscience for sin, then people want to get them into merry company, get a deck of cards, make them play a fit of music, go to some business in the world, put themselves upon business, one thing or another, drink down their trouble, play down their trouble. Thus, many have slight thoughts about their trouble of conscience.

When this is in their children, they cry out, "Oh! My child will certainly run mad, he is gone mad." Many carnal men and women, when their children begin to think of sin, they think they have begun to go mad.

I remember the story of Francis Spira. He said to his friends, because they thought it was a kind of frenzy and not a troubled conscience for sin, "Oh! I would to God it were frenzy, either feigned or real. If it were feigned frenzy, then I could put it off when I pleased. If it were a real frenzy, there would be a great deal more hope of God's mercy. I should not apprehend God's wrath as I do, but it is otherwise with me."

Brethren, those who have felt trouble of conscience for sin, upon whose hearts God has settled but the guilt of any one sin, what do you think of trouble of conscience for sin? They feel reality, they find that there is really unto them that which is a greater burden and grief and trouble than all the miseries of the world. Frances Spira has many dreadful expressions, which are most dreadful examples of horror of conscience for sin. "Oh!" said he, "I feel the very torments of hell within me, and this afflicts my conscience with intolerable pain. Oh! that somebody would let out this tired soul out of my body. Oh! that I were in the place of the damned, that I might be but free from fearing anything that is worse yet to come."

Though he acknowledged that there were greater torments in hell, yet he professed that he desired to be in hell so that he might be freed from the torture of his spirit which was still in fear of worse things to come. And, verily, it is a

most hideous story that shows the dreadfulness of a
wounded and troubled conscience for sin.

Certainly, if sin is all that which you have heard or read,
well might the Holy Ghost say, *A wounded spirit, who can
bear?* A man may sustain his infirmities, whatever his infirmities and troubles are in the world. It is no great matter to
sustain them; but a wounded spirit, who can bear? A
wounded spirit sees it has to deal with the infinite God, the
glorious, eternal Deity. And you must not tell such a one of
melancholiness and such grounds of trouble, for such a one
knows the arrows of the Almighty stick in his heart, and it is
another manner of business than so.

I might here have enlarged myself and spoken much to
those who have such mean apprehensions of trouble of conscience for sin, but I shall not at present. I shall wind up all
now briefly and prosecute it further in the next chapter.

Certainly, it is not melancholiness, it is another manner
of business than melancholiness. What do you think of the
Lord Christ Himself in His agony, who sweat drops of water and blood, which you see was the fruit of sin? Was that
melancholy? Certainly, that was of the same nature that the
troubled in conscience feel for sin.

The angels who sinned against God, the devils themselves, are not capable of melancholiness; they have no
bodies. And yet none have such horrors for sin as they have.
And so the souls of wicked men, many times, have horrid
apprehensions of the wrath of God for sin. But certainly, if
the souls of wicked men and women go out of their bodies
without pardon, the very first instant the soul is departed
from the body it has more horrid, dreadful, and dismal apprehensions of the wrath of God for sin than it ever had before.

I remember further that Luther had a speech concerning
trouble of conscience for sin in his commentary upon
Genesis. "It is a harder matter to comfort an afflicted conscience for sin than to raise one from the dead." This was a

speech of Luther's. He saw what was in an afflicted conscience for sin.

Further, surely it is not melancholy, nor timorousness, nor folly. Take just an example or two and I shall conclude. Take David. You shall find in David that he was a man most free from melancholy, for the temper of his body was a most cheerful disposition, and a warlike spirit, and very wise. And yet there is none in the Book of God more troubled in spirit for sin than he was.

First, I will show you what manner of man David was, and then what his troubles of conscience were for sin. Sure, he was no melancholy man; for, first, you shall find in 1 Samuel 16:12 that he, as for his bodily constitution, was sanguine and not melancholy. He was of a ruddy and beautiful countenance, and goodly to look upon. So that David, for the constitution of his body, was of a sanguine constitution. And then, for the valor of David, he was a mighty man of valor, 2 Samuel 17:10, *And he was valiant whose heart was as the heart of a lion.* This was the commendation of Hushai concerning David. And he was very cheerful. Who made as many Psalms, and who was as musical as David? He is called the sweet singer of Israel in 2 Samuel 23:1.

He had a sweet complexion, he was sanguine, he had a great deal of valor, and was the sweet singer of Israel. And for wisdom, he was like an angel of God, as the woman of Tekoa said to him. And yet, who ever was in such anguish and distress for sin as David?

You shall find this if you read his penitential Psalms. I cannot mention them all, but take a few. In Psalm 6, he is in trouble of spirit. Then you have Psalm 32, *When I kept silence, my bones waxed old through my roaring all the day long.* Mark it, David felt the weight of sin so upon his heart that his bones waxed old through his roaring all the day long. He did not find sin to be a light matter as some ordinary people do. In Psalm 38, there are notable expressions. Verse 2, *Thy arrows stick fast in me, and Thy hand presseth*

*me sore: there is no soundness in my flesh because of Thy
anger, nor rest in my bones because of my sin.* Verses 3 and
4, *My iniquities have gone over my head as an heavy burden, they are too heavy for me.* Verse 5, *My wounds stink
and are corrupt because of my foolishness.* Verse 6, *I am
troubled, I am bowed down greatly, I go mourning all the
day long.*

See what sin cost David. And I beseech you, take this
note along with you. You who make use of David's sin to
encourage yourselves with will say, "Why? Did not David
commit adultery and sin, this David who was a man after
God's own heart?"

Yes, but mark it, you who will make use of David's sin.
Make use of what David felt for sin. You see David's sin
cost him dearly and made the arrows of the Almighty stick
fast in him. It caused him to roar out in anguish and distress
of spirit all day long. He professed that he watered his couch
with tears.

Then we have Psalm 51, *Restore to me the joys of Thy
salvation, that the bones that Thou hast broken may rejoice.*
David's bones were broken through the trouble of his spirit,
that is, the strength of his spirit (not bones literally). As
bones are the strength of the body, so the strength of his
spirit was overcome by the anguish and trouble of his soul
for sin.

Thus it was with David, who was such a sanguine, such
a pleasant, such a valiant, such a wise man; yet he felt this
trouble of spirit, this trouble of conscience for sin.

You who have slight thoughts of sin and make a light
matter of it, Oh, you have brave, stout spirits! You will
scorn to be so afraid. What? Afraid of everything the minister says? I scorn to be such a fool.

You think you can be sermon proof, and can hear all this
dreadful evil of sin opened, without any fear and trembling.
Well, you who have such stout spirits, know that David's
spirit was as valiant as yours. His heart was as valiant as a

lion's, and yet the weight of sin broke his heart. And it will break yours too if God lays it rightly upon your spirits.

Oh! It is not timorousness that causes this trouble of conscience, for let God come and lay his afflicting hand on them, they can bear that as nothing in comparison to sin.

I remember hearing a story of a woman who had nine children, and had great pains with them all. Yet afterwards, having trouble of conscience, she said, "Oh! All the pains I have had with my nine children is nothing compared to the trouble of conscience I have felt in a short time."

So certainly, all pains are nothing in comparison to the pains of spirit when sin is settled by strong conviction upon your souls. You have many who are troubled for sin who could bear outward affliction who could not bear that. And you who speak of the valor of your spirits, you who are so valiant that you can bear trouble for sin as easily as you think, you who are so full of courage; when afflictions are upon you, your hearts are down and are poor, low spirits, white-livered, and can bear nothing, no cross or affliction. This shows that you have no true courage. You have courage to resist conscience and the motions of the Holy Ghost and the Word, but no true courage. It may be that you only have impudent spirits.

And mark one more example. One of the wisest men who ever lived upon the earth was greatly troubled for his sin all his days. And this is the example of Heman, who had such woeful trouble of spirit on him for sin. See Psalm 88. Read the whole psalm, and you shall see the trouble of his spirit for sin, especially verse 7, *Thy wrath lies hard upon me, and Thou hast afflicted me with all Thy waves.* And verse 14, *Lord, why castest Thou off my soul? Why hidest Thou Thy face from Me? I am afflicted and ready to die from my youth up.*

God was pleased to exercise him from a young man, and it is a blessed thing when God begins with young ones and makes them know what sin means while they are young, as

Heman did, *from my youth up*. While I suffer Thy terrors, I am distracted, and verse 16, *Thy fierce wrath goeth over me, Thy terrors even cut me off.*

Well, who was this Heman? For this is not a psalm of David. You shall see in the title that it was a psalm of Heman, and you will find that he was one of the wisest men who ever lived on the earth, I Kings 4:31. There it speaks of Heman. He was brought in the story among the most wise men who lived upon the earth. He is compared with Solomon. It is said of him that he was exceedingly wise and of excellent wisdom, *More wise than the children of the East country, for he was wiser than all men.* Heman was one of the wisest men of all, though Solomon excelled him. Yet next to him, Heman was one of the wisest. And how did he come to be this wise?

It is likely that one thing that caused him to be so wise was that he was afflicted and ready to die. From his youth up, he was troubled for sin all his days.

What is the folly of young people? They go up and down and take liberty in wickedness and sin, and never feel the weight of sin; but if God is pleased to begin with them and make them to see the evil of sin rightly, this is the way for them to come to have true wisdom. If God trains them up in trouble of conscience for sin, it is the way to make them wiser than their teachers, wiser than their fore-fathers, and to bring them to the wisdom even of the most wise.

Chapter 51

The former use further prosecuted. First, against those who have slight thoughts of trouble of conscience, which arises either from gross ignorance, atheism, or desperate slighting of God. Secondly, trouble of conscience is the beginning of eternal death. Thirdly, those who have slight thoughts of trouble of conscience can never prize Christ. Fourthly, those who have slight thoughts of trouble of conscience now shall one day alter their opinion. Fifthly, it would be just with God to let those sink under the burden of conscience who have slight thoughts of it now. Sixthly, those who have slight thoughts of trouble of conscience, those very thoughts take away a chief restraint from sin. Seventhly, slight thoughts of trouble of conscience for sin are (1) a high degree of blasphemy; and (2) a degree towards the unpardonable sin.

We have entered upon the application of all that has been said concerning the evil of sin. And you may remember, I have only named one use that arises from all that has been said about the evil of sin, and that we shall now prosecute.

The use is this, if there is as much evil in sin as you have heard opened unto you, beyond all the evil of any affliction, then we see that the wounds and trouble of conscience for sin is certainly no melancholy conceit. It is not a fancy or an imagination, as many in the world think of it. Many men have very slight thoughts about the trouble of conscience for sin and, when they hear of men or women troubled for their sin, they think "It is nothing but melancholy, or temptation, or some kind of frenzy, or madness, or folly, or weakness of spirit, or timorousness."

These are the thoughts men have of trouble of conscience and, according to the thoughts they have of it, such are the cures that they seek for it. I spoke somewhat of it in the last chapter, but now certainly, if these things are true, as verily they are the truths of God that have been delivered concerning the evil of sin, then we are not to wonder at men and women who have troubles of conscience for sin. I showed by some examples that trouble of conscience was not melancholy, especially in the example of Christ Himself who had the burden of sin, who had troubles of spirit. I cannot properly call it trouble of conscience, for there is a substantial difference between the wrath upon His soul that he felt and the wrath of God that others feel upon their consciences; but in effect, the wrath of God is the same that was upon Him by imputation of sin and upon others by reason of their own proper guilt. And it was not melancholiness in Him, nor in David, as I showed in the last chapter.

Now to proceed. There are two things I desire to proceed in.

First, I have many things to say unto those who have slight thoughts of trouble of conscience for sin; and, if there are any in this place who have wondered at men and women who have been troubled in their conscience for sin, let them attend to what they read. I have divers things to say unto them.

Secondly, I am to show you some differences between melancholy distempers and trouble of conscience for sin.

First, these thoughts of yours certainly come from either an abundance of ignorance, from atheism, or from a desperate slighting of God. They come from one of these three causes.

1. Ordinarily, these thoughts that men have of trouble of conscience being no greater a matter than melancholy conceits come from gross ignorance. You do not know God, you do not know what it is for a soul to have to deal with an infinite Deity. You never yet had a real sight of an infinite Deity with whom you have to deal. And it is a sad thing to think that men and women should live a long time and never, in all their lives, come to have a real sight of that infinite

Majesty and Deity with whom we have to do.

It comes from ignorance of the nature of sin. You do not know what sin is. God has yet blinded your eyes that you should sin, but not know what sin is. Certainly you do not know the Law of God, the spiritualness of it, and the dreadfulness of the wrath of God revealed against sin.

You do not know what eternity means. You do not apprehend what it is for a soul to be in hazard of miscarrying to all eternity. It was the speech of Frances Spira (as I opened in the former chapter), of which I shall make further use because it was such a notable example, "If I might endure the heavy wrath of God but for twenty thousand years, I should not think it much; but it must be eternal eternally. I must endure the eternal wrath of God." That lay heavy upon his spirit. Let any man or woman in the world, the most stout, the most proud spirit that lives upon the face of the earth, think what it is to miscarry to eternity, and this will make his spirit to be troubled. Therefore, it's gross ignorance in men that makes many have such slight thoughts of trouble of conscience for sin.

2. Again, if it is not from ignorance, then it is from atheism. For many men who seem to have excellent parts and are not ignorant dolts, yet have slight thoughts of trouble of conscience for sin. It is not so much to be wondered at to see a company of ignorant fools who know nothing of God and the principles of religion, that they should have such slight thoughts, and wonder what men mean to be troubled for sin; but men who have good parts, perhaps men of great gifts and pregnant wit, great scholars, yet have slight thoughts of trouble of conscience for sin.

Now, in these men, the usual cause is atheism, or slighting God. Woeful, desperate atheism is in the hearts of many great scholars, many pregnant wits, many who will speak much of religion, yet they are desperate atheists in their hearts. Therefore, from thence it comes.

Therefore, when you see learned men, understanding

men, go on in such and such sinful ways and slight all that is said concerning the evil of sin, do not wonder at it, for woeful desperate atheism may lie under an abundance of knowledge. There may be a great deal of knowledge, learning, wit and parts, and yet a slighting of sin.

This is the cause, atheism in their spirit. Compare these two Scriptures together, Psalm 14:1, *The fool hath said in his heart, there is no God;* and Proverbs 14:9, *Fools make a mock of sin.* That is, those fools who say in their hearts, "There is no God," make a mock of sin. They think lightly of all that has been said of the evil of sin, and why do we make such ado about the evil of sin? They can slight it and make light of it.

Well, it is such who make a mock of sin that say in their hearts, "There is no God."

If this is not the case, it comes from desperate wickedness, slighting of God. Perhaps men are not grown so far as to be plain, downright atheists, yet they have slight thoughts of God. Oh, what a slighting this is of the majesty of God! For any man or woman to think it is a light matter to sin against God! Or for trouble of conscience for sin to be a slight matter. Thus it will appear to spring from one of these causes.

Perhaps if you yourself are but crossed in anything, or anything comes to cross your will, you think it is a great thing and are woefully troubled and are in a rage. When you are crossed, you think it is intolerable. It must not be borne or suffered that anyone should cross you! But when it comes to crossing God and sinning against Him, you have slight thoughts of it and it is nothing to cross God. To sin against God is a slight matter. To cross you or to do any evil against you is insufferable.

What a slighting of God this is, that if you are crossed in your will it is so insufferable, and yet to have such slight thoughts of sinning against God. This is the first.

Secondly, you who have slight thoughts concerning

troubles of conscience, consider that what you have slight thoughts of, in itself, in its own nature, is no other but the very beginnings of eternal death, of the second death, the very beginnings of hell. The principal torment of hell lies in the perfection of that trouble now that, for the present, is upon the conscience, and yet you make nothing of this. You treat it as if it were only melancholy, as if the wrath of God that shall lie upon the damned in hell to all eternity were only a frenzy. Certainly, that which the Lord will, at the last, torment the souls of the damned with to all of eternity is of the very same nature with the wounds and horrors of conscience in this world.

It is true that God does, indeed, oftentimes, bless the horrors of conscience to the saving of the soul, to bring the soul to Christ, but horrors of conscience, in their own nature, are the beginnings of the second death. As pains and sickness of the body of a man or woman are the beginnings of the first death, so wounds and horrors of conscience are the beginnings of the second death.

The soul of man is a subject of larger capacity for torments than the body can be. Now the principal way that God has to torment the soul, that we know of, in hell itself, is by the horrors and wounds of conscience. I remember, therefore, the speech of Frances Spira, *I feel in me the wrath of God as the torments of hell*. And he was not mistaken, for they are the beginnings of the torments of hell. And therefore God, many times, to keep men from being swallowed up in those torments, makes them feel those torments. They have some sparks of these torments of hell upon their souls now that they may be delivered from the flames of hell to all eternity.

Trouble of conscience for sin is nothing else but God letting out some sparks of hell upon the soul. Now what a mistake is this for you to think that this is nothing but melancholy when, the truth is, it is nothing else but the sparks of hell upon the soul. This is the second.

Thirdly, you think this is a melancholy conceit. Certainly, it is impossible for such a man or woman ever, as long as they continue thus, to prize Christ or to love Christ. I say, whoever you are that has such conceits, if this abides in you, I dare charge you as from the Lord that you never yet, in all your life, have prized Jesus Christ or loved Him.

"But how does this appear?" you ask.

Thus: you never prized Christ or loved Christ rightly if you have this conceit, because you can never know what Christ suffered for you. The principal thing Christ suffered for sinners was the bearing of the wrath of the Father upon His soul. His soul-sufferings were more than His bodily sufferings. You hear sometimes of Christ's shedding His precious blood for you and dying upon the cross, but the death of His body, the shedding of His blood, was not the principal thing Christ suffered for you if you are saved. It was the suffering of the wrath of God upon His soul, when His soul was troubled, when He cried out, *My God, My God, why hast Thou forsaken Me?* And yet you have slight thoughts of these sufferings.

If you see a man or woman in bodily torture, in some disease, you think there is some reality in that; but for the sufferings of the soul, you have poor thoughts of these and cannot imagine what they should mean when they speak of the wrath of God to be upon the soul.

Now, if you have slight thoughts of the wrath of God upon the soul, it is impossible that you should prize Christ, because you do not know what He suffered. But a man or woman who has felt the wrath of God upon their souls in the wounds of conscience for sin, such a one has a little intimation of what the Lord Christ endured for them. Such a one can tell what Christ endured and can so prize Christ and love Christ. Such a one can reason like this, "What? Is one spark of the wrath of God upon the soul so terrible? Are the tortures so sore? How terrible, then, was the flame of God's wrath that was let out upon the soul of Jesus Christ?" For so it was.

If you have a little trouble of soul under the sense of sin now, know it is but as a spark of the fire that blazed out upon Christ. If you have one drop upon you, it is but as one drop of those flood gates let out upon the soul of Jesus Christ. The floodgates of God's displeasure were let out upon the soul of Christ.

This certainly is one reason why God will have sinners to be saved eternally, to feel trouble of soul for sin, that they may know how to prize Christ and love Christ more, and understand what the sufferings of the soul of Christ were for sin. As Christ suffered in His soul that He might be a merciful High Priest and have compassion on us and help us when we need (as 'tis a comfort to one who suffers in his soul to know that Christ suffered in His soul, and so knows how to feel compassion for such), so, on the other side, God causes poor souls to suffer trouble that they might be sensible of Christ's sufferings and so praise and love Him the more.

Fourthly, you who have slight thoughts of trouble of conscience for sin, whoever you are, this is a most certain truth. These thoughts of your heart shall certainly be altered one day, though they are slight now. This I dare affirm for everyone that has slight thoughts of sin and the trouble for it. These thoughts of their hearts shall be altered. You must come to know sin in another manner than you do now. You must come to feel what sin is in another manner than now you do.

I remember once I heard a credible relation of a scholar who was in jovial company and was very merry, yet had some enlightenings of conscience and, being very profane, was occasionally speaking of a wounded conscience. He pounded his breast and said, "One day this breast of mine must know what a wounded conscience means." He was conscious of an abundance of guilt in him, for he had light and was yet profane. His conscience told him that though he was merry now, yet one day that breast of his would have to know what having a wounded spirit meant.

So I say to you, is there any profane person this day before the Lord who has had, or still has, slight thoughts of the evil of sin and trouble of conscience for sin? Well, go your way and lay your hand upon your breast and say to yourself, "One day this breast of mine must know what a wounded spirit is, and must have other manner of thoughts about a troubled conscience for sin."

If your heart is not yet troubled for sin, if you do not feel the weight of sin now, it is a dangerous sign that you are reserved to feel the weight of sin in torment, to know what the meaning of sin is in the burden of it in torment. If you now have slight thought concerning trouble for sin, I say, take it as from the Lord this day as spoken to you, it is a fearful sign, a brand upon you that you are reserved to feel trouble for sin eternally.

God has time enough to trouble you for sin hereafter and, therefore, it may be He lets you go on in these slight thoughts for the present, while you bless yourselves in your own conceits. And God does not now convince you because He has time enough hereafter.

A fifth thing I would say to those who have slight thoughts about trouble for sin is this. If ever God should come in this world to awaken your conscience and lay the weight of sin upon your souls, it would be just with God to let you sink under the burden. I say, it would be just with God so to wound you for sin and to see you sweltering in your wounds and deny you compassion. Why? Because you have had slight thoughts of such a wound.

Certainly, brethren (observe what I say unto you), the very reason why men and women are so long in anguish of spirit for their sin, and under such sore troubles and distress of conscience by reason of their sin, and can have no comfort, is because prior to this they have had such slight thoughts of trouble of conscience. Perhaps then they were in their jolly and mirth they made a mock of it, they made nothing of it. They heard dreadful threats against sin and made light of it, and thought people were troubled more than necessary. Well, you once had such slight thoughts of trouble of conscience for sin. Now God comes upon you for it, and this hand of God lies upon you, and it is just with God that you should feel it to purpose, that you should smart enough; that God might instruct you and convince you of your error, and might now come and teach you after another manner.

What do you think now of trouble of conscience for sin? You had such and such thoughts of it heretofore. What are your thoughts of it now?

I remember there was a young maid not far from the place where I used to live who, hearing of many troubled in conscience for sin, in a kind of scorn and contempt, would feign herself as being troubled in conscience for sin. Oh, she was mightily troubled and in scorn of the ministers! Oh, these and these ministers must be sent for to comfort her, merely out of contempt and scorn. But afterward, God laid on in good earnest upon her conscience and then she was troubled to purpose so that she was at the very brink of making away with herself. And it was very much feared by all her friends that, indeed, she would have made away with herself. She attempted it many ways, but God wonderfully hindered it.

So those who have slight thoughts of perplexities of conscience for sin, when it does come, it may be just with God that it should be so heavy that they should not be able to bear it, but will sink under it. Then it will be so strange a thing to such as have slight thoughts of it that the very strangeness of trouble of conscience for sin will amaze them so that they will not know what in the world to do. This is a fifth thing. When trouble comes upon them, God may justly leave them under trouble.

A sixth thing I would say to such who have slight

thoughts about trouble of conscience for sin is this. These
thoughts of yours take away a chief restraint of sin and cause
you to disregard the authority of the Word. There are these
two fearful evils that follow upon your slight thoughts of
trouble of conscience for sin.

1. They take away that which is the chief restraint of sin.
There are many outward restraints to keep men and women
from sin, but all outwards restraints from sin are nothing to
the restraint of conscience. A man who has a tender conscience has the greatest restraint of sin that can be. There is
no restraint like it. But one who is so far from a tender conscience that he thinks trouble of conscience is a melancholy
conceit has no restraint (to purpose) from sin. He may have
restraints from outward and gross sins, but from close, secret sins he has none. Now it is a great evil to a man who
has the hindrances of sin taken away, and who gives himself
liberty in secret sins.

2. And then for the authority of the Word. It is a great
mercy for men and women to be in such a condition that
their heart should be continually under the authority of the
Word. However, you think it is a brave thing that you can
get your hearts above the Word; but certainly it is one of the
greatest mercies of God upon the earth for God to keep the
hearts of men and women under the authority of the Word.
But that man or woman who thinks lightly of trouble of conscience can slight the Word. They do not regard it. Let what
will be spoken, they can easily put it off because the main
hold the Word has upon the heart of a man or woman is
upon their conscience. The Word takes hold of their conscience and brings down the heart under the power of it. But
if the Word does not take hold upon the conscience, it takes
no hold at all. Let a man or woman come to know what
trouble of conscience for sin is, and what the power and authority of the Word is, and how then does the soul prize the
Word? No man or woman ever comes to prize the Word
until they have felt the power of the Word troubling their

conscience. Then they come to prize the Word.

You have a famous place for this in Job 33:16, *Then He opens the ears of man and seals their instruction.* That is, God, coming upon men in times of affliction, opens their ears and seals their instruction. That is, He makes the Word come with power and authority. A thing sealed comes with more authority than a blank page or a writing not sealed. "Sealed" is when the Word comes with power. Then, in verse 17, *That I may withdraw man from his purpose, and hide pride from man.* That is, having sealed instruction, He humbles the heart.

First, He causes the Word to come with power, and then He humbles the heart. *He keepeth back his soul from the pit and his life from perishing, he is chastened also with pain upon his bed, and the multitude of his bones with strong pains,* and so forth, and in verse 23, *If there be a messenger with him, an interpreter, one among a thousand, to show unto man his uprightness: Then he is gracious unto Him and saith, Deliver him from going down unto the pit.* That is, when God comes to seal instruction and humble the heart, and to cause pains to be upon a man and so make him sensible of his sin, then let a messenger, an interpreter, be found, one of a thousand. Such a one accounts a messenger and interpreter, who is able to declare the way of righteousness and show him a ransom how to be delivered from sin, to be one in a thousand. Whereas, if he should come before, he would be accounted as nobody, and the Word nothing but silly business; but now he is a man in a thousand. Oh, such a messenger, let such a one come and be welcome!

And therefore you have many men slight a conscientious minister in their health and prize those who preach slightly, but in their sickness, when conscience is open, they will not send for a slight minister. They will have those who have most preached to conscience. Those are the ones who will be most prized by them upon their sick and death beds. When conscience is awake, such a one will be one in a thousand then. This is the sixth.

Seventhly, and lastly, and indeed one of the most principal points. I desire all those who have had slight thoughts of trouble of conscience for sin to attend to it. It is this: those slight thoughts of yours about trouble of conscience for sin are a high degree of blasphemy against the Holy Ghost. If I make this plain, that they are guilty of a high degree of blasphemy against the Holy Ghost, then this should awe the hearts of men and women and should make them take heed what they do in giving way to these vain thoughts about trouble of conscience. I will not say it reaches the highest degree of blasphemy, yet I shall make it out to you that they come near it.

It is a high degree of blasphemy against the Holy Ghost, and that appears in this. Trouble of conscience for sin is a special work of the Spirit of God upon the soul of a man or woman wherever it is. Such a work of the Spirit of God as this has the denomination, so that he is called "the spirit of bondage." No, God has no denomination from any slight work. There must be some special and great work of God in which He has a denomination from it. In Romans 8:15, the Spirit of God has this denomination, it is called "the spirit of bondage." *For you have not received the Spirit of Bondage again to fear; but you have received the Spirit of Adoption, crying, Abba Father.* You have not received the Spirit of Bondage against to fear. It is as if the Holy Ghost should say, "There was a time when you had the Spirit of Bondage, and what was this Spirit of Bondage? It was none other than the Spirit of God revealing unto, and setting upon, the heart of a man or woman that bondage that they are in under the Law, corruption, and Satan."

This is the Spirit of Bondage, when God's Spirit shall come to enlighten a man and convince the conscience, and so lay this upon the conscience of any man or woman, "You are, by reason of sin, a bond-slave to the devil, under bondage to all the curses of the Law, by reason of sin. Yes, a bond-slave to your lusts." This is the Spirit revealing and making the soul sensible of this bondage, and is that which causes this denomination to the Spirit of God, to be called "the Spirit of Bondage."

Now for you to attribute to foolish, melancholy conceits that which is one of the special works of the Holy Ghost in the soul, is not this blasphemy against God? This is God's work, and it is a work of God's glory, for all the works of God are His glory. And that which the Spirit of God glories in, as that work proper to Him, you say is but folly and melancholy conceits. Is this not blasphemy and reproach to the Spirit God? Certainly, it is no other but reproach and blasphemy against the Holy Ghost in attributing the trouble of conscience to these other conceits.

No, further, it is a great degree towards the unpardonable sin if you do it out of malice and knowledge. By this, you come to the unpardonable sin. That this one place of Scripture for that, Mark 2. Compare the 22nd verse with the 24th verse. In verse 22, when Christ casts out devils, the text says that the Scribes and Pharisees who came out from Jerusalem said He had Beelzebub, *and by the Prince of the Devils He casts out devils.* They attributed the work of Christ's casting out devils to the power of devils. He casts out devils by the devil. But now, it was by the finger of God.

Well, Christ calls them to Himself and said, *How can Satan cast out Satan?* He convinced them that Satan could not cast out Satan, and told them it was by the Spirit of God that they were cast out. Mark how He goes on in the 28th verse, *Verily, I say unto you, all sins shall be forgiven unto the sons of men, and blasphemies, wherewith soever they shall blaspheme. But he that shall blaspheme against the Holy Ghost hath never forgiveness, but is in danger of eternal damnation.*

Because they said that He had an unclean spirit, Christ told them that other blasphemies shall be forgiven, but the blasphemies against the Spirit of God shall never be forgiven.

Why does Christ speak of this? How does it come in? The text says, *Christ spake it, because they said He had an unclean Spirit.* Mark, Christ was casting out devils, and the Scribes and Pharisees attributed this to an unclean spirit. Therefore, they sinned against the Holy Ghost because they attributed that which Christ did by the finger of God to an unclean spirit. Therefore, Christ tells them they sinned against the Holy Ghost and shall never be forgiven.

Now, brethren, see how near you come to this sin. The Scribes and Pharisees saw Christ cast out devils. They did it out of malice. They could not but know, and yet they said it was the devil. You see one who is troubled in conscience, which is something wrought by the Holy Ghost, and you say it is a foolish and mad spirit, sometimes an unclean spirit. But it is worse when you say it is a foolish and melancholy spirit. You blaspheme the Holy Ghost and come nearer this sin.

Oh, take heed and be humbled! Your condition is dangerous, you who have had, or do have any such low thoughts about trouble of conscience for sin.

OBJECTION. But we see, by experience, men and women troubled for sin who are very melancholy and heavy.

ANSWER. True, sometimes God may be pleased to sanctify even that humor of melancholiness so as to further such a work as this. Yes, God may cause a work on the conscience to be furthered by melancholy, and yet there is a great deal of difference between melancholy and this.

1. First, God may make use of melancholy to bring in trouble of conscience. For example, if it is not too prevailing, He may do it to dull men and women as sometimes it does. But if it is no more prevailing than to make men seriously consider and ponder and weigh things, then God makes use of a degree of melancholy to make men and women to know themselves, and sin, and the things of their

eternal estate, and such a melancholy is a blessed melancholy, and you have cause to bless God for it.

Melancholy, in some inferior things, is very useful. The philosophers say that the most eminent men in the world were melancholy because they were serious in their thoughts, whereas other men were of slight, vain, frothy spirits. Many who have never had melancholy conceive of things and they pass, They never lay anything to heart. They never knew what is was for one half hour to be serious in their thoughts all their lives.

Many who are sanguine are of a light, vain spirit. And it is a heavy judgment of God to be given over to a light, vain spirit that considers nothing. Now, God makes use of this particular degree of melancholy, to make men and women serious, and to consider what shall become of them another day, what the terms between God and them are. They ask, "What if I were to die now? What if I were to stand before God?" Then it is a good help to this work; but yet, because this work is a work beyond any melancholy conceits, we shall give you the differences.

But yet further, it must be acknowledged that, when God comes with trouble of conscience, it may be so mighty and strong that it may alter the body and consume the very spirits in the bodies of men and women. It may alter the temper of blood. It may be that strong and powerful. And so there may come melancholy in afterwards; but yet there is an abundance of difference between melancholy and trouble of conscience, and that will appear in these six particulars.

Chapter 52

Six differences between melancholy and trouble of conscience. Difference 1. Melancholy may be in those who are most grossly ignorant, but trouble of conscience comes with some enlightening work. Difference 2. Melancholy prevails on men by degrees, but trouble of conscience many times comes suddenly as lightning. Difference 3. Melancholy trouble is exceedingly confused, but troubles of conscience are more distinct. Difference 4. The more melancholy any one has, the less able they are to bear outward afflictions, but the more trouble of conscience, the more able to bear outward afflictions. Difference 5. Melancholy puts a dullness upon the spirits of men, but trouble of conscience for sin puts a mighty activity upon men's spirits. Difference 6. Trouble of conscience cannot be cured the ways melancholy can.

First, melancholy is many times in men and women where there is most gross ignorance of God, sin, and the things of their eternal estate. It may consist with gross ignorance. Many melancholy people are most ignorant and dull, and know nothing of the principles of religion. But troubles of conscience can never come without some new light of God darted in and settled upon the hearts of men and women. It always comes with some enlightening work of the Spirit. Melancholy is many times with a great deal of darkness within. The mind is dark where melancholy prevails and, many times, grossly ignorant. But there is never any true trouble of conscience without God coming in with some light. And, therefore, if any man or woman is troubled and says it is for sin, I put this to you. What has God revealed to them now more than before? What truths of God has He settled upon their hearts more than before? If they can give no account of other light let into them than before, or further truth let in upon their hearts than before, then indeed it may be suspected not to be trouble for sin, as many melancholy people have the name of being troubled for sin who only have fears of hell because of dark thoughts. But it is not the true work of the Spirit upon the soul unless it is with proof of new light, or settling some truth upon the soul more than before.

Secondly, melancholiness comes by degrees upon men and women. Alterations of the body are not sudden things. The temper of men and women's bodies cannot be suddenly altered to any extremity, only gradually from one degree to another. But trouble of conscience comes many times as a flash of lightning from heaven. Many men and women have come to the congregation with scornful spirits, profane, wicked, and ungodly persons who never knew what sin meant nor what trouble for sin meant; and God has met with them in the Word and fastened some sentence upon their hearts so that they fall down under the power of it. That sentence comes just as an arrow struck into their liver, and they could never get out of it and have gone away with horrors of soul. Therefore, this has not been melancholiness.

Certainly the humors of the body never alter the spirits of men so suddenly, but when God comes to work, when the Spirit of God and of bondage comes to work, it does not need any preparative matter before it, for the work of the Word is such that it works immediately without any preparation.

Therefore, many men who understood as little of trouble of conscience as ever any did in their lives, and yet God lets some truth reach them, fitted to their hearts and dispositions, find their own sin come to be revealed and they are smitten. This is as it is with the ignorant man from I Corinthians 14:25, who comes into the church and hears there the saints prophesy, *He is convinced, and falls down and said, verily God is among them, of a truth God is in them.* It is a remarkable text. Whatever he thought before, it may be he heard strange stories of the Church of Christ, of profane meetings. Perhaps he heard that, when God's people met together, they blew out the candles and committed uncleanness, wickedness. As there are notorious lies reported abroad of such sects in the world, for certainly there is no such sect in the world, but such reports are raised merely to make the meeting of God's saints odious in the esteem of others. As the Jesuit said, "If you malign someone strongly, some of it will stick though none of it true."

Well, whatever thoughts he had of the assemblies of the people of God (for it is like the heathens had strange thoughts), when he came in and heard what was done, he was convinced and he judged, and the secrets of his heart came to be revealed. The text says that the man falls down and worships God, and reports that God is among them.

So many people hear great relations of such men, and such preachers, and sermons, and they go to hear what they can say and see what they do. Perhaps they go with an intention to scorn, as I have known some come and sit close to a pillar with an intention to jeer and scorn. But, before they have been gone, God has darted some truth into their conscience, and they have been struck with the Word, and gone away with terrors in their conscience. This cannot be melancholy.

When God converted Paul, He came and met him with light from heaven, and struck him from his horse. Paul stood trembling and cried out, *Lord! What wilt Thou have me to do?* There is a great deal of difference between this and melancholy.

A third difference is this. Melancholy is exceedingly confusing to people. They are exceedingly confused in their thoughts and the trouble of their spirit. Many times they have troubles and sinkings, but they can give no account of it all. Yes, their troubles are beyond their ground; the grounds that they are troubled about are very confused so that they do not understand them themselves. But troubles of conscience are a great deal more distinct, and there the soul sees ground for the trouble beyond the trouble. As in melancholy, the trouble is beyond the ground of trouble, so in affliction of conscience the ground is beyond all trouble. I am troubled, indeed, but I see cause to be troubled more; and this is a great part of many men's trouble, that they can be troubled no more.

A fourth difference is this. The more melancholy there is in any man or woman, the less able they are to bear any outward affliction that befalls them. But the more trouble of conscience, the more able they shall be to bear afflictions that befall them.

Those who feel the trouble of sin is heavy account all other afflictions as being light. But melancholy people feel all afflictions are heavy. They cannot bear the least cross, their hearts are ready to sink upon anything; and the more melancholy increases, the more weak their spirits are and the less able to bear any cross. But now with trouble of conscience, the more sin and the heavier the burden of sin lies upon the soul, the more slight thoughts the soul has of outward crosses.

Alas, it may be that a man hears of some who have some grievous diseases in their bodies. "Oh," says he who is troubled in conscience, "if it was no worse with me than if it would be but a flea bite, but it is another manner of matter. If God would change my trouble, I could easily bear that."

Francis Spira had this expression, "Oh! Were I but released and set free as before from trouble of spirit, I think I could scorn all the threatenings of cruel tyrants, and with undaunted resolution bear all torments."

So that the height of this trouble makes the other one less. It was a good speech of a reverend divine of our time, when he heard anyone being impatient under their afflictions, "Surely the reason why affliction is heavy upon you is because sin is light." Those who are impatient under afflictions, it is a sign that sin is light because afflictions are heavy. Troubles of conscience would make all afflictions light, melancholy will not.

Fifthly, a principal difference above all that has been name is this. Melancholy mightily dulls the spirit of any man or woman. Wherever it prevails, it makes them heavy, dull, and backward. But now, trouble of conscience for sin puts a mighty quickness in men. It puts an activity, another manner of activity and stirring in the spirit than ever was before. You shall have many men and women sit dully under a minister many years, many years under the Word, and never act on it. But, when God comes to stir and awaken the conscience for sin, their spirits are active and stirring then in another manner than they were before. Poor people, overwhelmed with melancholy, sit moping and heavy, dull and lumpish, with no activity of spirit at all; but trouble of conscience is as fire in their bones. Jeremiah said that he would speak no more in the name of the Lord; but the Word of God was as fire in his bones and made him active and stirring.

So trouble of conscience makes people active and stirring. Now they can pray where they could not pray before. Now they are active and working.

In Acts 9:11, when God troubled Paul, the text says, *Behold, he prays,* as if Paul had never prayed before in his life. Certainly you who cannot pray, who never prayed, but read a prayer or prayers your mothers taught you; if God ever troubles your conscience for sin, then you will pray as if you were in heaven. There will be mighty prayers then! "Oh, for Christ. Oh, for pardon of sin and peace!"

So there is another manner of acting and stirring in the spirit than there ever was before; but melancholiness will not do it. It makes a man heavy and dull in the very act of prayer.

There is a notable example of the actings of spirit in troubles that come from sin whereas the other makes them dull. It is in the book of Ezra, chapter 9 verse 3 and 5. *When I heard this thing, I rent my garment and my mantle, and plucked off the hair of my head, and of my beard, and sat down astonished.* This, you will say, made him dull. Now mark what follow in verse 5, *And at the evening sacrifice I arose up from my heaviness, and having rent my garment and my mantle, I fell upon my knees, and I spread forth my hands unto the Lord my God, and said, Oh Lord my God, I am ashamed and blush to lift up my face to thee my God, for our iniquities are increased over our heads, and our trespasses are grown up to the heavens, etc.* Mark the prayer Ezra made at the evening sacrifice, when the time was come that he should stir and seek God. Then his spirit was mighty active and stirring, though he was astonished before. If it had been melancholy, his heart would have sat still then.

So trouble of conscience puts life in to the soul in prayer, and makes the soul active in meditation and contemplation. Melancholy people are dull and heavy, and do not know how to meditate, nor what to meditate on.

Those troubled in conscience, oh, what quick thoughts they have about God and Christ, eternity, the law, and sin! Their souls work about such objects that they can have no help from their bodies and senses, and yet their spirits are raised higher than before. And so, when they come to hear the Word, oh, how active are their spirits in catching the Word, in catching every truth!

I appeal to you who are troubled, what difference is there between your spirits now and what they were before you were troubled for sin, before you came to the congregations to see and be seen, when you wondered what men meant to be so earnest? Now you mark every truth and catch hold of every sentence. Now you mark the mind of God and understand what is said. Before you came and heard and never understood what was meant by such and such things. You saw the minister as earnest, but you would not conceive what the man meant in his earnestness. But now you see what he means in his earnestness, and you understand what weight is in those truths you hear revealed. This is something like when the spirit is thus stirred and active in prayer and hearing.

When you were in conference with good men before, your conference was dry and dull. You did not savor the things conferred on, but soon were asleep. But now, if you come where there is conference of God and His Word, of Christ and the like, your mind closes with this. If you were only melancholy, this would make you more dull and heavy, but this makes you more lively and active. Therefore, there is a great deal of difference.

Lastly, trouble of conscience cannot be cured like melancholy can. Melancholy, many times, is worn out with time and medicine can cure that; outward comforts and contentments can cure that. But trouble of conscience is a wound of a higher nature. As Frances Spira said, when they brought physicians and thought he had only trouble of body, "Alas, poor men, they think to cure me by medicine. Ah, it is another manner of malady, and must have another manner of medicine than plasters and drugs to cure a fainting soul and spirit for sin."

Conscience must have gospel antidotes. Therefore, you who thought you had trouble of conscience for sin and are now eased, or perhaps not so troubled as before, look back. What cured you? How does it come to pass that you are less troubled than before? Has time worn it away? Such a sermon and such apprehensions of a truth darted into you and troubled you. You had such troubles, but what cured you? Many times, one can give no account but this, "Sure, time has worn it away." If so, then it was not a right trouble.

It may be you took medicine. Your body was troubled before, but now it is lively. There is more blood in your veins, more spirit now, and perhaps your affliction is taken away and this has cured you. If there is no other trouble than this, certainly you do not know what trouble of conscience means, at least not in a saving way. Either it was not trouble of conscience at all, or else it is not cured rightly. It is rather like the thorn that lies rotting and rankling in the flesh. A thorn, when it first gets in, puts a person to a great deal of pain. Perhaps if it is left alone, the pain will be over for the time being, but it lies rankling and will put you to pain afterwards if it is not cured. So it is with trouble of conscience for sin. If nothing has cured it but these things, it is like the thorn in the flesh and will trouble you afterwards.

There is another manner of cure, for it is the greatest thing God can do to comfort a troubled conscience. It must be the blood of Christ applied by the Holy Ghost. It must be a plaster made of the blood of Jesus Christ and applied by the Holy Ghost to cure this. And therefore, I beseech you, consider what has been said about this argument. As the Psalmist said, "Blessed is the wise man who wisely considers the poor," so I say, blessed is the man and woman who wisely considers these troubles. Don't cast it upon your children and friends, "Oh, they are froward, or madmen, or melancholy!" Oh, do not say so!

You who are acquainted with storms and tempests think them dreadful. It may be some of your friends have lately known what dreadful storms there have been. Now if any of them should make an account of it, and another should say, "This is but a conceit and a fancy. This is no reality, it is a dream," would you think these men spoke like wise men? Certainly, if any storm you have met with at sea has terror in it, know that storms of conscience have a thousand times more terror than storms at sea!

Therefore, when you see any troubled in conscience for sin, fear and tremble. Let your conscience shake at it and make use of their trouble. I remember a story of one Vergerius, who came to comfort Frances Spira. He came to comfort him as other men did, but he saw such dreadfulness upon Spira that it struck terror in his soul. He left his bishopric and went to Basil and became a famous Protestant.

Thus, when you hear troubles of conscience, do not slight it. Rather, let the fear of God be upon you. Go and renounce sin. Oh, if some of our friends only knew what slighting of a troubled conscience was, it would make them do as Vergerius did! Though he had a rich bishopric, he renounced all. And thus we have completed the first use.

Chapter 53

A second use from the whole treatise, showing that a man may be in a most miserable condition, though he is delivered from outward affliction. First, if a man is prosperous by sin, if a man raises himself to a prosperous condition by any sinful way, let such men consider three things: (1) what is gotten by sin costs dearly; (2) what is gotten by sin is accursed to you; (3) what is gotten by sin must be cast away or your soul is cast away. Secondly, when men come to be more sinful by their prosperity explained in three particulars: (1) when prosperity is fuel for their sin; (2) when it gives men further liberty to sin; and (3) when it hardens in sin.

We are yet upon the great doctrine of the evil of sin, showing that there is more evil in sin than in any affliction. Many things, you know, have been delivered in the explanatory part of it, in which I have endeavored to set before you the vileness of sin, to paint it in its true colors as much as I was able. And, having set sin before you in its vileness, we have begun the applicatory parts of this point, to draw some collections by way of use from what has been said concerning the dreadful evil of sin. I have finished the first use, I shall now proceed to the second.

Use 2. And that is this, if there is such dreadful evil in sin above all evils of affliction, then it follows that a man or woman may be in a most miserable condition, a miserable estate, though they are delivered from affliction. I say, it is possible for a man or woman to be a most miserable creature, though they have no outward affliction. Their condition may be very miserable because there is enough evil in sin to make one miserable without affliction.

Most people in the world know no other miseries than that misery which comes by affliction, and they make afflictions to be the only rule and measure of a miserable condition. So much afflicted, so miserable is their estate. They think that those people who are delivered from affliction are happy people and those people who are under affliction are miserable people. "Oh, he has lost his estate, suffered shipwreck, has grievous diseases in all his body, is put in prison, and so lives miserably all his days!" Thus people look upon men and women in affliction as if they were only miserable.

Before I have finished this use, I hope I shall convince you that it is not affliction that makes us miserable, but only sin. Where there is most sin there is most misery, though there is less affliction. It is a great mistake for people to judge happiness or unhappiness by these outward things. You have many people who, when they see men and women who are poor, who have no houses, no clothes, no meat or drink, who are fain to work hard for their livings, or who are sickly and weak, will say, "Oh, they are in a pitiful condition!" But when they see others who have houses and land, who are gorgeously attired in fine clothes and who eat well, they will say, "These are happy men."

Now that point that has been opened to you will serve to rectify your judgments in these things, and not to make afflictions or the absence of afflictions to be the rule of happiness; but to make sin or the absence of sin, or less sin, to be the rule for judging the happiness of our condition.

It was a saying of Luther's, "One drop of an evil conscience is enough to swallow up all the joys in the world, all the prosperity in the world."

There is so much evil in sin that, though a man or woman had all the joys and prosperity that the world could possibly afford, yet one drop of an evil conscience, the guilt of one sin in an evil conscience, is enough to swallow up all and make this man miserable in the height of all prosperity. Let a man be raised up as high as the world can raise him. Put him on a throne, put a scepter in his hand and a crown on his head, let him have all the pomp and glory the world can afford, yet if he is sinful, if he has the guilt of any one sin upon his spirit, this man is a miserable man. But let any one be as poor as Job, sitting upon the dunghill scraping his sores, if he is delivered from the evil of sin, this man is a happy man.

I remember reading a speech of Anselm's. He said that he would rather be in hell without sin than in heaven with sin. He looked upon sin as so great an evil that to be rid of sin would make a man happy under the torments of hell; and being under the guilt of sin would make a man miserable though he was in heaven. Certainly, then, the guilt of sin makes a man miserable in all outward prosperity, and the deliverance from sin will make a man happy under all outwards afflictions and miseries. So, though a man is prosperous in his worldly estate, yet if he is sinful that has enough in it to make a man miserable. That is especially to be considered in this, if there are these two branches in it:

First, if a man is prosperous by sin. Or,

Secondly, if he is sinful by his prosperity.

Then he is, indeed, a miserable creature, notwithstanding all his prosperity. I beseech you to observe it, and it follows from the point that has been opened, that there is so much evil in sin.

First, if there is so much evil in sin, let a man be never so prosperous, if prosperity is furthered by sin, or sin furthered by prosperity, he must be a most wretched, miserable creature. For example, if any man raises himself to any outward prosperous estate in a sinful way, although the world may judge such a man happy, having his heart's desire satisfied, yet it is most certain that this man is a wretched man. Suppose a man gets preferment by a sinful way. Oh, his heart is eager and desirous to get up to preferment, to get livings and estates in the world, and he strains his conscience for it. And when there is a sin between him and his preferment, he will get over the sin. He will climb and scramble over this sin to get the preferment. Rather than lose the preferment, he will scramble over sin and go through sin to his preferment. So eagerly desirous are men of preferment that, though sin is between them and their preferment, they will break through. They will break through the hedge, but they will gain it.

Oh, how many scholars and others, especially such whose educations have been lowly, when they see any way of preferment, livings, or estates, though they have some sin between them and preferment, how have they gotten it, and think themselves safe when they have obtained them! Oh, these men are miserable, and therefore miserable because they are preferred, because they have prospered in their heart's desire! And so it is for men who get riches and estates other than by right means, who gain them by deceit and oppression, or in any sinful, wicked way.

It may be that they have gotten fair houses, well-furnished. It may be that they have means coming in, and they bless themselves and think they are now happy. Yes, and others also think that these are happy and live bravely in the world. But if you knew all, you would look upon these men as most wretched, cursed creatures. Certainly, those men will one day curse the time that ever they had such an estate, and will wish that they had begged their bread from door to door rather than to have gotten their estate by sin.

Seeing there is so much evil in sin, let these men consider these things. Such as have prosperity by sin, let them consider.

(1) This prosperity of yours has cost you dearly, exceedingly dearly. If you make up your reckoning and put all in that it cost you, you will find that you are no gainers at all. When men have gotten anything in possession, they usually reckon, "Aye, but what did this cost me? This much or this much?" And, if they see that the costs and charges are not as high as the benefits, then they applaud themselves as gainers. Well, you have gotten estates, preferments, and honors, let it be what it will in the world, but what did it cost you?

Some sin or another sin? Did you not strain your conscience in that benefit you received? And if you did so, certainly you must reckon this in, if there was in sin in it, you have gotten nothing in the bargain.

What hope does a hypocrite have, though he has gained? Though he may seem to have gained his heart's desire, yet if all is reckoned, put in what sin it cost and there is no gain at all!

If any of you should go to sea and suffer shipwreck, and are able to get home by boat, or some other way, saving your life; and, when you come home you have brought a toy or trifle to your wife, has this been a good voyage? Do you reckon this as a good voyage? Perhaps it was for a toy you suffered shipwreck and you bring this home. Do you think this will make the voyage good when you have counted up your reckoning?

How many men and women in the world, for trifles and toys, suffer shipwreck of a good conscience? When you look upon what you have received, it is but a trifle and a toy. You might have been happy without it, and you have ventured shipwreck of a good conscience for this. Do you think your prosperity is to be delighted in when you have gotten it in sinful and vile evil ways?

I remember the prophet, when he came to Ahab, when he had gotten Naboth's vineyard by most cursed, sinful, wicked ways, 1 Kings 21:19. God bade him go and meet Ahab and say, *What hast thou killed and gotten possession?* It is as if the prophet should say, "Oh, wretched man that you are. You have gotten possession of the vineyard, but have you killed to get possession?" So I may say to any wicked man or woman in the world who has gotten something by ways of sin, "What, have you sinned and gotten possession? Lied and gotten possession? Deceived and cheated and gotten possession? Do you think good will come from this? Are you happy in the enjoyment of this?" Well,

(2) Know that whatever you have gotten by sin is

accursed to you. You may look upon every bit of bread you eat as something you have gotten by sinful ways. Look upon it as having death in it. Look upon every draft of beer and wine you drink as having the wrath of the Almighty mixed with it.

You have gotten an estate. Perhaps you were poor and lowly before; but now you have wronged and cheated, and deceived others in sinful ways. And now you have your tables furnished and can go to the tavern and drink. In this meat and drink of yours, there is the wrath and curse of God.

Suppose a man had stolen a garment and it proved to be in a house that had the plague. Suppose a thief got into a house that had the plague and got clothes, perhaps the bed clothes of one who died from the plague. If someone tells him what they are, will he have delight in them? Perhaps he had them upon his bed, but the plague is in them. Certainly, whatever any of you, in all of your lives, have gotten by any way of sin, the plague is in it. That is a certain truth. There is the plague, the very curse of the Almighty in it.

(3) Therefore, whatever is gotten by sin, it must be cast away or else the soul is cast away. It must be restored again. There must be restitution made to the utmost of your power for anything gotten in a sinful way. There is so much evil in the way of sin that God will not have any man, by any means in the world, enjoy comforts that come that way. God Himself so hates sin, and He would have all His people so hate sin, that He would not have anyone in the world have any comfort by sin.

Therefore, as soon as ever anyone's conscience comes to be enlightened to understand what sin means, if they find that there is anything in the house gotten in a sinful way, they can never be quiet until they have rendered it back again. The sight of it strikes terror into them. They cannot endure to come into the room to see that which was gotten in a sinful way.

There have been some who have gotten much by ways of sin and, when they have lain upon their sick and death beds with their consciences awakened, Oh, they have cried, "For God's sake, take them from my sight!" They could not bear such things in their sight, those things they have gotten in ways of sin.

Judas got thirty pieces of silver. He had a covetous disposition and would have money. He would not be as poor as the other disciples, so he got money in a sinful way; but when his conscience came to be awakened and terrified, he went (and a kind of vengeance went with him) to the Scribes and Pharisees and threw the money down. Those coins were too hot for him, he could not endure the scalding of them in his conscience. They were even, as it were, melted in his soul. He could not keep the thirty pieces of silver, they were so terrible to him.

So, certainly, that's your thirty pieces: any household stuff, anything you have gotten in a sinful way. Oh, it will be terrible to you one day! I beseech you, brethren, take notice of it. Anyone who has gotten, by ways of sin, anything, it is not enough to the salvation of that soul that it has been never so sorrowful. All the sorrow in the world, and repentance you can have for sin, will not save your soul unless you restore. Unless you make restitution to the utmost of your ability, you can never have comfort and assurance that sin is pardoned. It is an old saying of an ancient, "The sin is not remitted until that which was taken away is restored."

There are many men and women who think, if they can get anything by sinful ways, they will repent and pray to God for forgiveness and be sorry, and yet keep that which was gotten in a sinful way. No, that will not serve the turn, all your praying to God with never so much sorrow. There must be restitution of what you have sinfully gotten to the utmost of your ability. Though the party is dead, you must not keep it.

Suppose the person you wronged is dead. You must not

keep it if they have any heirs or executors. Suppose you do not know them. Then you must give it to the poor. You must be rid of it. There is so much stain and evil in sin that anything that comes by way of sin must not be kept. And this is not so strange a thing; the heathens have been convinced of it.

I remember a story of a heathen who owed a shoemaker for a pair of shoes, and nobody knew he owed it. When the shoemaker died, this man thought to save it; but his conscience was so troubled, though the man was dead and nobody could charge him for the amount owed, that he could not sleep, rest, or be quiet. Instead, he rose with amazement and trouble in the night, ran to the shoemaker's house, and threw the money in and said, "Though he is dead to others, yet he is alive to me."

If a heathen had such convictions of conscience, that he must not keep that which was gotten by sin, if he could see sin as being so sinful that what was gotten by sin must be cast out, surely you Christians must be as wise! Oh, consider this! You are a multitude come together. Is there a man or woman's conscience, now in the presence of God, that tells them that there is something they have gotten by such a sinful way? Now this is the charge of God to you upon your spirits: if ever you expect to find mercy from God, you must go and immediately restore that which you have gotten by any sinful way. It will be your bane and your ruin. You venture your souls otherwise. That must be restored or your souls must go for it. And all your sorrow and trouble will not do unless these are restored; either these or some other thing in lieu of them. You must not think to live upon sin.

It may be that servants, in their master's service, pilfered and purloined. Whatever you got for yourselves (perhaps you have spent it), either your souls must perish or else you must, if God makes you able, restore it though it is all of your estate. You are bound to cast up those sweet morsels you have taken.

There was once a man who had wronged another man for five shillings. And fifty years after that wrong had been done, he sent to these hands of mine those five shillings and asked me to restore it. Conscience so stung him that he could not enjoy it.

So, though it is forty, fifty, or sixty years ago, when you were young that you did the wrong, you are bound, if you expect mercy from God, to restore what you have wronged, because there can be no prosperity come in by sin, no good, because there is so much evil in sin.

This is the first. When a man comes to be prosperous by sin, then he may be miserable, notwithstanding his prosperity.

Secondly, when a man comes to be sinful by prosperity. As when a man comes to prosperity by sin, so when sin comes in by prosperity. And for this, there are three considerations also. Sin, sometimes, comes in by prosperity. A man is more sinful because he is more prosperous. Certainly this man may be miserable, notwithstanding his prosperity. As,

First, when prosperity is fuel for sin.

Secondly, when it gives them further license and liberty to sin.

Thirdly, when it hardens them in sin.

Certainly this man, though he is freed from afflictions all his days, is yet a most miserable man because he is delivered from afflictions.

1. He comes to have prosperity be fuel for sin. That is matter for sin to work upon, so that prosperity nourishes and fattens up sin. Many men's sins, because they have prosperity, grow to a mighty height by prosperity. Prosperity is fuel for lusts; it fattens your malice and occasions pride. Were it not that a man had such an estate as he has, and a healthful, lusty body, then he could not be guilty of so much lust, uncleanness, drunkenness, pride, or so malice and revenge. The more God delivers a man from afflictions, sickness,

poverty, the more fuel he has for sin, wickedness, and the lusts of his heart to burn upon and grow up to a flame. As it is with a body, those humors of the body are matters for the disease to grow upon and feed the disease. They are no good to the body, but are mischief to it.

Some men have great big arms and legs, but what bigness is it? A bigness that comes by disease or dropsy. Their bodies are full of these humors; they feed the disease of the body. Now are these humors any such things that we should rejoice in ? Do they make for the good of the body? They make for the bigness, but not for the goodness of the body.

So any man's estate that makes for matter to feed his lusts upon, and nourish and grow upon this, such a man is so much more the miserable by how much more prosperous he is. Usually, wicked men, through the malignity in their hearts, make all their prosperity to be nothing else but nourishment for lust to breed upon. As a gracious heart will turn all things it enjoys to be a matter for grace to work upon, and to further the work of grace, so a wicked heart will turn all he enjoys to be a matter for his lust to work upon, and to further his lust. The excellency of grace appears in the one, and the malignity of sin appears in the other.

Now, if sin is so great an evil, then whatever a man enjoys, if it is a furtherance of sin and nourishes sin, it makes him the more miserable, a miserable creature. Though he is a prosperous man, yet this man is miserable because his prosperity makes him more sinful.

2. If his prosperity gives him further liberty to sin. For example, many men who are poor, are quickly restrained. They have many restraints. Alas, they are afraid the law will get hold of them if they are drunk or unclean. It may be that they dare not do something for fear of the displeasure of some friend they depend on. A hundred things keep men in affliction from taking their liberty in sin, which otherwise his heart would have committed. Whereas a man who is prosperous in the world takes liberty, and who will control him?

He will be drunk and unclean; he will break the Sabbath, and who dares control and speak to him? And I beseech you to observe this: many men account that the greatest happiness of prosperity to be that, by this means, they may come to have their wills, their sinful wills, that they can live without control in the satisfying of their sinful lusts. This they account the happiness of prosperity.

This is a most abominable, cursed happiness, to account the good of prosperity to consist in this, that it gives us more liberty to sin. Oh, it is a most malignant power that enables one to do mischief, to hurt one's own soul, or the soul of others. So this is a most cumbersome estate and condition, that gives a man liberty to satisfy his lusts all the more.

Brethren, consider this. It is a most dreadful curse of God upon a man that God will let a man go on smoothly in ways of sin without control, that he shall have liberty without control. If there is any brand of reprobation that one may give, this is it. This is as black a brand as can be given, that God suffers a man to go on smoothly in sin without any control so that he can have full liberty. It is a speech of Barnard's, "Therefore doth God spare the rich, because his iniquity is not found only to displeasure, but to hatred." Because God is not only now angry, but He *hates* him for sin. Therefore, God spares the rich and delivers many wicked men from affliction because sin is grown to the height, that it is above God's displeasure. God may be displeased with His children for sin, but He does not come to hate them. They are not children of hatred because of infirmity, but now when God suffers a wicked man to go on smoothly without any affliction in his way of sin, and so to take liberty in sin, this man's sin, it is to be feared, has grown to the height that it comes to the very hatred of God, not just to His displeasure.

I remember Barnard, in another place, calls this kind of mercy in God, to deliver men from affliction in a sinful way, more cruel than any anger, and prays God to deliver Him from that kind of mercy, that is, that he should go on prosperously in a wicked way. And if you knew all, it would be one petition to God (you in a prosperous way, it would be one petition you would put up to God) every day, "Oh Lord, never let me prosper in a sinful way and course. Oh Lord, rather let any affliction be upon me than that my smoothness in my way should make my sin more smooth and delightful."

I appeal to you mariners. Suppose you were failing near rocks or sands, and were deprived of wind for your sails. So you come near the rocks, and then a wind comes upon you and fills your sails to the fullest. Your sails are all up, and a wind comes that fills them fully with wind. But this wind carries you directly upon the sands or the rocks. Would you not rather have the wind a little more still? Would you not rather have a half wind? Or a side wind? Would you not rather have your sails down? Or not half so much filled as they are when they carry you upon the rocks and sands? So it is here. It is just as if you should see a man rejoice that his sails are filled with wind, and all his sails up, when another who stands by knows it carries him upon the sands that will undo him.

So it is with a man who rejoices in the prosperity that carries him with full sail to wickedness. God fills their sails, their hearts are filled to the full with all that their hearts can desire, and they are filled with all their bravery, but this (like the sail) carries them on further to sin and wickedness, upon the rocks and sands to eternal destruction. It would be better for these men that their sails were down and all under the hatches. That would be a thousand times better than to have all the liberty to sin.

I beseech you, brethren, observe the difference between God's dispensations and dealing with the wicked and His dispensations and dealings with His children. In this one thing it is very observable. With the wicked, God deals this way. In just judgment, He suffers stumbling blocks to lie in the way of religion so that they stumble therein and find an abundance of difficulty when they have some good stirrings of their affections, and good motions, and affections. But there is such a stumbling block at which they are offended, and such a thing lies there and hinders them and makes the ways of religion difficult; but when they come to the ways of sin, there all their ways are smooth. There's no stumbling block lies there but all is clear, and God suffers them to prosper and go on a pace. They way of life is full of stumbling blocks, but the way to destruction is clear. That is how God deals with the wicked.

But with His children, God will make the way to life and salvation to be very smooth and clear. *The way of the upright is plain.* If the heart is upright, those things others are offended at and stumbled at, they are delivered from. Gracious hearts find the ways of godliness to be plain, comfortable, and smooth ways. But now the ways of sin to God's children are full of stumbling blocks, and there God is pleased to lay stumbling blocks. When God sees His children hanker after sinful ways, God makes this hindrance and that hindrance, this affliction and that affliction; they shall find, in God's providence, one thing or another to stop them in their way.

A most excellent promise for this to the children of God you have in Hosea 2:6-7, when God was in a way of mercy to them. *Therefore behold, I will hedge up thy way with thorns, and make a wall that she shall not find her paths.* Mark it, when God intends good to His church, He promises to hedge up the way and wall it up, that is, the way to idols, so that they should not find it as easily as they did before.

Oh, take notice of this all ye servants of God! When you have found your hearts hankering after evil ways, how good God is that He has laid stumbling blocks in the ways of death, whereas others, when they have come to the ways of death, all is clear and smooth before them, and they have their heart's desire. This is the difference between God's dealings with His people and the wicked.

3. As prosperity is fuel for sin, and gives liberty to sin, so it hardens the hearts of men and women in sin. As it is with the clay, when the sun shines upon it, it grows harder with the shining of the sun, so wicked and ungodly men have their hearts grow hard in the ways of sin with the shine of prosperity upon it.

As iron is soft when it is in the fire, but harder out of the fire, so it is with men and women. In affliction, they seem to be soft, but they are the harder when they are out again. We have a notable place for this in Job 21:7-14. There is a description of the prosperous estate of the wicked. Now at the 14th verse, see how their hearts are hardened. *Therefore they say to God, depart from us, we desire not the knowledge of His way.* This was because He had said of them before, *Their houses are safe from fear, neither is the rod of God upon them. Their bull gendereth and faileth not, their cow calveth and casteth not her calf. They send forth their little ones like a flock, and their children dance. They take the timbrel and harp and rejoice at the sound of the organ. They spend their days in wealth.*

They live merry, brave lives; therefore their hearts are hardened in sin so that they say to the Almighty, "Depart from us, what need do we have of the knowledge of God? What need do we have of so much preaching? And so much ado? We do not desire these things."

I beseech you to mark and observe what kind of men these are who slight the Word of God and hold it in such low esteem. In their carriage and actions, they say unto God Himself, "Depart from us," for so it is. Though they may not think so, when they do not esteem the Word and ordinances, it is as if they should say to God, "Depart from us, we do not desire the knowledge of Thy ways."

I say, observe what kind of men these are. They are not men under God's wrath or afflictions. These are men in authority, men who flourish, men who have delights and contentments in their flesh. These say, "Depart."

I confess, when poor people who know nothing of God and who are mere atheists, who live all their days in mere atheism, say these things, we do not wonder; but I am speaking of enlightened men. Let all such men know, who are so ready to say, "Depart from us," who let the Word and ordinances depart, who slight God in His ordinances, who enjoy comforts and brave lives, who have the world at will, that though they may bless themselves, and though the world may bless them, yet woe to them when God says, "Let them prosper in sin." Hosea 4:14, *I will not punish your daughters when they commit iniquity.* God threatens it as a judgment not to afflict them.

I remember that Origen, commenting upon this text, had this note, "Will you hear the terrible voice of God? God speaking with indignation? I will not visit when you sin." This he calls the terrible voice of God speaking with indignation. This is the most extreme of God's anger, when thus He speaks.

And so Luther had such an expression, "Woe to those men at whose sins God doth wink and connive, and who have not afflictions as other men."

And so Jerome, writing to a friend who prospered in wicked says, said, "I judge you to be miserable, because you are not miserable."

So certainly, those men are therefore miserable because they are not miserable, and it would be a thousand times better for these men to lie under some heavy and dreadful affliction in this world.

And this is the second use. If there is so much evil in sin, then a man may be a miserable man though he is not an afflicted man, because there is enough evil in sin alone to make a man miserable without affliction.

Chapter 54

Use 3. If there is so much evil in sin, then it's a mighty mercy to get the pardon of sin.

If there is so much evil in sin, as you have heard, then it must follow that to get pardon of sin is a mighty mercy. It must be a wonderful thing to have the pardon of sin, to be delivered from that which has so much evil, from that which is so dreadful. It must be a thing very hard to be obtained. Grievous diseases are cured with great difficulty.

Certainly, brethren, those men and women who think that to get pardon of, and power against, sin is a little or slight matter, I dare to charge them as in the presence of God, they never yet knew what sin means. And all that I have delivered about the evil of sin has been but beating the air to them to no purpose, no purpose to them who yet make light of the great work of procuring pardon for sin and making peace with God for their sin.

If all the world was in confusion, turned into chaos, we would think it a great work of God to bring all in frame and order again. Certainly it's a greater work of God to deliver the soul from the evil of sin than it would be to raise up the frame of heaven and earth again.

Therefore, in Numbers 14:17-19, where Moses speaks of pardon of sin, see how he speaks of it there, *And now I beseech Thee, let the power of my Lord be great, according as Thou hast spoken, saying.* What was this concerning which God had spoken, that He would show His great power therein? See the 19th verse, *Pardon I beseech Thee the iniquity of this people, according to the greatness of Thy mercy.* Mark it, let the power of my Lord be great, and then pardon the iniquity of Thy people.

It is as if Moses should say, "Oh Lord, this requires great power. The Almighty power of God is required for pardoning iniquity as well as the infinite mercy of God."

Oh, consider this, you who think lightly of getting pardon of sin. This is the greatest business in the world, and certainly that soul which God sets in good earnest about this work, to get the pardon of sin, is the busiest creature in all the world. Never was the soul taken up about a more blessed work since it had a being than this one. If it understands what it is about it takes up the whole strength of soul and body when the soul is about so great a work.

Therefore, you who come to have some enlightenings to show you the evil of sin, and you are about that work of getting pardon, Oh, you must work mightily and strongly indeed! For know this, you are about the greatest business, the greatest work that ever any creature was about in the world. There is no creature in all the world who was ever about so great a work as you are. When you are about the business of getting pardon for sin, you need to mind it and follow it, and not have your heart taken up about other things, for it is the great work of the Lord that infinitely concerns you.

Oh, that men and women had clear apprehensions about the sweetness of this work. 'Tis true, God's mercy is above all our sins, and He is ready to pardon and to forgive; but the Lord will have His creatures know that it is the greatest work that ever he did. Yes, and the justification of a sinner is as great a work as ever God did. The means that tend to it and the work of a soul procuring pardon is the greatest work that ever the soul was about. So you must understand it, and you cannot but understand it if you understand what has been delivered. This is the third use.

Chapter 55

Use 4. If there is so much evil in sin, this justifies the strict-
ness and care of God's people against sin. Two directions to
those who make conscience of small sins. First, be even in
your ways; be strict against all sin. Secondly, be very yield-
ing in all lawful things.

If there is so much evil in sin, then the strictness and care
of the people of God against sin is justified. They are afraid
of every sin. They dare not be as bold in the ways of sin as
others are, but they tremble. When any sin is presented to
them, they are afraid and tremble. Others go on boldly and
presumptuously, and laugh at such as are afraid. "Oh, such
scrupulous consciences! Oh, they dare not do such a thing
because they say it is a sin! Oh, they dare not, by any
means, because they dare not sin!"

Thus others laugh at them because they think they are
more scrupulous than they need to be. They should be afraid
to do things as little as they think these are.

I beseech you to observe the perverseness of men's
hearts. You can see that when men offend the law of man,
those who are in authority, the commands of men, in things
that they themselves will profess to be very little and small.
Then they will cry out of such things that it is rebellion, that
they are rebels against authority, and they are not worthy to
live. They would have the most severe punishments that can
be against those who will not obey man's authority in little
things; but mark, these men urge small things and, where
they are small, they say that the disobedience is worse in
small things. Yet they seem very conscientious in such
things when they see men afraid to offend God, who dare
not do little things if they are sinful; dare not speak an idle
word, dare not be sinfully merry like others are, afraid of
intemperance and every small thing. These men will jeer,

"What a horrible sin is this?"

What! Urge man's authority in small things and jeer those who are conscientious to God's authority in small things! What! Shall the authority of man put weight upon small things, and shall not the authority of the Almighty put weight in small things?

Well, whatever they think, brethren, go on and make conscience of small things, and never call any sin little because you have heard of so much evil in it. Go away with this impression of the evil of sin on your hearts, "Well, by this I have heard of the evil of sin. I have learned to account no sin small, though never so little in the eye of the world."

Is it a sin? If so, then never allow for it. If it is a sin, abhor it. Let this temptation never prevail with you. What? Will you not do this? Then you may do worse. This I would advise those gracious and godly who do, indeed, make conscience of small sins and do well in making conscience of small things. I give you these two instructions to carry along with you as you make conscience of small things. And you do well in it because there is so much evil in sin.

THE FIRST INSTRUCTION. Be sure your conscience is even this way, that as you seem to make conscience of some things small, so make conscience of all. Do not let the men of the world who observe your ways find you tripping and have just cause to say, "These men seem scrupulous in small things, but in other ways they give themselves much liberty. And, though they will not swear, they will lie."

Through such aspersions, and sometimes through malice, the men of the world cast doubt upon your profession. But I speak to you in the name of the Lord. Take heed that you do not give occasion to the men of the world to say so, to say "Aye, these are so scrupulous in their ceremonies, and so nice in these things." Certainly we are bound to be so, for God is a jealous God and, if in anything we are to be conscientious, we must be in His worship, but then you need to be so much the more careful that they find you exact in everything you do.

You servants, perhaps you inquire after the worship of God; perhaps, also, you young people. It is a great mercy of God that He stirs up young ones to inquire after the true worship of God and not to worship God in that ignorance that your forefathers did. They took up everything because of custom, or the tradition of the parish they lived in; but it is not the common practice, or the command of some authority, that makes something lawful if it is not warranted by the Word. Well, perhaps many young ones now begin to inquire after the ways of God's worship, and perhaps your masters, or parents, or maybe your husbands are angry and vexed, and wonder what has become of you, because you have grown so scrupulous in these things.

Now, I say, you need to be very exact in your master's family so that you may not be found tripping in other things. You wives need to be very exact so that your husbands do not find you faulty in other things. You children need to be very respectful to your parents, careful of your duties to them, because they are more apprehensive of any failings in that which is due to them than they are of anything in the worship of God. They know God ties you to the practice of those duties.

Suppose you are a servant, and cannot join in their practice, and do such superstitions as your masters do. If you servants are unfaithful in your service, and are careless, stubborn, and stout in answering back, this will harden your master's heart against this way of worship. You make conscience of superstition because it is sinful, and is this not a sin as well as that? Is it not a sin to be unfaithful, stubborn, and stout? If you make conscience of one sin, why not of another?

Therefore, all you who seem to have more tender consciences than others, and are more afraid of the least sin than others, be sure you walk exactly, and especially have a care of your duty towards men before whom you walk, because they can spot you immediately if you trip.

A SECOND INSTRUCTION. I commend to those who make conscience of little sins, of the least sin, this: be sure you are as yielding and compliant in all other things as you possibly can be, in all things lawful. I ground it upon this, because those whose consciences are tender and dare not commit the least sin, cannot but stand out rather than commit some evils. Some things they are required to do they dare not do because they are sinful. It cannot but be that in some things they must stand out because they are convinced that it is a sin.

Now the world judges this as being stout and proud. You make conscience of it, but they think it is pride and stoutness of spirit. Why? Cannot you do this as well as others? When, alas, God knows, and your consciences tell you, that you would with all your hearts, but cannot. You would sin against and wound your own consciences. Therefore, let them do what they will, you cannot do what is required by them. Let masters rage and be angry, let husbands be displeased, you cannot yield; your conscience will not allow you.

Now, the question arises, how shall this be known that it is conscience and not stubbornness? For we cannot see into your conscience. I give you this note to reveal it to them. Be more pliable and yielding in all other things. Go beyond all other women, children, or servants in this respect.

For example, suppose there is a woman whose conscience cannot yield to some things, and her husband is displeased because he believes it is defiance. Now, so that her husband may believe it is conscience and not defiance, it concerns that woman to observe whatever gives content to her husband in everything else, and to be more yielding and pliable, and docile and, in those things, to deny her own will. This should give content to her husband in other things, and hereby he will be convinced that she is not defiant and stubborn in other things. Why? Because in this he finds her more pliable, yielding, and willing than before.

So, servants, if you cannot yield to your masters in one thing, strive to give him more content in other things. Children, to your parents, in other things be more dutiful, and one neighbor to another. If neighbors would have you do that which is against your conscience when you cannot do that, yield in other things to convince them that, in what you do not yield, it is merely out of conscience and not from stubbornness. That is the fourth use.

I might have gone further, and (if there is so much evil in sin, I would) have labored with men and women to come to be sensible of all the evil of sin, and to have stopped sinners in their sinful ways and courses. I would likewise wished to have drawn sinners to Christ, and to have made men and women to prize Jesus Christ, by whom all their sins may possibly come to be forgiven, who is the only ransom and propitiation for sin; for this, brethren, is the ground of all I have said. All I have said is for this aim, that we might be made to esteem Christ and prize Christ. And, in this regard, though what I have said seems legal, yet, certainly, it is a fond mistake in people who think Christ is not preached unless the word "Christ" is named.

But know that all that has been said about the sinfulness of sin has been a preaching of Christ, for it has been in a way and order to bring souls to Christ, that I might cause souls to fly to Christ, and to go to Him who is the only propitiation for sin, and the only ransom for souls.

And certainly, brethren, once these things I have delivered concerning the evil of sin come to be apprehended, and the soul is made sensible of them, Oh! how sweet, and precious, and dear will Christ be to such a soul! And the name of that great God will be honored in such a soul. But I shall prosecute this in the following discourse.

Chapter 56

Use 5. If there is such evil in sin, then the dreadful things spoken in the Word against sinners are justified.

There is more evil in sin than in all affliction. That's the argument we have been long upon, and we have made some good entrance into the application of it. There have been four uses made of this point already that have flowed naturally from the evil of sin. There are yet several more uses which are of great concern, wherefore we proceed to them.

Use 5. If there is such dreadful evil in sin, then the Word of God that speaks such dreadful things against sinners cannot but be justified of all those that know what sin is. There are very severe and fearful things revealed in the Word against sin. Now, those who do not understand what the evil of sin is are ready to think of them as being very hard. Indeed, it is only by the Word that we come to understand wherein the true evil of sin lies. Paul, in Romans, tells us that, before the Law came, he did not know what sin was. And had I preached these sermons concerning the evil of sin before the Athenians, the wisest of philosophers, they would have said as they did concerning Paul, "What, something new? What strange doctrine is this?"

And so it is like it has been unto all those who have no other rule to judge things by than carnal reason and sense. Those who are not acquainted with the mind of God revealed in His Word have, perhaps, strange thoughts concerning all that has been delivered, and think I have been at hyperbole all this while. But, certainly, those who judge things according to the Word see that there is a reality in all that has been delivered, and they justify the Word in everything. Yes, they justify the severity of the Word against sin when they see it even against themselves for their own sins. That's a good sign, when the heart of a man or woman not only justifies

the Word in general, but when the Word comes most powerfully and sharply against his own sins. Still he lies under the
power of the Word and says, "It is good and holy and righteous, the Word of the Lord," even though it speaks bitterly
against his own sins.

There are many men and women who have some seem-
ing good affections, some tenderness of spirit, and who
would seem to melt at a sermon when some truths are delivered to them; but when the severity and strictness of God's
justice in the Word is presented before them, their hearts fly
off and they seem to be very hard things.

We have a notable example of this in Luke 20. If you
read the story, you shall find the people spoken of were
quite stirred with many things they heard in the Word; but in
the 16th verse, Christ told them He would come and destroy
those husbandmen who had treated the messengers who
were sent, and the king's only son, too. *He shall come and
destroy those husbandmen, and give the vineyard unto others, and when they heard it, they said, God forbid.*

Oh, God forbid that there should be so much severity.
Those people, in this particular story, discovered a slight-
ness of spirit. Though they were people who seemed to have
tender hearts, and were quite stirred, and whose hearts
melted at some truths delivered, yet when they heard of the
severe judgments against evil men, they had more compassion in them than God had. They said, "God forbid that
things should be so hard. What? Is God not a merciful God?
We hear of nothing but severity. That there should be so
much severity in God so as to utterly destroy? God forbid!"

Thus people nowadays, when they hear arguments of
God's goodness and mercy, their hearts are ready to melt
and yield. They are affected and stirred; but when they hear
of the severity of God's justice against sin, Oh then, "God
forbid that there should be such hard things. God forbid that
these things should be true."

Certainly, brethren, you cannot have any true meltings of

spirit wrought in you, nor work of God's sanctifying Spirit, unless you find such a principle in your hearts as causes you to fall down, and tremble, and yield unto the justice of God and the severity of the Word against sin, unless you find a willingness to justify God and His Word in all the severity that He reveals against you in your owns sins. This is the fifth.

Chapter 57

Use 6. If there is such evil in sin, it shows the miserable condition of those whose hearts and lives are filled with sin.

Another use is this. If there is so much evil in sin, then what a miserable condition are those in who are full of sin, whose hearts and lives are filled up to the brim, to the very top, exceedingly full of sin. Is there all this evil (that I have spoken of) in the nature of sin? In one sin? Such dreadful evil in the least sin? Oh Lord, what a condition are those in (I say) who are guilty of an infinite number of sins?

It is said, Ecclesiastes 9:3, *The hearts of men are full of evil, full of sin.* It is true of all the sons and daughters of men in the world that their hearts are full of sin. A toad is not so full of poison as the heart of every man and woman in the world is full of sin. And that which you are full of is such an abominable thing in the eyes of God as you have heard. Yes, and as their hearts are full of sin, so they are fully set to do evil, Ecclesiastes 8:11, *Because sentence against an evil work is not speedily executed, therefore the hearts of the sons of men are fully set in them to do evil.* This is true of all. In their natural condition, their hearts are full of evil, and their hearts are fully set in them to do evil.

All the actions that you ever do, all the thoughts of your mind, all the words of your mouth, all the actions of your life ever since you were born, have been nothing else but sin, if you are in your natural estate. This we dare avow and speak as in the presence of God. Every man and woman not yet converted never had any thought, never spoke any word, never did any action all their lives but they sinned against God. And if sin is so evil, what an evil case are those men in who are so full of sin? Yes, their best actions, how full of sin are those? And how miserable is their condition in that regard who have given themselves up to follow sin with greediness?

Are there not some of you before the Lord whose consciences cannot but tell you that you have given up yourselves to follow the lusts of your own hearts with greediness? To satisfy them to the full? And all your grief has been that you could satisfy them no more.

This has been the condition of many who have lived in a course of sin all their days, yes, and it may be against conscience also; who have been guilty not only of multitudes of sin, but guilty of such multitudes with woeful aggravation against light, against means, against vows. Certainly, if sin is such an evil in its own nature, if God should set the least sin, a sin of thought, upon a man's heart as He may do, He would sink the most stubborn heart down to the bottomless gulf of despair.

Then what will become of you if God comes to settle all your abominations upon your heart altogether? *The floods of ungodly men hath made me afraid,* said David in Psalm 18:14. The word "men" there is not in the original. It is translated by some, "The floods of wickedness have made me afraid." Certainly, if God reveals floods of those wickednesses that your consciences tell you that you have been guilty of, it cannot but make you afraid. If God comes and sets all those sins in order before your face, it will be a most dreadful object and spectacle.

Let me make use of that phrase in Job 6:12, *Is my strength the strength of stones? and my flesh of brass?* So may I say unto those who have woeful guilt of sin upon them. What? Is your strength the strength of stones and is your flesh made of brass so that you can bear the weight and burden of so many horrible transgressions as you have been guilty of, when you hear that there is so much evil in one sin, and that in the least sin?

We read, in Leviticus 16:22-24, of the scapegoat. When Aaron and his sons the priests should come and lay hands upon it and put the sins of the people upon him, he was to

go into the wilderness, into a desolate place among the wild
beasts there, to note the woeful condition of a sinner who
has the guilt of multitudes upon him. He is like that
scapegoat who is to go into the wilderness among the wild
beasts, who are ready to tear him apart. Your condition is
worse unless you are delivered from the guilt of sin.

I speak of one under the guilt of sin. It is likely to be
worse with you than if you were to live among tigers, and
bears, and dragons who were ready to tear you apart.
Certainly, your estate is far worse. If your body were full of
sores, you would think your condition was very sad. It
would cause much dejection of spirit; but for your soul to be
full of sin, to have so much sin, is worse than if you had
plague sores upon your body from head to foot. If you
should see a man full of plague sores from the crown of the
head to the sole of the foot, you would think that man was in
a sad condition. Certainly, the state of every unconverted
man in far worse because he is all over full of sin, which has
so much evil in it.

As for that doctrine of the sinfulness of sin in the heart
and life of man, that will require another and larger treatise
by itself. Therefore, I do not intend to fall upon that doctrine
of how man is full of sin in his heart and life. That may be
done hereafter. But for the present, to present this meditation
before you, I say this. If there is so much evil in every sin,
then the fullness of sin must put a man or woman in an evil
and sad condition. God says, Psalm 73:10, *We will wring
out to the wicked a full cup of wrath,* to those full of sin. In
Job 20:11, it is spoken of the wicked and ungodly, *That
their bones are full of the sins of their youth.*

Your life is full of sin, your bones may be full of the sins
of your youth. Many youths, many young people, run on in
great iniquities in the times of their youth and multiply sins
and add sin to sin. Well, know that your youthful sins may
prove your aged years to be a terror; and you who are so full
of sins when young, given up to all kind of sin now, here-

after your bones may be full of the sins of your youth.

Thus much for this use, because it would require another doctrine by itself. I proceed to another.

Chapter 58

Use 7. If there is so much evil in sin, how dreadful a thing it is for men or women to delight in sin.

If there is as much evil in sin as you have heard, mark then further what follows. What a dreadful thing is it for men and women to delight in sin, to rejoice in sinful ways, to make a sport of sin? What infinite impudence is this, for a creature to make merry and rejoice in sin against God? Have you nothing to be merry with? Have you nothing to rejoice in but sinning against the Almighty?

What? Shall there be so much revealed to you concerning the dreadful evil of your sins, and yet you are so far from being convinced that there is so much evil in it that you look upon sin as having more good in it than there is in God Himself, Christ, heaven, and all the glorious things of eternal life! So does every man and woman who makes any sinful way their chief joy. I say, they are so far from being convinced of the evil in sin, as has been declared, that they rejoice in it as if there were more good in sin than in God Himself, or Christ, or anything revealed in the Word concerning the treasures of the riches of the grace of God in Christ.

This is a horrible wickedness. It is a horrible evil in your heart, that such an evil as sin should be so suitable to your heart; that there should be any suitableness between your heart and so great an evil as sin is.

Yes, note that you have a very cursed heart who can be so suitable to that which is so evil; a very poisonous heart that there should be so much agreement between that which is so poisonous and the temper of your heart. True, a toad will take poison and is suitable to it. It lives upon it and takes delight in it as you do meat and drink.

Now those who can make sin their meat and drink (as

Christ said, *It is meat and drink to do the will of My Father*), so it is meat and drink to many ungodly men and women to do wickedness. Now hereby you are declared to be a toad, to be of a venomous nature, who has such a suitableness between your nature and sin. Surely, nothing but a venomous toad can delight in poison; so nothing but a heart more venomous and loathsome than a toad is to the daintiest lady in the world (think of putting a toad's head in the mouth of such a lady), none but such a heart could take delight in a sinful and ungodly way.

Suppose there were a suitableness between the corrupt humors in your soul and sin. Yet now you have heard so much of the evil of it, it is a cursed madness in you to take delight in it because it is suitable to your nature. What, can you delight to drink poison because the poison is sweet and comes to be suitable because of its sweetness? If you know it to be poison, and strong poison at that, what madness would it be for you to drink a full draught merely because it was sweet!

There is the same madness in all men and women in the world who can take pleasure in sin, simply because there is sweetness in it and is suitable to their corrupt nature. There is not only a difference, there is a contrariety between your heart and a godly man's. A godly man or woman would rather suffer all the torments in the world than endure that which you would make your chief joy. What a contrariety to God and the nature of God! What a difference between the nature of God and you! That which is a burden to me, Spirit of God, is the most delightful thing in the world to Thy Spirit.

Yes, what a desperate heart you have, in that the thing which murdered Christ, you can delight in! Certainly, where there is delight and pleasure in sin, sin increases infinitely. There must be a most desperate increase of sin. For, as it is with grace, those men and women who have gracious hearts, and come to make the ways of godliness their delight grow up in godliness. No men and women grow up in god-liness as these do who come to make the ways of God their delight. If you would grow up in grace, make the ways of God your delight, and then you will grow in grace.

Contrarily, those men and women who come to make any ways of sin their delight, and the joy of their heart, grow up in sin in a most dreadful manner. And let it be known to you that, according to the measure of your delight in sin, so shall the bitterness and torment be that you shall endure hereafter. In Revelation 18:7, it is said of Babylon, *So much as she hath glorified herself; so much torment give her.*

So God will say of all sinners who have taken pleasure in unrighteousness. As much as you have rejoiced in sin, so much torment will your soul have. Yes, the time will come when God will take as much delight in your destruction as you have delighted in sinning against Him. Proverbs 1:26, *God will laugh at their destruction, and mock when their fear cometh.*

Is there never a man or woman here in this congregation who has committed sin and laughed at it? Or made some others commit sin and laughed at it? I speak to you as in the name of God, is there not one man or woman whose conscience tells them, "I have sworn an oath, or told a lie, and laughed at it. I made another drunk and laughed at it." Do you laugh at sin? Rejoice at sin? Take heed, come in quickly. You need to fall down and mourn bitterly at Christ's feet. Otherwise, certainly, you are the man or woman at whose destruction God will laugh another day.

It would be your wisdom rather to howl and cry out in anguish of spirit because of sin, rather than to make it a matter of jollity and joy. Let us all take heed of making ourselves merry with sin. We must not play with edged tools.

There is a notable place we have in Proverbs 26:18-19, *As a mad man, who casts fire brands, arrows, and death, so is the man that deceives his neighbor, and saith, Am I not in sport?* I beseech you to consider this text. Many of you will deceive and cheat your neighbors and, when you are done, make a jest of it. So the Holy Ghost speaks to such a man, and this Scripture singles out that man or woman, whoever they are, who ever deceived their neighbor and afterwards, when they came among their companions, laughed about it. As mad men or women, mark what the text says, who casts firebrands, arrows, and death, so is the man who deceives his neighbor and says, "Am I not in sport? It is only a joke, it is nothing." Mark, this is a madman who casts firebrands, arrows, and death.

Oh, that God this very day would cast a firebrand, arrows, and every sentence of death upon your heart if you are guilty of this and have not been humbled to this day for it. Oh, it is the fool, as I have showed, who makes a mockery of sin. What? Can you commit a wickedness, be drunk, be unclean or filthy, and then afterwards go and tell your companions and make a sport of sin or mock it? You are one of the fools in Israel, and God this day casts shame in your face. You have shame cast in your face by the Almighty this day out of His Word.

Certainly, brethren, if we understand what the evil of sin is, when we are in any company where men and women are never so merry, if there was but one willful sin committed among them, any one apparent sin, it would be enough to dampen all the joy that day; and, indeed, it should be so.

We read about David. When he carried the ark, a gracious work, and there was but one sin committed, that of touching the ark unadvisedly, and it dampened all the joy. And certainly, it was the sin from which there was more cause of dampening the joy than from the punishment, for there was more evil in the sin than in the punishment.

Now you will have many men and women in merry company who are merry, eat, drink, and laugh. Well, an abundance of sin is committed in that company, but not one whit is dampened all that day. They can go on in their mirth, tales, and laughing; go on as freely and fully as if there were no sin committed. Be it known to you this day from the Lord, any of you who have been in any company, merry and jolly, and yet sin has been committed before your eyes and you have heard it with your ears. If it has not dampened your joy and mirth, know that your hearts are not right with God, and it is a sign that your hearts have been vile, cursed hearts when you can see sin committed in your company and yet you can go on with joy.

Suppose in your company that, in the midst of your mirth, someone were to take a knife and stab himself in the heart. Would you go on in your mirth still? When you are in company and hear someone swear, if you had eyes, you would see them stab themselves in the heart. There is more evil in this than in the other, and yet you can go on in your mirth and joy, though since you sat down there have been forty oaths sworn there.

So, if your hearts are right when you are in company and hear one swear, or blaspheme God's name, or speak against religion, it would be as much as if one were stabbed in the room. All the mirth of that day would be gone if your hearts were right.

And do not think this too strict, that sin committed by others should dampen your joy. Certainly, the thing is most reasonable and apparent as can possibly be to convince any man's conscience who understands what the evil of sin means. And yet many of you have not only continued your joy, but have been joyful and jocund *because* sin is committed in your company.

Suppose someone makes a joke about religion and scorns profession. You laugh with them and make merry with them. When one tells a lie about religion, you can laugh and be merry. Oh, certainly, if you have any conscience at all, you cannot but this day be convinced of horrible sin against God.

Suppose you were in merry company and should hear for certain that the tide is in and your ship is cast away, and that you have lost all that you ever ventured in that ship. Would you not say it is time for me to go now? And do you not account the hazard of your own soul more than that? The soul of your brother? Than of your goods? Certainly, your heart cannot be right with God.

Oh! Take heed in your merry meetings. We do not deny that men and women may be joyful and eat and drink together, and delight themselves in the creature. But it must be so that it must be without apparent sin. I know there will be natural infirmities in any action, but I am speaking of open and apparent wickedness. Joy must not be there when there is apparent wickedness.

You think godly people are not for society and good fellowship. Indeed, you cannot expect them to be joyful and merry, but that they should rather be melancholy, heavy, and sad in your company when they see so many sins committed there.

What, would you have them merry when they see the company soak their hands in their Father's blood? Would you have the son be merry when the company soaks their hands in his father's blood? Certainly every godly man or woman, when they come in company and see so many sins committed, they actually and really see you stab and soak your hands in God's blood. When you rejoice in the Lord, they can be as merry and joyful as any of you, and have sweet comfort in your company; but now when sin is committed there.

Many of you, when you have been in merry company and then departed, can say, "Oh, today we were in such a place, and we had such merry company. It would do one's heart good to be among them. We were so merry and jocund; we have a brave time." Well, but was there no apparent wickedness committed in your company? Never an oath sworn? No excessive drinking? No ribald talking? You never think of that. You act as if that were nothing at all. It did not abate the least of your joy. Certainly, your heart is not right. You do not know what sin means. You must know it after another manner.

One particular more, because it is useful and these merry times (this was preached at Stepney on the 26th of February) are most pleasing among the younger people. When they come abroad in company, they will make a sport of sin and think nothing of it. I will apply one text of Scripture to that sport of young men, when they seek to make one another drunk, or swear, or speak wickedly and rejoice in it. It is just like that sport mentioned in 2 Samuel 2:14, where Abner said to Joab, *Let the young men arise and play before us,* and observe what this play was. *Then there arose and went out twelve men of Benjamin, which pertained to Ishbosheth the son of Saul, and twelve of the servants of David, and they caught every one his fellow by the head and thrust his sword in his fellow's side, so they fell down together.* This was their play.

So it is with young men. Many times young profane men come together to play and make sport, but it is to further sin in one another; and they take the sword, as it were, and thrust it into one another's bowels, doing what in them lies to their ruin and eternal destruction forever.

Chapter 59

Use 8. If there is so much evil in sin, then every soul is to be humbled for sin.

If there is as much evil in sin as you have heard, then the consideration of what has been delivered should cause your hearts to be humbled for the sins your conscience tells you are guilty of. Not only those who are so full of sin, but every women's child has cause to apply what has been said, and to be humbled in their souls before the Lord for that woeful guilt they have brought upon themselves. And now I speak to every soul, for there is no one here who does not have much sin they are guilty of.

Now, Oh you sinner, whoever you are, charge upon your soul what you remember concerning the evil of sin. Charge it upon your heart. Labor to bring it with power upon your own spirit. Bring your sin with all the aggravations of it that you possibly can, and lay it upon your heart. Labor to burden your heart, to make your spirit sensible of it. Open your conscience and let in all these truths you have heard. Suffer the Law to come with power and, though it slays you (as Paul said, "When the Law came, sin revived, and I died"), though it slays your soul, open your bosom and let it come. Go to the very pit's brink that sin endeavors to plunge soul and body in eternally. Be willing to go to the brink of the pit and see what is there.

Upbraid your own heart for the hardness of it, and think to yourself thus, "Lord, what a heart have I! I can be troubled for every little loss and affliction, but oh the hardness of my heart. I cannot be affected for sin. My heart does not yield and stir for that. But for any petty loss, or if anyone crosses me, what a disturbance there is in my spirit then! But little or nothing for my sin! Oh, what shall become of this heart of mine? What shall I do with this heart of mine, thus hardened from the fear of the Lord? What? Will sin bring confusion upon the whole creation? What shall then become of my soul if I ever come to answer for my sin myself?"

Certainly, my brethren, God must have glory, and therefore we must be humbled for sin, seeing there is so much evil in it. It cannot possibly be but that God must expect to see all His poor creatures who have been so guilty to lie down abased and humbled as poor, wretched, miserable, forlorn, undone creatures by reason of sin. It is a mighty dishonor to God that ever we have sinned thus against Him as we have done. But, that we should not be sensible of it adds as great a dishonor unto God as the former sin did.

When a man or woman commits sin, they dishonor God in that. But not being sensible of it after it is committed is a greater dishonor to God than the commission of it was; and the longer they continue insensible of their sin, the more desperate their sin against God grows, for if you do not have any sense of sin, but go on, in a little while you may come to be past feeling. The Scripture uses the phrase, "being past feeling."

So it is with many men and women. At first they begin to not be troubled for sin and put it off. At length, they come to be past feeling. And if your heart is insensible of the evil of it, then sin grows exceedingly. So the Scripture says, Ephesians 4:19, *Being past feeling, they give up themselves with greediness to all lasciviousness, and wantonness.* What is the reason men and women give up their souls to sin, to lasciviousness and wantonness with greediness? Because they are past feeling. Oh, the hardness of the heart in sin! The stone in the heart is worse than the stone in the bladder.

OBJECTION. But you will say, "If I labor to bring the weight of sin upon my soul, you have told us there is so much evil in sin that, if God should but bring and set it upon my heart, it would sink my heart and bring me to despair. We need to labor to put off the weight and burden of it. Yet now, after you have told me the heavy weight of it, do you labor now to bring the weight and burden of it upon our souls?"

ANSWER. Yes, brethren, to bring the weight and sense of sin is what I labor for. Not to bring more guilt, but the sense and burden of sin; and this is not the way to bring you to despair. First learn what I mean by this, that you may learn not to be so shy of bearing the weight of sin as you have been before; but to be willing to take up the burden, for there is no danger of despair in this.

If despair comes, it is rather when God shall force the burden of sin upon your souls, but if God sees a man or woman free and willing to lay the weight and burden of sin upon themselves, to that end that they may be humbled before the Lord and give glory to God, certainly God will take care of that soul. It shall never sink under the burden of sin.

This now, in the name of the Lord, I pronounce to you. Every soul that is willing to bring the weight of sin upon himself to the end that it may be humbled and give glory to God, my life for that soul, that soul shall never sink under the burden of sin. Certainly God will take care of such a soul so that it shall not sink under that burden. Therefore, be as willing as you will to let as much weight of sin upon your heart, and the more willing you are, the greater is God's care over that heart that it shall not perish.

It is the way to despair if you, upon hearing these things, come to be shy of meditating upon sin, and are loath to entertain those meditations that may work the weight of sin upon your souls. Now it is just with God, when He shall come and force the weight of sin upon you and lay the burden of it upon your spirits, to let you sink under the burden of it, for God to behold you sweltering under the burden of it without pity and compassion. And your own conscience will be ready to tell you so. "Yes, now the weight of sin is upon me, but is forced whether I will or not."

Now God may justly let it lie. This is a sad and sinking thought, and if anything lets sin lie upon the soul so that it shall never be purged, it will be this. When the Spirit would have brought the weight of sin upon my conscience, I put it off. Now God puts it upon me and, therefore, it troubles me thus. Therefore, be willing to be humbled, and know, if you are willing, Jesus Christ was appointed for that end: to raise you up. And there is as much power in the gospel to raise your heart as there is in sin to press your heart down, if you are rightly burdened with it.

Chapter 60

Use 9. If there is so much evil in sin, this should be a loud cry to stop men and turn them from sin.

Another use is this. If there is so much evil in sin, then the consideration and meditation of all that has been said should be a mighty cry unto all to turn back and stop in the ways of sin. Oh, you sinner! Whoever you are, in whatever place of the congregation you are, God has brought you by His providence to hear or read these sermons concerning the evil of sin. Know that all these sermons which have been preached unto you are all one loud, loud cry to your soul, "Stop! Stop!" Oh, sinner, in your sinful courses, stop here. Turn, turn! Oh, sinner, out of your sinful ways, turn, turn! Why will you die? Why will you die? Oh, wretched, sinful soul! You are lost, cursed, undone, and will perish eternally in the way you are in. Turn, turn while you have time.

God cries, His Word cries, His ministers cry, conscience cries. All those who have known what the evil of sin means cry to you. Unless you will destroy yourself, undo yourself eternally, stop in that way, for it is a dangerous, desperate way you go in. It is the very road way to the chambers of eternal death.

When you are on your sickbed, in the anguish of your soul, you will then cry, "Now, Lord, have mercy on a poor, wretched, sinful soul." You would be glad that the Lord should hear your cry upon your sickbed or death bed. Now, then, if ever you would have God hear your cry when you are in the great anguish of your souls upon your sickbed, when you see death before you, be willing to hear the cry of God to your souls at this moment. Know, if you do not hear the cry of God that cries to you to stop you in your sinful ways, then these very words I have spoken to you at this time may come in your mind when you cry for mercy. Then you may think, "Oh wretch, now I cry to God for mercy, but do I not remember such a time? Was there not a loud cry in my ears and conscience from God that I should stop my sinful ways and courses? And was not I then charged in the name of God that if ever I expected God should hear my cry in such a time that I should hear His voice?"

Oh, it will be dreadful for you to hear such a voice as this, "Because you would not hear Me, therefore I will not hear you." Therefore, behold, I cry again in the name of God, "Stop, stop! Turn, you sinful soul! Alas! Where are you going? You are going from God, from comfort, from life, from happiness, from all good whatsoever!"

I call heaven and earth to record that these things I have delivered to you concerning the evil of sin are the truths of God and have been the truths of God. And certainly, what I have delivered and you have read concerning the evil of sin, will come and rise up one day against every sinful man and woman who go on in any known way of sin, and it will be as scalding lead in your conscience. Every truth you have heard, every chapter you have read concerning the evil of sin, if you still go on in any one known way of sin, it will one day be as scalding lead in your conscience. Dropping scalding lead into the eyes of a man will not be more terrible to him than dropping these truths will be in your conscience another day.

Now it is a sad thing, my brethren, if God should send me among you by His providence only to aggravate any of your condemnations. God forbid that there should be this messenger sent among you, that any of His messengers should be sent for this end: to aggravate your consciences. This is that which is the prayer of my soul, that this may not be the errand I am sent for, if possible; not to seal the condemnation of any one soul. But this I know, unless there is great reformation among many, certainly the very errand God intended in the conclusion (though I do not say it is the primary and first end, but it is that which will prove so in the conclusion), through the stubbornness of the hearts of sinners, that will prove the aggravation of their consideration.

Wherefore, yet let me labor with your souls. Who knows whether any of you shall hear me preach one sermon more? Whether God will call after you any more? Whether you shall hear the Word again? Perhaps God will sear your conscience and say to him who is filthy, "Let him be filthy." God now speaks to you and cries after you. If you harden your hearts now, it is more than angels or men know whether you will ever have one more cry. Therefore, let me abide here. Tell me, oh sinner, what is it that you get in ways of sin that makes you want to abide there? What is it the world has to draw your heart from the strength of all these truths delivered in these sermons? Surely it must be some mighty thing when such truths as these, backed with arguments from Scripture and strength of reason, cannot restrain you. Surely it must be some wonderful thing that must outweigh all these sermons and all these things.

What, have you such a heart that is set upon any sinful way, any secret haunt of sin, that you find such good in? That by it all these truths are outweighed? Certainly there is no such good in the world. If all the creatures in the world should join together to give some comfort, to balance these truths delivered concerning the evil of sin, all the creatures in heaven and earth could not give such things as would balance it.

Therefore, certainly, you are deceived. Therefore, return, return, oh Shulamite! Return, return! Oh, that the truths delivered in this point might be as that sudden, amazing light that came to Saul when he was going on in courses of sin, Acts 9. There was an amazing light that came and stopped Saul in his course. Oh, that God would cause the light of these glorious truths, delivered concerning this argument, to be as an amazing light to your soul, to stop you in the ways of sin.

OBJECTION. But you will say, "We cannot stop. You

are putting in our power that which God alone must do."

ANSWER. First, for that act (I have told you), what power God gives, though you have none of your own. God gives power for the bare outward act. Do not say you cannot do this. You know what arguments you have had of that, therefore, say no more that you cannot. And though you cannot, yet God uses to convey power through the Word while God calls upon sinners to stop and mend. God's way is, then, to convey power. But, in the meantime, though there is no saving work of grace come in, yet this much, by an ordinary and common work of God's Spirit, may be done. God may cause a sinner to resolve, whatever comes of it, "That way of sin I dwelt in, I will never meddle with." And so there may be a sequestration of the heart from sin, though a full possession of God's Spirit does not come upon the soul.

For example, it is many times with God and the sinner as it is with man and man. A man is in debt and unable to pay. An arrest comes on his goods and there is a sequestration of the goods so that they lie in other men's hands. Though they are not quite taken away from the debtor, they are out of his power. He can have no use of them for the moment until the debt is paid. But whoever will come and pay the debt shall have the goods.

So it is with the heart when the sinner comes to venture upon Christ for pardon of sin. The sinner sees that he cannot overrule his self, sanctify his heart, or overcome his lusts. However, God sequesters the heart for the moment so far from them that he will not go on in these ways again. He will not follow that company again. There is a forbearance of those acts of sin so that, though the heart cannot sanctify itself, still it lies before the Lord and says, "Oh, Lord, pardon, come in, and oh, let Christ pay the debt for my sin and let Him take possession of my heart; but, in the meantime, Satan shall not use it as before. And those ways of sin, those gross ways I will forbear, though I die for it. I would rather sit still all my days and never stir off my seat than go to such wicked company. I would rather never open my mouth again than swear and speak so filthy. But, Oh Lord, discharge my soul and take it to Thyself." And then comes a sanctifying work of God to sanctify the soul and save it.

But, oh! That I might prevail this far with you, that there might be a sequestration of the soul from sin this day. Though sanctification does not come in, though the Holy Ghost does not come to rule in your soul, yet that there might be a sequestration, that the heart might come in and lie down and say, "Lord, come in and take possession. As far as those delights and contentments I took in sin before, I am resolved that, though I perish forever, I will not go on in them hereafter."

Here would be a good stop in the ways of sin. A man who goes in a dangerous way must make a stop before he turns and consider, "Oh, Lord, where am I? Where am I going? Is this my way?" and then he turns. Now this I endeavor, if possible, to make a stop in sinful ways so that you might consider, "Oh, Lord, where am I? What am I doing? What will become of me?"

Oh! that you might go away with such thoughts in your bosoms. And then follows the next.

Chapter 61

Use 10 and 11. If there is so much evil in sin, then turn to Christ, and bless God for Christ.

Use 10 is to labor to drive your hearts to Christ. Oh, then, fly to Christ! Here you have revealed to you that which one would think would terrify the hearts of men and women and make them fly to Christ. One would think that which has been revealed concerning the evil of sin would make the heavens ring with cries to God for Christ. Oh! None but Christ, none but Christ!

What would become of all your souls if it were not for Jesus Christ, were it not for that glorious Mediator sent to be a propitiation for sin and to make an atonement to the Father for sin? Christ is set up as that brazen serpent, that all those stung in conscience with the venom and poison of sin might look up to the brazen serpent and be saved.

Is there any soul that, by all I have said of the evil of sin, finds itself stung with the poison of sin? Know that Christ is that brazen serpent who is set up for you to look upon. If you find sin as the avenger of blood pursues you, oh now, run to Christ! If your heart burns and scorches in the apprehension of sin, as the deer pants after the water brook, so let your heart pant after Christ. There are cooling and refreshing waters. Then, indeed, shall that which I have delivered be useful for the souls of poor creatures.

When the soul has been before the Lord, crying mightily to heaven for pardon and part in Jesus Christ, if so be after I have preached all these sermons, if God shall hear souls getting alone in their closets and crying out, "Oh, Lord, I never understood what the meaning of sin was! Oh, what a wretched creature have I been all my days? Now, Lord, unless Thou hast mercy in Thy Son, in the mediation of Jesus Christ through His blood, His heart's blood that was shed for sinners, I am a lost and undone creature forever! Oh, Lord, that which is done can never be undone. Oh, Lord, let me find favor in Thy Son. Here I am, do with me whatever Thou please, only a pardon, a pardon in Jesus Christ, to deliver me from the guilt and uncleanness of my sin."

Yes, now will God say that something has been done, when sinners' cries come up to heaven. What has been happening in this congregation? What is the matter that you come crying for Christ? Heretofore, your hearts were never stirred after Christ, what is the matter? Why do you stir so? Who has told you anything?

When God called to Adam, Adam hid himself and said, *I was afraid because I was naked.* God said, *Who told you that you were naked?* So, when poor souls cry to heaven for Christ, God may say to the poor soul, "Why? What is the matter? Who has told you anything?" As Christ said to the Pharisees, *Who hath forewarned you to fly from the wrath to come?* So God will say, "Why? What is the matter? Who told you this?"

I hope some poor soul will experience this. When you go to pray for Christ and you pray in another manner than before, when your prayers shall be cries to heaven, when God shall say, "Why? What is the matter? Why do you cry more than before?" I hope some poor soul can give a good account of it and say, "I see myself lost and undone without Christ. It is better to be a dog, or a toad, or anything than a man if I do not have Christ, because they are not capable of sin, and my heart is full of sin. I have heard the evil of it, and therefore give me Christ or I am undone!"

Oh, such a soul will be exceedingly acceptable unto God. And therefore, to such a soul, I propound in the name of the Lord, the doctrine of life, salvation, and peace. Let it be known, therefore, to you that God the Father, looking upon the sinful children of men, and seeing them all in a perishing condition by sin, out of infinite bowels of tender compassion, has provided a glorious way of mediation, of propitiation for sin. And, to that end, He has sent His only beloved Son out of His bosom, who has taken man's nature upon Himself, united in a personal union to the end that He might be a fit Mediator to stand between a provoked God and sinful souls. And this Christ has borne the full vials of the wrath of His Father, the curse of the Law due to sin, satisfied infinite divine justice, and made a full atonement between God and sinful man. Upon these terms alone, now, He tenders and offers to every poor, wearied, distressed soul all that His Son has purchased by His blood, all His merits, that they might be an atonement for sin, a propitiation for your soul to discharge all your sins, that you might come through Him to stand acquitted before the Father for evermore. This is the sum of the gospel, and this I present and preach and offer to you, and this I offer not only to the least sinner, but to the greatest sinner in the world.

This I present as in the name of God, as the message we have in the name of God to deliver unto you. And now, whatever your sins have been heretofore, God only requires that your souls should now stand admiring the infinite riches of His grace in His Son, and that your souls should be taken off from the creature and sin to live upon Christ, surrender your souls to Him, and cast your souls on that infinite, rich grace of God in Him; and upon that instant, every one of your sins, though never so great and heinous, yet I pronounce in the name of the Lord, every one of them is pardoned and all is done away with as if they had never been committed. This is the sum of the gospel unto those who come to see their sins and are sensible of their need of Christ by their sin.

OBJECTION. But you will say, "This makes all you have done a little matter. If sin may be thus done away with, what need is there of all this discourse of the evil of sin if it may thus be washed away?"

ANSWER. Ah, poor carnal heart that speaks thus. Is this a light or little matter? True, it is in a few words in the end of a sermon, but let it be known to you that there is more in these words I have spoken to you in this last quarter of an hour, there is more of the glory of God in them, than in heaven and earth beside; not because they come from me, but because I have spoken that which is the sum of the gospel. In truth, in one sentence of the gospel, there is more of the glory of God than in all heaven and earth beside. You must be convinced of this and know it is so, and if ever you come to be partakers of the good of the gospel, you will see it to be so.

Oh, brethren! In that which I have said, there is the glorious mystery of godliness. Great is the mystery of godliness, God manifest in the flesh. The great counsel of God, working from all eternity is in this, in the sum of the gospel. The greatest work that God ever did was in sending His Son, and in the offer of His Son to sinners that their sins might be pardoned. Therefore, do not think it is a small thing, and hear when I call upon sinners to come and cast their souls upon Christ.

It is one of the most glorious works ever done for a sinful soul to come and close with Christ the Mediator; and once you come in, your hearts will be so full of the glory of God that immediately all the glory of the creature will be darkened in your eyes and you will be so filled with the glory of God that you will come to see the filthiness of sin this way as much as in any way. All the sermons I have delivered concerning the evil of sin will not set out the filthiness of sin to you as much as the glory of God will that will fill your hearts as soon as you come to close with God in this mystery of the gospel. Perhaps it is not so apparent to every soul, but wait awhile and there will be more of the evil of sin revealed this way than in any other way.

USE 11. And then the use that I shall make of it is this. If there is such evil in sin, then bless God for Christ. *Blessed is that man and woman whose sin is pardoned,*

Psalm 32. Oh, blessed is he whose sin is forgiven! Certainly, it is a blessed thing that sin should be forgiven. This requires a whole sermon by itself. I shall but name it now, because I shall hereafter speak of this particularly, of the great blessedness of the pardon of sin. Only take notice of it now. Any who has a comfortable assurance of their sin being pardoned, go away rejoicing. Son, daughter, rejoice that your sins are pardoned. And there is enough in that word to bring comfort and joy to your souls.

Chapter 62

Use 12. If there is so much evil in sin, then it is of great concern to be religious early, and thereby prevent much sin.

Again, one use more. If there is such evil in sin, then it is great use to begin to be godly and religious early, for young ones to come to be godly speedily. Why? Because they may come to prevent so much evil and so much sin. Oh, happy are those who begin to be godly when they are young. You prevent a thousand sins that others commit by their not knowing sin early. True, if there were no other use of godliness than merely to bring you to heaven, then you might stay until your sick and deathbeds and then be religious, it would be enough. But besides bring you to heaven, there is use of godliness to keep you away from sin and ungodliness, and there is enough in that to outweigh any pleasure.

Suppose you young people abstain from some pleasure or joy that others have. The truth is, you have greater and better pleasures; but suppose you had none but keeping your souls from sin. This would be enough to outweigh whatever you suffer in the ways of sin.

There are many who were converted when they were old, and what would those give to be delivered from the guilt of some sins committed when they were young? When they look back to their lives they think, "Oh, this sin I committed in such a family, and when I was an apprentice in such a place. Oh, that I were delivered from them! Oh, they lie upon my heart! Oh, that vanity and wickedness! Oh, those oaths I swore in such company, among young men! Oh, those Sabbaths I broke! Oh, those lies I told and the drunkenness I was drawn to! Oh, I cannot look back to these without thinking that I could tear my heart from my belly! To think what a heart I had, to sin against God and to multiply sin against Him."

Thus, at best, when God awakens their hearts, they would give ten thousand worlds to be delivered from the sins of their youth. And therefore, now, you young ones, seeing there is such evil in sin, oh, prevent it! You know how the sins of youth lay upon David, *Remember not against me the sins of my youth.* Therefore, now, prevent those sins that otherwise will lay so heavily upon you so that you will be forced to cry out, "Oh, remember not against me the sins of my youth!"

It is a happy thing to see young ones good, and it is the greatest hope that God will show mercy to England in that God begins to draw young ones in the ways of godliness, so that we hope there will not be so many sins committed in the age to come. We have cried out for the sins of young ones, and one generation that has followed another has been like the kennel. The lower and further it goes, the more filth it has gathered. And so, the lower generations have gone, the more filthy they have been. But we hope God intends to turn the course, and to make godliness as much honored as it has been dishonored before, and that there should not be as much sin in the next generation.

Before this, when young people had days of recreation, what did they do but multiply sin? What abundance of wickedness was committed by youth then? And on Shrove-Tuesdays, an abundance of wickedness was committed by the youth then. And so the generation was filled with sins of youth. But now God is pleased to stir up the hearts of young ones who, instead of multiplying sin, have gotten together on such days to fast, to pray, and to make days to attend upon the Word, and so avoid sin. It is that, certainly, that encourages the hearts of God's people to pray to Him and to seek Him for mercy, that God gives hearts to young people that they do not multiply sin as before.

If there are any here who have begun this, Oh, go on in that way! And, when others multiply wickedness upon such days, get alone and attend upon the Word. Recreate your souls in the Word and in holy conference. True, God gives liberty to recreate, but let it be as it used to be with the companies in London. Though they recreated, they would have their sermons, too. So, instead of horrible wickedness that used to be upon those days, as I suppose some of you can remember, upon Shrove-Tuesdays infinite wickedness was committed in the city and thereabouts. We hope that, instead of wickedness and joining together in wickedness, there will be joining together in the ways of God. And, thus doing, you will encourage us in the ways of God, and peace and mercy will be upon you.

Chapter 63

Use 13. If there is so much evil in sin, then it is a fearful thing for any to be instrumental in drawing others into sin.

We are now to finish that treatise on the greatness of the evil of sin. It has been an argument that has increased much in our hands like the bread that Christ broke to the people, which in the very breaking multiplied, and so has this argument done. But now we are to put a period to it.

Many uses, you know, have been made already, as corollaries and consequences from that great doctrine of the evil of sin, that sin is a greater evil than affliction. The last day, the special aim and intention of the application was therefore to drive sinners to Jesus Christ, seeing there is so much more evil in sin than in affliction. Oh, what need do we have (who are such great sinners) of Jesus Christ, who is the Propitiation for sin? I have only one note to add further on that, and we shall proceed.

It is an excellent expression I find in Luther. He said, "There is a great deal of difference between the legal consequence and the evangelical consequence." There is a consequence of the Law, and that is this: you have sinned and, therefore, you must be damned. But the consequence of the gospel is this: you have sinned, therefore go to Jesus Christ. That is the argument the gospel uses from sin. But passing by all we have said concerning that use, we proceed to further applications that are behind. Four or five uses we are to speak of, and then we shall have done with the point. I will be brief upon the first two or three, and the last two we shall stick most upon.

Use 13. If there is such evil in sin as you have heard, then it is a fearful thing for any one to be instrumental in drawing others into sin. All that has been said in the opening of the evil of sin must speak very terrible unto all who have ever been in any way instruments to draw others to sin all their lives. Now, oh that God would speak to every man's and woman's conscience in this congregation who are conscious of ever having been the cause of drawing others into sin. Is there not one whose conscience immediately tells you, at the naming of this, "Well, now, God speaks to me, for certainly there have been some who I have drawn to sin, who I have been a means to further in sin."

If any one of you has ever been a means by counsel, or advice, by approbation, by persuasion, by encouragement, by abetting, or by joining in with any in some sinful course to draw them into sin, know that God speaks to you.

First, God tells you this. If you had been born to do mischief, you could not do a greater mischief than this is. If you had been the means to undo men and women in their outward estate, it would not be as much. But you have, what in you lies, been a means to undo an immortal soul, yes, and to cause them to sin against an infinite God; so that you are guilty of every sin you have been a means to draw others into, and you are worse than those who have sinned, for your act in drawing them to it is a dreadful evil, and then that which they have done is yours, too.

Have you not sins of your own enough to answer for before the Lord? Must you have the sins of others also? Do you know what you have done in enticing others to sin, either to uncleanness, drunkenness, keeping bad company, breaking the Sabbath, and other sins? Perhaps you have brought them to pilfering and purloining, or to many other particulars and ways that might be named. For, indeed, if we should enlarge ourselves at this point, it might well require another entire treatise. But we must contract our thoughts.

It may be that there are some in this congregation who have been a means to draw others to sin, and they are now in hell at this instant for that sin you were a cause of. What a sad thing is this, for any man or woman to have this to lay on their heart? "I know I have drawn such and such to sin, I have been a means (at least) to further sin in them. Well, they are dead and gone, and they manifested no repentance before they died and, therefore, for all I know, they are now in hell, and now being tormented for that very sin I was the cause of, and if the Lord gives me wages according to my works, I must go there to them. What? Shall they be in hell for the sins I brought them to, and will I escape? Is it any way likely and probable but that I must follow, when they are there for the sins I brought them to? What, shall the accessory be condemned and executed, but not the principal? I am the principal and the other is only the accessory."

Certainly there needs to be a mighty work of humiliation, for you are in exceeding danger who are the cause of bring another to sin. That must lie exceedingly heavy on the soul of any man or woman. If God ever gave you a sight of this, certainly you would perish. But suppose God gave you the sight of so great an evil and you began to be humbled. Oh, this very meditation will cause your humiliations to be full of bitterness, and will cause it to be very hard for you to lay hold of mercy and pardon when you think like this, "Ah, were it for my own sins that I were to answer for, I might have greater hope. But there are other sins I drew some into, and they are condemned, perhaps, and in hell. How shall I escape condemnation myself?"

I do not say there is no possibility of pardon, for the grace of God is infinite. And, were it not infinite, it would be impossible for such a soul to perish while you are saved. I say, there is a possibility, but it is as if it were through the fire if you ever do escape. Consider what it would be for you do die in impenitency also, as the other did, and you went to hell. When you two met at the day of judgment, and he saw you, the one who drew him into sin, Oh! what a grief it would be to you. How he would curse you and the day he ever saw your face, that he ever lived in the same family as you!

It may be that some parents have been a means to draw,

by counsel and advice, their children to sin. Oh, when the child sees his parents at the day of judgment, how he will curse the time that ever he came from such loins, from such a woman's womb! He would rather have been the offspring of a dragon, the generation of a viper, then from the loins of such a man or woman. "You encouraged me to such and such ways of sin, to opposition, and hatred, and speaking evil against the people of God, the servants of God who were strict in their way. And now you and I must perish eternally."

Surely, in hell, they will be ready to cast fire brands in one another's faces who have been the cause of sin in one another in this world. And so husbands and wives, who lie in one another's bosom, if they are the cause of any sin in one another, it may cause woeful terror in them and appear worse than if a serpent had lain in their bosom, for those who draw others to sin do worse mischief than any serpent or viper in the world can do.

You need to look to it quickly. (I shall wind it up with this one note.) Whoever has been the cause to draw others to commit any sin, know this: the least that can be required, if God gives you a sight of your sin and you are humbled for it, if you go away from the presence of God as having an arrow darted into your bosom for this, then I say go away with this one note - you are bound to make some restitution in a spiritual way as much as you can.

For this you know (I showed before) in a man's temporal estate, when you have wronged, you must make restitution. If you will have mercy, you must make up the wrong as you are able. Much more here, when you have wronged someone in their souls. A soul wrong calls for spiritual restitution as well as a body wrong, or estate wrong, calls for a bodily or estate restitution.

QUESTION. What do you mean by this "spiritual restitution?"

ANSWER. I mean that if those are alive that you have

drawn to sin, you are bound to restitution, that is, to go to them and undo what you can of what you have done; and now to tell them of the evil of that sin, and to do them all the good you possibly can for their souls. You must show them how God has convinced you, and what the work of God has been upon you, and how heavy and dreadful sin has been made to you. You must beseech them, for the Lord's sake, to look to themselves and to consider their estates, and to repent of their sin that you were the cause of bringing them to.

And so, if there are any means in the world whereby you can do good to their souls, you are bound to do it, yes, to them, to their children, to their friends. You are bound to make restitution unto the next friends and heirs of those you have wronged with regard to physical things, if the wronged person is dead. So, if those should be dead you have drawn to sin, you are bound to do good to the souls of their children. Suppose when you were young, you drew such a man to drunkenness, adultery, or the like, and they are dead and gone. You are bound to do good to the souls of their children, for know that, according to the nature of the wrong, so must the restitution be.

One text is observable to show that, according to the nature of the wrong, the restitution must be to the utmost it can be. Exodus 22:5, *If a man shall cause a field, or vineyard to be eaten, and shall put in his beast and shall feed in another man's field, of the best of his own field, and of the best of his own vineyard shall he make restitution.* This is the scope of the Holy Ghost in this text of Scripture, that if any one shall wrong another in his vineyard or field, he shall make restitution. And mark what the text says, not in any slight manner, but of the best of his field or vineyard.

He must not say, "My cattle did not do any harm, they only ate a little of the worst. So I will make restitution of the worst."

No, he must make restitution of the best of his field and vineyard. So, if he has wronged his neighbor's field, he must not go and say, "I will give a part of the common crop," but of the best of his field he must make restitution. If he has wronged another's estate, he must give of his estate. And if the wrong is to the soul, the restitution must be to the soul according to the wrong done.

I beseech you to be convinced of this. All the sorrow in the world in not sufficient unless you make restitution. This is so clear out of the Word, and even by the light of nature and conscience, that whoever doubts this may easily convince themselves. Nothing in religion is more clear than this. Therefore, restitution is required by God of you if ever you expect to find mercy.

This argument, if God is pleased to set it home, will make many men and women, who were ringleaders when they were young to bring others to wickedness, to be ringleaders to bring others to good now. I pronounce it as in the name of God. You can have no assurance of the truth of repentance unless there is some endeavor in some degree to be as forward for God now as you have been in the ways of sin before.

If you have been ringleaders to the sin of Sabbath-breaking, you must be ringleaders to draw others to keep the Sabbath. If you have been ringleaders to ungodliness, you must be forward to draw others to godliness.

Oh, take heed of this. It is a woeful thing to draw others to sin, seeing there is as much evil in sin as there is.

Chapter 64

Use 14. If there is so much evil in sin, then there ought to be no pleading for sin.

If there is as much evil in sin as you have heard, then surely there ought to be no pleading for sin. There is too much evil in it for anyone in the world to plead for it, to make any excuse or any plea for it. If there is a notorious, wicked house where much evil is done, we account it a great disgrace for anyone to plead for it. If it is in question, and any justice of the peace pleads for wicked ale houses, it is a blot on his record. If there were not sin committed in it, it would not be much but, if it is a notorious house for sin, to plead for it is accounted a great blot.

And now, you who have heard of the great evil of sin, will you ever open your mouths to diminish and excuse sin? And yet how ordinary this is in the world. Some go to evil, wicked company and, when they spend their time in drinking, they plead, "Why, they must have recreation!"

I pray, what work do they tire themselves with who need so much recreation? What service do they do for God in which they spend their spirits, and the strength of their souls in serving God that they need so much refreshing? And so, when they spend whole days in drinking and eating, why, they are only rejoicing in the use of the creature. May they not keep company with such men who are honest men?

And so, to these people, wicked, ribald talking is but mirth; notorious covetousness is but providing for their family; horrible pride is but handsomeness. They will have something to say, pleas and excuses, for almost any sin.

Certainly, brethren, if we understood the nature of sin, we would say as did Jerubael, *Let Baal plead for himself.* So let sin plead for itself. Never be heard opening your mouth to plead for sin in others, much less in yourself. Those who are so full of excuses and pleas for sin give an evident argument that God never revealed the evil of sin to them yet. He never caused the weight and burden of sin to lie upon their conscience, nor what we have mentioned of the evil of it.

Oh, you must know that you have to deal with an infinite God! It is a matter of your soul and your eternal estate. Do not think to put it off with vain pleas and excuses, but set yourself in the presence of the eternal, infinite God. Indeed, if you have to deal with your mothers or friends, you may put them off with excuses for sin, but if you would set yourselves in the presence of God, and there set sin before your eyes, you would not so easily put it off with excuses as you do.

Chapter 65

Use 15. If there is so much evil in sin, then of all judgments, spiritual judgment are the greatest.

If there is as much evil in sin as has been revealed, then above all judgments, spiritual judgments are the greatest. Oh! What a dreadful thing is it, then, for God to give men or women up to sin. This is the most fearful judgment that can befall any man or woman in the world, unless God should send them down quickly to hell. Yes, it may be that, if God should send them quickly down to hell and cause hell's mouth to open immediately, it would not be as great a judgment as to give them up to sin. And yet the Scripture speaks much of God's wrath burning this way. God hardened the heart of Pharaoh. God gives men up to a reprobate sense, *he that will be filthy, let him be filthy still.* He gives men up to their own counsels.

I might show you divers texts of Scripture for this, but there are two things in this point that require large discussion.

1. How can God, who is so infinitely good, have a hand in sin that has so much evil in it? We must clear God, and show that He is not the cause of sin in any, but to show how far God has a hand in sin would require a long time to open, which I cannot take.

2. To show how much dreadfulness there is in this misery of being given up to sin, to open to you the dreadfulness of spiritual judgments, will require a long time also. Therefore, because I have resolved to make an end of this at this time, I must reserve these two things to larger discussion. For the present, let this be the prayer of every one of you, "Oh Lord, whatever judgment you send upon us, do not deliver us up to spiritual judgments! Lord, do not give us up to sin. Do not punish sin with sin, but rather punish sin

with any affliction than with sin."

When God comes to punish sin with sin, the condition of that man or woman is a very dreadful condition, because there is so much evil in sin.

Chapter 66

Use 16. If there is more evil in sin than in affliction, then when sin and affliction meet they make a man most miserable.

Now we come to the last two uses. We must insist a little longer upon them, especially the last, as having several branches.

Therefore, if there is more evil in sin than in affliction, what a miserable condition those are in who have both these evils upon them, and that in a high degree. Sense teaches men and women that affliction makes a man to be in a very sad and miserable condition. Everyone accounts those men and women who are under great afflictions to be in great misery. Well, but now you have heard in these many sermons how there is another evil greater than all afflictions.

Now, then, what if both these evils come together and concur together to make a man miserable? Then he is a miserable man in every way. Then he is a miserable man both to sense and to reason in the judgment of the world. He is a miserable man in the judgment of the Holy Ghost, too; in the judgment of God and the saints, and in the judgment of the Word. When sin and affliction come and join together to make a man miserable, surely these are miserable persons indeed.

If a child of God sees a man in affliction, he will not immediately judge him miserable because he does not know. It may be that he is godly. If he is godly, he is not miserable though he is afflicted. On the other side, the world does not judge him to be miserable, though he is sinful, if he is not afflicted.

On the one hand, the godly man judges that man in affliction as not being miserable if he is not sinful. On the other hand, the world judges that man not miserable who is not afflicted, though he is sinful. But now, when these two are together in one man, all judge this to be misery. And what a company of most miserable wretches we have in this world!

How many are in woeful straits and bodily extremities? How many, in their estates, lack bread, lack clothes, lack housing, lack heat, lack all the necessities that can be? Their bodies are diseased, full of pains, their bodies are deformed. Their very parts of nature are exceedingly loathsome and unfit for service in every way. By all outward appearances, their estates are extremely miserable. Yet, with all this, they are extremely wicked also, extremely sinful.

Go into their houses. There is nothing but poverty and misery there, and there is as much wickedness and iniquity as poverty and misery. It may be that these poor creatures who are this miserable have hearts full of atheism. They live without God in the world; they do not know God. They do not know Christ. They know nothing of their immortal souls. They know nothing of another life. They live just like brute beasts in all filthy uncleanness. It may be that they suffer for their wickedness before men and are whipped, put into the stocks or a cage, lie in dark dungeons in cold, nakedness, and hunger, and all for their sin and wickedness.

What woeful creatures these are, and how many hundreds, nay, thousands you have of this kind of creature here in Stepney who are such objects of pity. I think this should make your hearts bleed when you consider them. How many you have of them in this place! I confess, if the charge of souls in this place should lie upon me, I think I would have enough work to do with such poor creatures as these if I were to live all of Methuselah's days and should make the number of hours in a day to be more than twenty four. There would be work enough for all my time. I would think I had little time for any refreshment any other way, knowing how many poor souls are in such a condition who, perhaps, are not only outwardly miserable but inwardly poor. But their outward misery increases by their inward misery. The one increases the other.

As it is a great evil for sin to bring affliction, so it is a great evil for affliction to increase sin as their affliction does. Their affliction puts them upon swearing, lying, profaneness, and deception. It keeps them from sanctifying the Sabbath, and they seldom come into the congregation.

I am convinced that there are thousands who belong to this place who have scarcely ever heard a sermon in this place. They scarcely know whether Christ was a man or a woman. They scarcely know more than if they had lived among the Turks, and yet these poor creatures live miserable lives every way for their bodies.

Alas, I suppose there are very few of these I am preaching to now, who are hearing me now. Perhaps God may have some love to some poor creatures who may come creeping into this congregation and may hear me. This exercise was intended for such poor people who might come in the morning, for many of the richer sort would rather take their ease and give them room. They might supply the lack of their room, and yet how few of them come here. They may be at home (many of them) mending their clothes, or perhaps at some worse exercise on the Sabbath, and thus have neither God nor the world. They are miserable here and will, likely, be eternally miserable.

If Parliament had given to this place, or any other, such money so that every Sabbath morning sixpence should be given to each person, or even two pence, we would have an abundance, whereas now scarcely anyone comes. And as there are not many mighty, not many rich or noble who come, so there are not very many poor and outwardly miserable who come.

I think when any of you look upon their condition, you should have your hearts raised to bless God that he has made a difference between you and them. And when you are crossed in your families, think to yourselves, "Why should I be discontented just because I have this or that cross? Does not God make my condition a thousand times better than many hundreds who live near me? Do I not, every day, every hour, in the streets see hundreds of people I would never want to change places with?"

And who has made the difference? Who has put a difference between you and them? You who have estates, and comfortable spouses, and children about you, who have your tables spread, and houses furnished, and lodging, and good friends, and to whom God has made Himself known, and given His ordinances unto you, and hope of eternal life; oh, what a difference there is between you and such wretched creatures as these are! And yet there are many such poor creatures, thus afflicted, who look upon themselves and acknowledge that they are miserable creatures in regard of affliction, but never think themselves miserable in regard of sin. They do not understand that misery.

But now I speak to you who have heard these sermons of the evil of sin, or have read them. I hope, by this time, that you have come to understand what a great deal of evil there is in sin so that you may put both together, woeful affliction and sin. If there are any here who account themselves miserable by affliction, as I suppose (though you are not yet in that extremity of poverty that others are) many think themselves miserable by affliction who do not think they are miserable by sin all this while. No, some maybe have thought themselves so miserable by affliction that they have made out and measured God's intentions of good to them hereafter by that. They have their hell here for the present, and therefore think they shall have heaven afterwards.

This is the great argument many men and women have. Because they have a hell here, therefore they shall have heaven afterwards. But let it be known to you, if together with your affliction you still remain sinful and wicked, you may have a hell here and a hell eternal hereafter also. Mark what is said of Sodom, unclean and filthy Sodom, that lived in all manner of filthiness like brute beasts. It is said of them in the 7th verse of the Epistle of Jude, *Even as Sodom and Gomorrah, and the cities about them in like manner, giving themselves over to fornication, and going after strange flesh, are set forth for an example, suffering the vengeance of eternal fire.*

Mark, Sodom suffered the vengeance of eternal fire, and yet Sodom suffered the vengeance of present fire. Fire came into this world and brimstone, and consumed them for uncleanness who burned in lust, and yet for all the fire and brimstone upon them in this world, the Holy Ghost said that they suffered the vengeance of eternal fire. They were sent down from fire in this world to eternal fire in that world to come.

So certainly, many people are sent from misery in this world to eternal misery, and all the miseries on them in this world are but the beginnings of misery, are as the pre-boiling of flesh to the roasting hereafter. They have a little heat of misery here, but it is only as the pre-boiling to the roasting in hell hereafter.

Know, therefore, that all those who are miserable here and are sinful and wicked, the justice of God is an infinite stream, and there is never a whit less to run because of all that has run before. His hand is stretched out still, as in Isaiah 5:25. After God had spoken of dreadful wrath against His people, He said, *Therefore is the anger of the Lord kindled against His people, and He hath stretched out His hand against them and smitten them, and the hills did tremble, and their carcasses were torn in the midst of the street; for all this His anger is not turned away, but His hand is stretched out still.*

Mark it, God's wrath is so terrible that hills and mountains tremble at it. So, though God has manifested some displeasure, or brought woeful misery upon your body, estate, or name, yet your heart is not brought to the true work of repentance for all this. The hand of God is still stretched out, eternally against you if you do not return from sin.

For you to think that there will be an end at last, because you have endured hard things, is just like a fool I read of. He sat by a stream and would have gone across, but he thought he could not do so yet. He had seen a great deal of water running by, and so sat still, hoping it would run out before night. His thinking was that, since it had run a great deal, it would run dry. He never considered that it was fed by a fountain and was a running stream.

Such is the folly of many people who think that because they suffer something now, before long they shall suffer no more. Do you not know that God's wrath is an eternal stream, fed from an eternal fountain?

Some reason like this, "Because I prosper, therefore I hope God loves me." And others reason like this, "Because I am afflicted, I hope He loves me." But both these reasons will certainly deceive you.

Oh, that I had many of these people here to speak to! I would enlarge myself to them, for my soul bleeds over them. Oh consider, you who are under great afflictions (if God has brought any such poor creatures to this exercise) and are sensible of them. If you were only delivered from sin and wickedness, the greater part of your misery by far would be gone and over. What would you do to deliver yourself from misery? You are in woeful poverty, in painful diseases, and in grievous extremities. Oh, if one should come to help you, he would be a good master who could deliver you from your woeful pain, your miserable poverty, and your extremity.

We know that if God gives you a heart to turn from sin, the greatest of your misery would be gone, and you would immediately be in a better condition than the greatest emperor, monarch, or prince in the world who is still in a sinful condition. I would only put this to any of those poor sinful creatures who are sensible enough of their misery by affliction. Suppose you were quite delivered from outward misery, and you had an estate given to you so that you could live elegantly, and in as great a pomp as any gentleman or knight. You, who were in great poverty and misery, now come to live like a man of fashion. Would you not think it a woeful evil for you all of a sudden to be put in the same poverty you were in before, in rags, and having to beg for a farthing? If your estate were now changed and you could ride in your coach, having all that your heart desired, would you not account it a woeful condition to be immediately put into that woeful poverty and penury you were in before? This would sink your heart!

Know that the commission of any one sin is a greater misery than if there should be a change of your estate. If God should give you a heart to turn from sin, perhaps your affliction might be taken away, for it's a punishment for sin. And, as you know, David said in Psalm 37, *I have been young, and now am old, yet never have I seen the righteous forsaken, and his seed begging their bread.* And truly, what he has said, I truly believe most of you may say, that in all your lives, you never saw one who you had good evidence of being truly godly and gracious having to go up and down as common beggars in that woeful perplexity. I do not say that godly, righteous men may never be in want or in need, but, for my part, I never knew any godly and righteous person who, but one way or the other, God stirred up someone to relieve them. Or, if they have been forced to seek relief of some, they have gone and made known their condition to their neighbors, and so they have commended them to others so that eventually they are relieved.

But to go in such an extravagant way, from door to door begging for bread, I hardly think you can give examples of any godly who have been forced to do so! And if God would but turn the heart of some poor, wretched, miserable creatures so that there might appear godliness in them, God would provide for them. It's true, though there is not godliness, we should not let them perish. God forbid! Let them not lack that which is absolutely necessary. Let them not starve! Yet the Scripture says that those who will not work are not to eat. Let us not do more than the Scripture commands, to give liberty in such ways as will increase sin. And let us not nourish that which nourishes sin, but let us inquire after those who are godly and give them relief. And if poor people would depend upon God in His ways, He would provide for them. And know, if your afflictions are not taken away, if your sin were gone, you would be far more able to bear your affliction, for a man who has a sore shoulder cannot bear a burden, but if the soreness is gone, he can bear it better. So your affliction would not be so heavy, if you were godly, as it is now. No, it would be sanctified to you, and you would bear it better.

I confess, it is hard to convince those who are ignorant of God and the nature of grace, but certainly there is a truth in these things. Therefore, it is rare for God to come in with His saving grace into the heart of such as are miserably afflicted; though it is true that their affliction does not hinder, for if it were not for their wickedness, they might be happy. I would not make their affliction greater than it is. They might be happy were it not for their wickedness, but we see it so rarely because their education is such that there is no good principle in them and nothing to work upon in them, being bred in atheism. Therefore, it is very rare.

But because it is so rare, so much the greater will God's grace be, if God has some of these poor creatures in this congregation at this moment and speaks to their hearts. How much more rare would it be because it is not often seen? What if God passes by great, rich men, noble men, princes, and shall look into your cottage, and on your miserable estate, and shall convert your soul and show mercy to you? What! For God to set His heart upon you and give the blood of His Son for you! To make you an heir with Jesus Christ! To give you an inheritance in the kingdom of glory and in life! To make you come and reign with Him eternally! Oh, the infiniteness of God's grace, that God should ever set His heart upon such a poor creature as you are!

Therefore, go away with these thoughts, "Oh wretched creature, how have I lived without God in the world and looked for nothing but a little bread and drink and thought myself happy if only I could get this or that. Thus I have lived miserably here, and I confess I have thought myself a miserable wretch all this while, but God has told me at this moment that there is a greater evil than all this: the evil of sin I have been full of all my life. Put both together, and how miserable I am! Therefore, the Lord is merciful to me."

If God strikes your heart, know that your soul is as precious in God's eyes as the richest man in the world, as any king or prince. The greatest noble man in the land is not more precious in God's eyes than you are.

Yes, and the ministers of the gospel are sent by God to preach Jesus Christ to you, as well as to preach to the richest and greatest in the world. Christ came to shed His blood for you, as well as for the greatest in the world, and the kingdom of heaven is opened as wide to you as to the greatest and the richest. Though you cannot deliver yourself from outward affliction, yet you may deliver your soul from hell as well as the greatest in the world. Therefore, do not be miserable here and miserable hereafter, but look after God and Christ and eternal life.

Though you are not likely to be great here, yet who knows but that you may be crowned with glory eternally hereafter! There is fullness of mercy in God.

Poor creatures, if they see a coach come, and they think a gentleman or a nobleman is there, how they run and cry out, "Oh, my Lord," or "Oh, your worship," and lift up their voices for alms.

If an ordinary man comes, they will desire relief and beg them for a half penny or a farthing; but if a rich and great man passes by, then they cry and lift up their voices. Why? Because they think there is more to be had.

Oh, know that there is fullness of riches and grace in God to turn your misery to eternal felicity! There is mercy enough in God to raise you from your low, weak, miserable estate to the height of glory and happiness. And if God causes His Son to prevail with your soul, you may go away with the best portion you ever had in all your life. And thus much I thought to speak to those poor people who were both sinful, miserable, and afflicted.

Chapter 67

Use 17. Being of reprehension to six sorts of people. First, it reprehends those who are more afraid of affliction than sin. Secondly, it reprehends those who are careful to keep themselves from sin, but merely for fear of affliction, for: (1) this may be without change of nature; (2) your obedience is forced; (3) you are not released from yourself; (4) you are not likely to hold out. Also, two answers to an objection of those who think they avoid sin for fear of hell: (1) your sensitive part may be most stirred by fear, but yet your rational part may be most carried against sin as sin. (2) Those who avoid sin merely for fear never come to love the command that forbids the sin. (3) They are ignorant of many sins. (4) Those who avoid sin, and not out of fear, even when they fear God will destroy them, then they desire that God may be glorified. (5) Those who avoid sin out of fear do not see the excellency of godliness so as to be enamored with it. Thirdly, it reprehends those who will sin to avoid affliction. Fourthly, it rebukes those who, when they are under affliction, are more sensible of affliction than of sin. Also there are five discoveries whether men's affliction or sin trouble them. Fifthly, it reprehends those who get out of affliction by sinful courses, and yet think they are doing well. Sixthly, it reprehends those who, after being delivered from affliction, can bless themselves in their sin.

We come now to the last thing. The last use is this (I will but show what might have been said, and so wind up all). There are six sorts of people who, from this point, are reprehended. You shall see all naturally follow from the point in hand that there is greater evil in sin than in affliction.

First, this reprehends such people as are more afraid of affliction than of sin. There are many people who are very shy of affliction, and solicitous to prevent affliction, but not to prevent sin. Many reason like this, "I need to have a good husband and to lay up something before I die, because I do not know what I may meet with before I die. I may have wants before I die." Many are penurious and covetous, and will not enlarge themselves to good uses when God calls because they are afraid they and their children may lack before they die. Who knows what they will meet with? And thus they are careful to prevent affliction.

But, as for sin, they do not lay up to prevent that. We should be very solicitous least we should be drawn into temptation and, therefore, we are taught to pray, *Lead us not into temptation,* as well as *Forgive us out trespasses.* True, God keeps me from such and such sins, but what if God should leave me to temptation? What a wretched creature I would be if ever this corrupt heart of mind should prevail against me! I have cause to fear because I find such wickedness boiling and bubbling up. I find such proneness to such and such sins. If the Lord is not infinitely merciful to me, I shall break out to the dishonor of His name, the scandal of religion, and the wounding of my conscience, and this, God knows, causes the most solicitous care I ever had lest my heart should break out against God to the scandal of that holy profession I have taken upon me.

Oh, is it thus with you? Oh, this would be a happy thing, indeed!

When men hear of one who is broke, they will inquire as to the reason. He had such an estate, why is he broke? One man may say, "He trusted his servants too much, and that caused him to break. This will cause him to see to it that he never trusts his servants too much."

Another may say, "Because he lived above his means, and this will make it so he does not live above his means." And another will say, "He wanted his country home, and his servants rioted at home while he was abroad." And yet another says, "He trusted too much."

Now we will be wise to take heed of that which brings

others to afflictions. So it should be with us when we see any fall into sin. Professors who make a show of religion, and afterwards fall afoul, inquire now, "Why is this man broke? He broke his conscience, what is the matter? He was one who had such admirable gifts and made such a profession! Oh, maybe all this time he had a proud heart. Therefore, I will keep my heart humble. Oh, he had excellent gifts and enlargements in prayer; but he had a slight, vain spirit. Oh, let me take heed of this root of bitterness in my soul. He is broke now, but what is the matter? Oh, he began to be sluggish and cold in closet work and such duties in his family. Oh, let me take heed and keep up communion with God in secret in my closet and in my family. He is broke, indeed, but how? Oh, some secret sin he kept in his bosom. There was some secret sin he let his heart hanker after, and now God has left him to it. Now, by God's grace, I will look to myself. I will, by the grace of God, take heed of secret sins."

Thus, brethren, if we were sensible of the evil of sin, we would be thus careful to prevent the evil of sin as well as the evil of affliction.

Many will provide for their children but, if you were apprehensive of the evil of sin, you would provide for their souls as well as their bodies. Therefore you would say, "Oh, let me put him in a good family, and there he may learn to prevent sin."

This is the first, to reprove those who labor to prevent affliction but not sin.

Secondly, it reproves those who are careful to keep themselves from sin, but it is merely for fear of affliction, and only upon that ground, as if there were not enough evil in sin itself, but all the evil was in affliction. Certainly, those men and women do not understand that there is more evil in sin than in affliction. If you did understand and were sensible of this point I have treated, you would find enough arguments from sin itself to keep you from sin, even though no affliction should follow.

You abstain from sin. What is the reason? Not because of any great evil you see in sin, but because of affliction. Your conscience tells you it will bring you to trouble and into affliction, and this keeps you away from sin. It is true, it is good for men and women to avoid sin upon any terms, and this is one motive God propounds to avoid sin by, but the fear of affliction and trouble is not the chief motive. Your conscience tells you that God will get even with you and that the wrath of God will pursue you. Very few come so far as to have such apprehensions of the evil consequences of sin, and to avoid them on such grounds. But you should labor, not only to avoid sin from the evil consequences of sin, but for the evil of sin itself, for if you avoid sin only from the evil consequences of sin, know:

(1) This may be without a change of nature. A man or a woman may be in such an estate as they may not dare to commit some sin out of fear of trouble that may follow, and yet not have their nature changed. A wolf that is chained up may be the same as he was before he was chained up. His nature is not changed.

(2) If you forbear sin merely for fear of trouble, then know that your service and obedience is forced service and obedience, and so is not acceptable when it is merely forced.

(3) If you avoid sin merely for fear of affliction, then you are not yet loosed from yourself, not quite taken off from yourself.

(4) If you avoid sin merely to prevent affliction, then you are not likely to hold out. That is a principal of nature. Nothing is perpetual that is violent, and this is violent: to avoid sin merely for fear of affliction. Such men and women will not hold out if there is no other principle than this. They will fall off at last. They will abate at last, and so they will come to fall off.

But you will say, "Oh Lord, this is my condition; I am afraid!"

There are, I suppose, many in this congregation who apply these things, and it strikes to their hearts to think, "Lord, then I am afraid I have no grace at all. This is true, I have avoided sin, and have not gone on in the same sins others have done; but for my own part, for all I know, I have done it merely out of fear of hell and affliction and the trouble that will follow, rather than from any other evil in sin. What, is there no grace in me so that I avoid sin for fear of affliction?"

To help them who apply it otherwise than it should be, and conclude that they have no grace at all,

(1) Know that, though the sensitive part may not be so much stirred from beholding the evil of sin as opposed to affliction, the rational part may yet more work against sin as sin than from the affliction that follows. How will this follow that the rational part is not ordered by the sensitive? If I put my finger in the fire, there will be more pain to sense than if I endured that which is a hundred times worse.

Suppose a prince should lose his kingdom. That is a much greater evil than to have his finger burned a little; yet there would be more to the sense for the instant than can be in the other. But if he comes to the rational part, to choose which he will take, he will rather take that which is most painful for the moment. So were the troubled soul, though sense finds more from the fear of evil, given a choice, it would choose affliction rather than sin. So the rational part fears sin more than affliction. If you had a choice to commit sin without any affliction or affliction without sin, which would you take? Certainly, the soul, in its rational part, will choose the affliction without sin rather than the sin without the affliction.

But yet I have here more to say to these, to satisfy the consciences of those who are troubled, and who say they are afraid that they avoid sin from fear of affliction.

(2) Know, therefore, that man or woman who avoids sin merely from fear of affliction, though they avoid the sin,

they never come to love the command that forbids the sin. They are weary of God's commands. But now a soul that does not only avoid sin through fear, but has a love to that command that binds his spirit as well, if you find it thus with you, that you have a love to the command that forbids that sin which you avoid, certainly you do not merely avoid sin from fear of affliction.

Those who avoid sin merely from fear of affliction do not commit sin because they dare not; but, in the meantime, they would be glad if there were no command against it. This is like the speech of one who cried out, "Oh that God had never made the seventh commandment." He had an enlightened conscience, but a filthy heart. Conscience now stood in his way, therefore he hated the command that forbade the sin. "Oh, that this commandment had never been made!" he said. So those who refrain from sin merely from fear of trouble and hell, though they keep from the sin, yet they never love the command that forbids the sin. But if your heart closes with the command and says it is good, holy, and righteous, and if your heart blesses God for this holy Law, peace be to your soul. It is not the case that you avoid sin for fear of affliction, but for fear of sin itself.

(3) To satisfy those consciences, those who avoid sin merely from fear of affliction are willingly ignorant of many sins. They willingly turn their eyes from the Law of God that forbids sin. True, they do not dare go on in the commission of those sins directly against conscience. Conscience will not suffer them. Now, because they have a mind to sin, they wink with their eyes and are loath to be convinced that it is a sin, because they have a heart delighting to close with the sin. There is a great deal of deceit this way.

But now, when a man or woman's conscience tells them this, "It is the desire of my soul to know any sin and, if I find there is a sin I am ignorant of in the way I walk, I could spend night and day until I come to know it. And when I have found it out, I hope my soul will come to rejoice that God has revealed to be sin that which before I did not know was sin." But now one who avoids sin for fear of affliction, if he does not know it to be sin, he can go on quietly and is willing to go on in ignorance. Therefore, he is loath to take pains to know a sin to be sin. If he has any fear of, or any suspicion that such a gainful way, or such a pleasant way is sin, if he fears it, he says, "Give me time to examine whether or not it is sin," and he is willing to pass over examination so that he may go on and enjoy his lust without fear.

But now, when the heart is right, if there is any suspicion that a way is sinful, though you have gotten never so much by it, yet it must be left off. I must, if this is sin, come to live lower than I have done. Yes, my conscience tells me that, if this is found to be sin, I must come down. Yet my heart tells me that I would with all my heart know it, and ask counsel of them who know the mind of God, and beg God that He would reveal to me whether this is a sin or not. But those who avoid sin for fear, when they ask counsel, will be sure to ask advice of those who are of the same mind as themselves.

(4) Those men who are willing to avoid sin not out of fear, but because of the evil of sin itself, find this disposition in their souls. At such a time as they are even afraid that God will destroy them for sin, even then they desire that God may be glorified. "Though I perish, let God be glorified." But those who avoid sin out of fear, when they apprehend there is no hope, they are ready to fly in God's face. "No, if I must be damned, I will be damned for something. If I must perish, I will perish for something." But the soul that fears sin for the evil of it says, "Well, though I perish and am damned, yet let God be glorified." Certainly, these do not avoid sin merely out of fear!

(5) Again, those who avoid sin out of fear do not see the beauty and excellency of godliness in others so as to be enamored with it. Some avoid sin out of a dislike and hatred of

sin. Do you see a beauty in these, and do you say, "Oh, that I were in such a condition!" Those who can see the excellency of grace in others, and can love and prize it in others, certainly there is some seed of that grace in their souls. So now, they who have no grace envy others who have grace; but they that have grace rejoice in those they see who have any grace. This is the second particular, rebuking those who sin merely out of fear of affliction, together with satisfaction to that case of conscience, because I know it lies heavy upon men's and women's souls.

Thirdly, the consideration of this point rebukes those who are so shy of affliction that they will fall into sin to prevent affliction. Certainly, this is a foolish choice for any to be so afraid of affliction that, to prevent affliction, they will rather venture upon sin. It would be like a man who sees a craggy way, and will rather turn into a puddle, all mire and dirt, rather than endure one that is hard and craggy. You see the ways of God as hard and craggy, and so you turn into the puddles and dirt of sin to avoid that hard, craggy way. Well, if God loves you, He will bring you back again, and you must go that way which you will not now go!

Augustine had this expression in his "Confessions." He said, "When God first convinced me, I was convinced of the rightness of God's way, but I saw the trouble in it, and I cried out, it pleaseth not me well to go in such troublesome ways."

So many men and women are convinced of God's ways, but they shall suffer such trouble in them, and they must go through such straits and, to prevent this, they will choose sin. Certainly, brethren, it was not long since there was a time that those who made conscience of sin were subject to many troubles and suffered much, a time when, if a man departed from evil, it was enough to make him a prey. I beseech you, see if you did not (to prevent some suffering) commit some sin. Some of you, when brought to be sworn vassals to those courts that were never by God's institution, had you not some remorse in conscience? (I mean the church wardens, as they called them.) And, when you were put to such oaths, had you never inward regret in your consciences? But yet you must be excommunicated if you did not take the oath, and if you did, then you bound yourselves not only to be their vassals (which were not of God), but besides, you bound yourselves to be persecutors of the saints by it. Certainly, the fulfilling of their canons was merely persecution, and yet you were their sworn vassals, and yet because you were afraid of trouble, you ventured and made bold with your consciences.

Oh, look back to these things. If you will say, "Now ministers speak against such things, you should have done so two or three years ago." For my own part, I did. Two, three, four, five years ago, and was of the same mind then that I am now. And through the strength of Christ and God's mercy to me, I ventured somewhat, and therefore I may speak more freely and boldly now. It was not merely to keep from danger that I have spoken no more, for I did speak before this. But now look back at what regret of conscience you had, and yet merely for fear of affliction, you passed through that regret of conscience. It would be just with God to make affliction more sore and heavy, and those who will avoid the affliction by sin, God may justly bring back that affliction. But this would be a large argument, to speak to those who will not venture upon suffering, but run upon sin.

Fourthly, this rebukes those who, when they are under affliction, are a great deal more sensible of afflictions than of sin. This is against the point that says there is more evil in sin than in affliction, and yet, when you are under affliction, you are more sensible of the evil of affliction than of sin. There are divers sorts of these, and divers things to be said to these.

1. One such group is profane, wicked men who commit horrible wickednesses. It is a wonder their conscience does not fly in their face and tear their heart out of their bosom for

the woeful guilt upon them, and yet they are never stirred. But when God's hand is upon them in some grievous sickness, they cry out in pain; yet they are not one whit sensible of sin. That never comes into their minds, but their pain and disease does. When their friends come, they complain of grievous nights, and what heated fever they are in, how they burn and have been tormented by their illness, but not a word about sin. All their guilt, their Sabbath-breaking, oaths, keeping bad company, opposing goodness, none of these lies upon their conscience at all. Oh! These are wretched creatures; dull, guilty, hard-hearted, left by God to the day of His righteous judgment.

2. Others, when they are under God's hand, lie fretting and vexing, murmuring and repining. As Solomon said, Proverbs 19:3, *Man perverts his way, and his heart frets against God.* First he perverts his way, and yet when God's hand is upon him, he frets against God's way. You should fret against your own heart for sin, but you fret against God for affliction.

3. A third sort, and these are the ones to whom I principally intend to speak, are those who, when they are in affliction, will complain much about sin, and seem to put all the trouble upon sin. But, in truth, their trouble is more for affliction than sin. Now I would find these out (though it will require time). I suppose I could point out a great many who, it may be, make great complaints of sin and yet, the truth is, that which lies at the heart and pinches there is affliction rather than sin.

How do you know this? If a man comes and complains, "Oh, this wretched heart of mine! Pray, help me against it!" How can you tell it is for affliction and not for sin? Perhaps they have had great losses at sea, brought their names into disgrace, lost such a friend, are pinched with poverty, and then come and lay all upon sin. Whereas, it is the affliction that lies in the heart; this pinches them the most. Many men and women account it a kind of shame to complain of affliction. They think this is a disgrace and, therefore, that they might not have the disgrace of complaining of affliction, they turn all upon sin; and it is sin that troubles them. Now I would find them out thus.

(1) You shall find many who come and complain of sin. Who do they complain to? To strangers, who know little of them and their condition, rather than to others who are acquainted with all their ways and their whole course of life, though it is those people who are most able to help them. There is a great deal of superstition in that, for certainly, if your heart is right, you will make complaint to those who know most of your ways and courses. But those who are strangers, you can go and complain to in some general way. Perhaps some of these may be, some way, able to help and relieve you in affliction, but you will not complain to those who may be able to help you against sin, if they are not able to help you otherwise.

(2) Another sort is this. Those who make complaint of sin (and, indeed, not true) it is affliction, not sin. You may know it by this. Though they complain of sin, it is in general terms. Oh! They are vile, sinful creatures, but they never come to rip up the secrets of their hearts to those they complain to. But now, any secret sins that might cause shame are kept in and never opened. This is your general complaint: you are vile, sinful creatures; whereas, if it was sin that lay upon your heart, you would come and open all your secret sins to those who are faithful and willing and able to help you, if you judge them faithful. If you do not judge them to be faithful, why do you complain to them? If you think they are faithful, you will be willing to open all your sins to them. But if you are always speaking in general terms, it is a dangerous sign that it is affliction and not sin that troubles you.

(3) Again, many complain to others, but very little between God and their own souls in secret. Their complaints are more large when they come to others than they are between God and their own souls in their closets. Now, if it is

for your sin that you complain, then your chief complaint
will be to God at the throne of grace, and it is there you will
pour forth your soul in the bitterness of your heart. Many
come to the minister and complain that they are wretched
sinners, but scarcely will go to God in secret. Or else they
will content themselves with some prayers, just as they are
in the prayer book or the like, but they will never pour forth
their souls in secret for sin. That is another sign that it is for
affliction rather than for sin.

(4) Another note is this as to whether it is for affliction
more than for sin. Anyone who has grief upon them, according to that grief, they are ready to aggravate that grief. For
example, suppose a man or a woman was troubled for the
death of their father, or husband, or wife. Oh, such a one's
dear friend is dead, their father is dead, their husband or
wife is dead. Well, they are mightily troubled and perplexed
for this. Now if anyone comes and speaks anything to aggravate their sorrow, they close with it immediately. They do
it like this, "You complain of sorrow for your father. Aye,
he was a loving father." And they immediately close with it,
and this aggravates their sorrow. Or you might hear this,
"So, you have lost your husband? Oh! Never has a woman
lost as precious a husband as I have." So that which is spoken to aggravate that which already lies upon the spirits of
men and woman they are ready to close with.

So now, if you would know what lies upon your spirits
and, if you would know what lies upon the spirits of men
and women who are troubled, here is the trial: what are they
troubled for? Here is the art of a minister of a Christian, to
find out what lies upon the spirits of men and women. Some
say it is sin. Well, but it may be that it is not that. How shall
we find out? Like this: whatever lies upon the heart that
troubles them, they will be very willing to acknowledge
anything said to aggravate that which most lies upon their
spirits. A Christian may come and tell them of the evil of sin,
and he may aggravate it and say, "This is an evil condition,

and you must be humbled for it," and thoroughly apply the Word of God to them, to show how deeply they are to be humbled, and lays sin before them in its right colors. If sin troubles them, they join with it and say, "It is evil, indeed. The Lord humble me and show me more of this evil of sin." And they like that Word of God that lays home the evil of sin most.

But if it is not sin that they are troubled for, by these speakings against sin, their hearts are hardened and their hearts rise against the aggravation of sin. If it is affliction, they will want you to come, and pity and console them and say, "Alas! You have such sorrows and troubles." And "Oh! Poor creatures, it is a pity so that some others should help you." Aye, they take this, and this aggravates their sorrow.

It is observable that, when David fled from Absalom, he was ready to entertain anything that might aggravate his sorrow. When Ziba came and accused Mephibosheth, though it was very unlikely, he immediately embraces it. So, when a man is under affliction, he will readily hear and embrace that which will aggravate his condition, and a man who is under trouble for sin will readily embrace that which will aggravate his sin. This is an excellent note to come to know where the burden pinches, whether it is sin or affliction.

(5) The last note to try whether sin or affliction troubles you is this. There is, according to the trouble of the heart for sin, a savoriness of Spirit to the contrary good. Your heart will, in some measure, have a love to, and a savor and relish of, that spiritual grace which is contrary to that sin of yours of which you are complaining. But now you have many who complain of sin, they say, but yet their hearts are still as unsavory, and they no more relish spiritual and heavenly things contrary to that sin that they complain of than they ever did before. Therefore, the burden and weight does not lie upon sin, but affliction. Take heed; examine your own heart. There is much deceitfulness in the spirits of men and women. You take the name of God in vain when you come

and complain of sin, and the truth is that your affliction is upon you. And if your affliction were gone, you would be well enough. Perhaps you are crossed in your family. If that were taken away, you would be well enough for all sin. Therefore, be sure you are faithful with God and your own soul.

A fifth sort of people to be reprehended are those who get out of affliction by sinful ways and think they do well. But, if there is more evil in sin than in affliction, then it must be a woeful getting out if by way of sin. Many people are in straits. If they can get out any way, by hook or by crook, they will do it. They do not care how they do it. What! Have you gotten out of prison by sin? You have broken out of prison!

If a criminal breaks out of prison, there is a hue and cry sent after him, and the constable pursues him. And if he is captured, he is laid in the dungeon, and bolts are put upon him, and he is treated more harshly. So I say, if you are under any affliction, you should lie there until God lets you out. But, if you break out before God lets you out, hue and cry will follow you and you will certainly be overtaken. The remedy is worse than the disease. This is to skip out of the frying pan into the fire. Like a man in a burning fever, if he drinks a pint of cold water to ease himself, it may ease him for awhile, but he is scorched and parched with heat afterwards.

This is like a man who runs from a little dog that barks at him and runs into the mouth of a lion. There is just as much difference between sin and affliction. It is as if you should say, "God will not help me and, therefore, the devil shall." Every man who takes sin to help him says just that, "Well, I see God will not help; therefore the devil must."

What God does, He does by lawful means, and if you cannot have it by lawful means you must say, "Well, then I shall not have help." Yet you will have it and, therefore, you go to the devil for it. Certainly, if you knew all, you would have little comfort in this. Will you break your bonds in sinful ways to get out of affliction? Many apprentices, because their masters chastise them, run away into many hardships. So many men and women, because they have crosses with their spouses, break away and will not live together.

There are a hundred other particulars that I might use to show how men break from affliction by sinful ways, but I must hasten. Only take that place for this in Jeremiah 28:13, *Go tell Hananiah, saying, thus saith the Lord, Thou hast broken the yokes of wood, but thou shalt make for them yokes of iron.* When God sent a yoke of wood to declare what affliction the people should bear, Hananiah broke it. Yes, said God, has he broken them? Go tell him that he shall have a yoke of iron. You break of the yoke of affliction? Know from God that you shall have a yoke of iron.

Sixth, this reprehends those who, after deliverance from affliction, can bless themselves in their sin, though they are not delivered from it. There was such a sickness you had, and there you laid in anguish of spirit, and everyone thought you would die. You thought, then, that you would go to hell. Well, you are delivered and are as bad as ever, as unclean as ever, as covetous as ever, as malicious and profane as ever. Oh, know your condition is woeful!

I remember Austin had this saying, "You have lost the benefit of affliction as well as you have lost the affliction." Oh, it is a heavy loss to lose affliction without profit, for this is the last means God usually uses and, therefore, you are worse than before.

It may be that you were troubled with the stone. And you have the stone cut off, but you have as hard a heart as ever. What, is the stone gone from the bladder and the stone still in the heart? Oh! It may be that God sent this to cure your heart, and you are delivered from the one, and you are glad of that. Oh, know that you are in a woeful case, for sin, by this means, has gotten a firmer root because it has withstood affliction. The arrows have been taken out; but the venom still remains.

Now all I shall say is this. The Lord seal all these truths about the evil of sin upon your hearts, all I have said of the evil of sin. I must be brought at the day of judgment to avouch and justify what I have delivered. And know that every one of you here, at that great Audit Day, must be brought to answer for what you have heard, and how you have heard, and for what effect it has had on you all. Consider what has been said, and the Lord give you understanding in all things.